THE FIRST TYCOONS

Adolph Zukor and Jesse Lasky

AMERICAN MOVIES: THE FIRST THIRTY YEARS

THE FIRST TYCOONS
by
Richard Dyer MacCann

THE SCARECROW PRESS, INC.
Metuchen, New Jersey & London

in association with

IMAGE & IDEA, INC.
Iowa City, Iowa

© Copyright 1987 by Richard Dyer MacCann.
List of permissions begins on page viii.

All rights reserved.

Printed in the United States of America.

Other Books by Richard Dyer MacCann:

Hollywood in Transition (1962)
Film and Society (1964)
Film: A Montage of Theories (1966)
The People's Films (1973)
The New Film Index (1975)
    (with Edward S. Perry)
Cinema Examined (1982)
    (with Jack C. Ellis)

In Preparation:
The First Film Makers
The Stars Appear
The Comedians
Films of the 1920s

Film/Video Works:
Degas: Master of Motion (1960)
How to Build a Freeway (1965)
How to Look at Freeways (1965)
Murder at Best (1981)
The Quiet Channel series (1983)
American Movies: The First 30 Years (1984)

Library of Congress Cataloging in Publication

MacCann, Richard Dyer.
    The first tycoons.

    (American movies)
    "[Published] in association with Image & Idea, Inc., Iowa City, Iowa."
        Bibliography: pp. 253–259
        1. Moving-picture industry – United States – History.
    I. Title.   II. Series.
    PN1993.5U6M188   1986   384'.8'0973   86-22064
    ISBN 0-8108-1949-X
    ISBN 0-8108-1950-3 (pbk.)

Contents

1 Introduction. Business First.

11 Chapter 1. The First Exhibitors
   13 Tino Balio. The Kinetoscope.
   17 Terry Ramsaye. First Night on Broadway.
   20 Bosley Crowther. Marcus Loew Is Willing.
   24 Terry Ramsaye. The Screen Theatre Arrives.
   27 [Moving Picture World]. The Nickelodeon.

31 Chapter 2. Earliest Production Companies
   34 Robert M. Henderson. Biograph.
   37 Paul C. Spehr. Pathé Frères.
   40 Robert Grau. Help from Overseas.
   43 Richard Griffith and Arthur Mayer. The Men Who Owned the Business.
   46 John Drinkwater. The Trust Fight.
   50 Robert Sklar. New Producing Companies.
   54 Robert Grau. The Growth of Universal.
   57 Attilio H. Giannini. The First Loans.
   60 Benjamin B. Hampton. J. Stuart Blackton.
   62 Albert E. Smith. Vitagraph.

71 Chapter 3. Enter Lasky and Zukor

    73 Adolph Zukor. I Felt the Freedom in the Air.
    80 Adolph Zukor. Nobody Would Make Big Pictures.
    87 Will Irwin. Waiting at the Theatre.
    89 Daniel Frohman. Edison Is Agreeable.
    92 Kenneth Macgowan. The Coming of the Feature Film.
    97 George Pratt. Multiple Reel Films.
   100 Ben M. Hall. The Strand Theatre.
   104 Terry Ramsaye. Lasky Rents a Barn.
   107 Jesse L. Lasky. *The Squaw Man.*
   114 Louis Reeves Harrison. *The Squaw Man.*
   118 Will Irwin. The Low Spot.
   124 Terry Ramsaye. Hodkinson and Paramount.
   126 Jesse L. Lasky. "So We Combined."
   131 Adolph Zukor. Operating in a Turmoil.
   133 Samuel Goldwyn. A Bitter Chapter.
   136 Jesse L. Lasky. The Power and the Glory.
   140 Jesse L. Lasky. Production Problems.
   143 Jesse L. Lasky. Cruzing Over the Santa Fe Trail.
   149 Bruce Bliven. *The Covered Wagon.*

153 Chapter 4. The Big Five

   156 Kenneth Macgowan. The Triangle of Griffith, Ince, and Sennett.
   160 Benjamin B. Hampton. The Rise of First National.
   168 Mae D. Huettig. The Battle for Theaters.
   174 Albert E. Smith. It Was a Rugged Era.
   179 Michael Conant. Bankers and Theaters.
   182 Norman Zierold. The Films' Forgotten Man: William Fox.
   188 Benjamin B. Hampton. William Fox Improves His Position.
   194 Arthur L. Mayer. The Origins of United Artists.
   200 Tino Balio. United Artists Takes Shape.
   206 Bosley Crowther. Loew Buys a Studio.
   211 Bosley Crowther. The Saga of *Ben Hur.*
   220 Albert E. Smith. A Handshake with Harry Warner.

223 Appendices.
    223 A. Author's Note About Motion Picture History.
    233 B. Arthur Knight. The Machine for Seeing Better.
    238 C. Howard T. Lewis. Paramount Famous Lasky Corporation.
    243 D. Selected Companies of the Silent Period: A Chronological List
    238 E. Brief Biographies of Early Film Executives
    243 F. A Few Business Events Covered by the *New York Times.*
    253 G. Bibliography.

Illustrations

Frontispiece	Adolph Zukor and Jesse Lasky.
Page x	*The Covered Wagon* (1923).
Page 9	An early kinetoscope.
Page 10	*The Great Train Robbery* (1903).
Page 23	Marcus Loew
Page 30	Albert Einstein visiting Carl Laemmle at Universal.
Page 70	*Queen Elizabeth* (1912) and *The Squaw Man* (1913).
Page 152	*Ben Hur* (1925) With Francis X. Bushman and Ramon Novarro.
Page 222	The Roxy Theater.

ACKNOWLEDGMENTS

This book has been in preparation for a long time, but it got under way during a research leave granted by The University of Iowa in 1976. It has benefited from study at what was then the Motion Picture Section of the Library of Congress, but even more from the remarkable and extensive holdings of film books and magazines in the University of Iowa library. My thanks to all who have helped me at these places and at the Academy of Motion Picture Arts and Sciences in Beverly Hills.

Special appreciation goes to the graduate and undergraduate students since 1979 who have given me comments, pro and con, on many specific selections used in class. I remember a special session of advice from Francine Blais, Jim Gilmore, Doug Kelley, Chai-Kim Lee, and Carl Robinson. Also I am grateful for helpful and cheering conversations in recent years with Phil Brown, Jeff Carpenter, Henry Jenkins, Pieter Pereboom, Brad Pouleson, and Tom Schmidt. Michael Kolinski provided research assistance during one semester.

I'm especially in debt to Ron Mottram for reading the entire manuscript at an early stage, giving me not only critical advice but an encouraging judgment that film study would benefit from its publication. Also to Wes Gehring for an early reading and certain suggestions, and for placing a substantial portion of the introduction in a film-related issue of the Indiana Social Studies Quarterly (autumn 1981) which he edited and which included pieces by other former students of mine.

May I call the reader's attention to the fact that there is no Preface or Foreword in this book to delay an immediate plunge into the introduction, the chapters, and the readings. There is, however, a rather extensive "Author's Note About Motion Picture History" among the appendices which may more comfortably engage attention after acquaintance with the readings.

R.D.M.

Acknowledgment is made of the following permissions to use material from copyrighted works:

Excerpt from introduction to Part I, "A Novelty Spawns Small Businesses, 1894–1908" (herein titled "The Kinetoscope"), from *The American Film Industry* by Tino Balio. Excerpt from "United Artists Takes Shape," from *United Artists* by Tino Balio. Both books copyright © 1976 by University of Wisconsin Press. Reprinted by permission of publisher and author.

"First Night on Broadway," "The Screen Theatre Arrives," and "Lasky Rents a Barn," from *A Million and One Nights* by Terry Ramsaye. Copyright © 1925, 1956 by Simon & Schuster. "The Men Who Owned the Business" and "The Fighting Independents" from *The Movies* by Richard Griffith and Arthur Mayer. Copyright © 1957, 1970 by Simon & Schuster. Reprinted by permission of Simon & Schuster, Inc.

Excerpt from "The Background" (herein titled "Biograph") from *D. W. Griffith: The Years at Biograph* by Robert M. Henderson. Copyright © 1970 by Robert M. Henderson. Reprinted by permission of Farrar, Straus, and Giroux, Inc.

"Pathé Frères," from *The Movies Begin* by Paul C. Spehr. Used by permission of the Newark Museum, Newark, N.J.

Excerpt from "Edison's Trust and How It Got Busted" (herein titled "New Producing Companies") from *Movie-Made America* by Robert Sklar. Copyright © Robert Sklar 1975. Reprinted by permission of Random House, Inc.

"A Myth Is as Good as Milestone" (herein titled "Multiple Reel Films") by George Pratt in *Image* November 1957. Used by permission of George Eastman House, publisher.

"A Wonderful Audience in Costly Togs" (herein titled "The Strand Theatre"), reprinted from *The Best Remaining Seats* by Ben M. Hall. Copyright © 1961 by Ben M. Hall. Used by permission of Crown Publishers, Inc.

"The Squaw Man," "So We Combined," "The Power and the Glory," and "Cruzing Over the Santa Fe Trail," from *I Blow My Own Horn* by Jesse L. Lasky. Reprinted by permission of Jesse L. Lasky Jr.

"The Battle for Theaters" from *Economic Control of the Motion Picture Industry* by Mae D. Huettig. Copyright 1944. Used by permission of author, Mae Churchill.

"Bankers and Theaters," from *Antitrust in the Motion Picture Industry* by Michael Conant. Copyright 1960. Used by permission of University of California Press.

"The Films' Forgotten Man: William Fox," from *The Moguls*. Copyright 1969 by Norman Zierold. Reprinted by permission of the Putnam Publishing Group. Originally published by Coward McCann Inc. and in England by Hamish Hamilton.

"The Origins of United Artists" by Arthur Mayer. Reprinted by permission of *Variety*.

"The Machine for Seeing Better," reprinted from *The Liveliest Art* by Arthur Knight. Copyright © Arthur Knight 1957. Reprinted with permission of Macmillan Publishing Company.

"Paramount-Famous-Lasky Corporation," excerpts omitting diagrams reprinted from *Harvard Business Reports* by Howard T. Lewis. Copyright © 1930. Used by permission of McGraw-Hill Book Company.

Excerpts from *Behind the Screen* By Samuel Goldwyn. Copyright 1923 by George H. Doran Co. Printed by permission of Doubleday & Company Inc.

The Covered Wagon (1923)

Introduction

Business First

Suppose you were going to organize a motion picture studio. Who would be your dominant factor? Would you have a man of my type who was a visionary, half a dreamer and only half a business man, who was keen about the quality of the product and might well lose touch with the cost? Or would you put at the head a thoroughly trained business man? — Jesse Lasky

In these days of everpresent imaging—with color pictures flashing by satellite from anywhere to everywhere, night and day—it may seem antiquarian to slip back into the past, into that simple, quiet time of pictorial pantomime we associate with the silent screen.

Yet the vast design of modern telecommunications has its roots in the first thirty years of the movies, when the pioneers built, step by step, the image industries of yesterday. Whenever network, cable, and videocassette titans clash today, there are echoes of those early years when nobody knew what form of organization was going to be most successful.

Those who have seen a few "old movies" may have an impression of jerky action and dim lighting, or remember some comedies of Chaplin. But there was more, much more. The formative decades of the American cinema (about 1896 to 1916) were full of intriguing promise. The broken shards and imposing temples surviving from those ancient times—from *The Great Train Robbery* to

1

2   THE FIRST TYCOONS

Intolerance—are still fascinating to look at. And the 1920s contain one of the richest periods of drama and comedy in the history of cinema.

Motion picture history is primarily the history of an art and its artists. There would be little interest or value in recounting such history if there were not a variety of marvelous works still surviving—worth remembering, worth looking at again. Such works, we have to admit, are of a higher order of value than more prosaic products. Bulldozers and bicycles, cosmetics and file cabinets no doubt have their charms and their histories. The human race is far more concerned, and rightly so, with a medium which intensely examines human personalities and emotions. Movies are powerful, omnipresent, and wonderful—and they are about us. Therefore we care about almost any aspect of their history.

This book is about the businessmen and production executives who provided management support for the artists and the works of art in the first thirty years of American movies. Such men are significant because of what they allowed to happen (sometimes in spite of themselves). But they are also interesting in their own right. They are the earliest of those bosses we still talk about today, with mingled nostalgia and disdain, as "real showmen." Unlike some of the current conglomerate financiers, these first tycoons were deeply involved in every major decision and loved the whole process of making and selling movies. After all, they had consciously chosen motion pictures as a way of life.

Six men in particular had a major influence on the movies and the movie companies of the silent era and therefore on the entire "golden era" of Hollywood (1920-1960). Four of them had been immigrants before they were twenty years old, and the other two were second and third generation Americans who had to make their own way. Rockbottom poor, all of them, they had little time for education and had to work full time before they were well into their teens. Yet every one of them had already made a success of some other business—and gave up that security—when they were attracted into the uncharted paths of the silent screen.

Birthplace, business, first investment in movies	Age in 1912	
Adolph Zukor (Hungary) fur salesman	1903, at 30	39
Marcus Loew (New York) fur salesman	1904, at 34	42
William Fox (Hungary) cloth manufacturing	1904, at 25	33
Carl Laemmle (Germany) retail clothing	1906, at 39	45
Jesse Lasky (San Francisco) vaudeville booker	1913, at 33	32
Sam Goldwyn (Poland) glove salesman	1913, at 31	30

There is no human history without personalities on the one hand, and material conditions on the other—limitations of time and place and physical possibility. The American motion picture industry certainly drew on the preliminary contributions of countless inventors and technical developments, of a business-oriented society and a capitalistic system of investment, of an audience acquainted with popular novels and vaudeville, eager for a mixture of realism and romance.

But against this background there came on the scene some daring entrepreneurs. It could be said that they were better fitted than others to conform profitably to the business circumstances of their time. They were also, all of them, energetic and persistent salesmen, ready for the long chance.

These influential pioneers were preceded by a first wave of small-time shopkeepers who were aware only of the short-range curiosity of the audience—of the desire for momentary surprises and spectacles and perhaps a single twenty-minute exploration of the common life. These first businessmen provided a screen as cramped and circumscribed, as nervous and diverse as vaudeville or current events.

The men who took over leadership around 1912 and guided the new medium to a peak of popularity and achievement were businessmen of more passion and commitment. They were aware of deeper and broader audience yearnings, a readiness to sit in a theater for as long as an hour or more. These newer corporation executives provided a screen made transparent for extended dramas of human emotions.

The characteristic business practices of the American film industry were formed during the silent years. These practices were not unlike those of other industries of the time. The tendency toward vertical integration was a familiar pattern of corporate enterprise, against which the trust-busting crusades of Theodore Roosevelt and other national leaders made slight headway. There was too much logic, too much advantage in top-to-bottom control. Standard Oil—refiner, distributor, and retailer—stood as a model of organization, and John D. Rockefeller's aggressive tactics of salesmanship made mincemeat of lesser competitors.

The Hamiltonian tradition had always been to trust private industry to work for the best interests of the nation. Adam Smith, Thomas Hobbes, Charles Darwin, and William Graham Sumner

4   THE FIRST TYCOONS

were potent sources of philosophy for primitive self-help and the idea of more power to the powerful. Hamiltonianism was coming into its greatest time of acceptance in the late 19th century with the rising power of finance capitalism and industrialism – big factories, far-flung marketing, widespread chains of sales outlets.

The Jeffersonian ideal of many small, independent and especially agricultural enterprises was losing the battle in real life by the end of the nineteenth century. It was hard to conceive of a blast furnace as a cottage industry, or the distribution of its products as a gentlemanly regional activity.

Adolph Zukor, founder of the company which became Paramount Pictures, looked on and learned – and approved. The technological complexity of movie-making, even in the silent days, suggested a comparison with other large industries instead of a comparison with the visual arts, theatrical performances, and museums. The large-scale investment required, whether for the sets of *Intolerance* or for the salaries of temperamental stars, meant that a lot of conservation of scarce resources had to be contemplated. Income from successful pictures was needed if new pictures were to be made. Or else, more and more often, bankers had to be brought in. Capital of the short-range, high-cost type, had to be borrowed.

The higher mathematics of all this was not readily apparent to all concerned until the high costs of sound equipment hit the budgetary bottom lines in the 1930s. But men like Carl Laemmle, William Fox, and Adolph Zukor, after the first flush of battle with swords and spears against the patents trust (1908–1915), became aware quite early that the movie business was a large enterprise which profited from close controls.

In a capitalistic country, it was surely a capitalistic enterprise. Of course in a free country it involved a lot of competitive contests for public attention, too, and the screen had to reflect the interests of the audience. But there was bound to be a great deal of forceful maneuvering behind the scenes to get a hammerlock on the best theaters in the biggest cities. Movies might be a democratic art in the sense that they depended on the boxoffice. But nothing would reach the paying customer in the first place until someone risked and planned and organized and put it on the screen, expecting to get back the money invested.

The theory behind this was only in the first instance Darwinian. The best man might win and the best form of organization might become the leading factor in the marketplace, by virtue of healthy competition of an individualist dog-eat-dog variety. But after a while the participants discovered that survival of the fittest was not a good working hypothesis. It seemed the most convenient environment would be one in which there were few competitors—embattled but cautiously polite—and nearly automatic profits.

The entrepreneurs of the film business were more than once tempted by dreams of monopoly. Both Edison, in the first decade, and Zukor, in the second, faced with intransigent competitors, settled instead for oligopoly. Still, the strong surviving companies, the "Big Five," were those that were vertically integrated, like Standard Oil.

Terry Ramsaye, near the close of his book, *A Million and One Nights* (1926), put it in his own summary way—a paragraph of brisk and sweeping amateur economic theory which is about as helpful as any of the heavy reinterpretations of determinism served up recently by capitalists, Marxists, or structuralists:

> The motion picture industry is controlled by entirely automatic forces of growth by which it is evolving increasingly complex specimens of the so-called vertical trust. This is not the especially conscious plan of any one man or group of men but the following of basic laws of structure. It is as inevitable as the course by which the tree elaborates its organic processes complete from soil to nuts. The pattern, only slightly obscured by differing details, may be observed in all the arts, religions, and other industries by which the alleged human race lives and reconciles itself to living. Everything that grows grows the same way. Nobody can do anything about it.

Yet this "automatic" process was initiated, developed, revised, and adjusted by individuals. There was a moment in the late 1920s when Fox thought he had M-G-M by the throat. By dint of a big fee to Nicholas Schenck, Marcus Loew's successor, he was about to take over Loew's Inc. and its prestigious studio. Such a move would have put Fox in a dominant position in the industry. But the crash of 1929 evaporated the water out of his stock values and turned him into a nobody almost overnight.

Zukor was more cautious, and luckier. At the height of his power over production and sales in the industry (a position he reached in 1917 largely because of his contract with Mary Pickford) he was confronted by First National, a grouping of theater owners aggrieved by his block-booking practices and intent upon entering film production on a competitive scale. Famous Players-Lasky then fell back to a position of one among a few. Zukor began buying more theaters as a counter-thrust in 1919, but he never reached the same relative position of dominance again. In the same year, the founders of United Artists (Mary Pickford, Douglas Fairbanks, D. W. Griffith, and Charlie Chaplin) ranged themselves against the established distributors to sell their wares directly to theaters. This was going back to star power instead of corporate integration.

Thus the grind of competitive egos and companies went on, seeking advantage and profits. Surely one of the more poignant voices to be noted among our case studies in the film business of the silent era is the voice of Albert Smith. Like W. W. Hodkinson, he held to the view that he should do the job he knew best. Hodkinson wanted to be a distributor and nothing else. He would leave production to those who knew how. This lofty theory put him out in the street. Famous Players-Lasky took over his distribution company, including the name he gave it: "Paramount."

Smith, for his part, wanted only to run a little production company named Vitagraph, one of the last remaining firms of the Edison group. He thought it was his right to have access to theaters. Zukor did not share that view at all. Paramount-Famous-Lasky, greedy for profits, privately sneered at Smith's films and warned Paramount's best customers not to book them. It was a war to the death instead of fair competition.

It may be said that Smith was naive, that his Jeffersonian principles (if he was aware of them as such) were outdated and self-defeating.

On the other hand, it seems likely that if Smith had gone into the business of exhibition, if he had undertaken with his limited capital a campaign to buy theaters on his own, he would have done badly. His picture-making, too, would have suffered. His function in society was probably well chosen. His alternative, unfortunately, was not to function at all, and that was what happened to him when he sold out to Harry Warner in 1925.

Zukor would have been just as lost if he had had to spend his days on the details of production and nothing else. It is characteristic of such a man to add up his overhead costs first, and from that decide how many pictures to make. Zukor was the archetype of the cool executive who had few values beyond profits and the public pulse. Before he went into business for himself he spent two or three years watching and listening to film audiences. Such sales consciousness was neither stupid nor condescending. Enter-

tainment for the masses is a valuable commodity for society, and Zukor fulfilled that need for many years. But he became the model for all those movie executives who could never say "yes" to an artist just on a hunch, without worrying about the profits.
It is difficult to determine to what extent Zukor was involved with detailed creative decisions. Apart from the power to say "no" on budgets, the inevitable prerogative of "the New York office," he apparently did carry on extended conversations with Jesse Lasky about projects and stories, if not about scripts. No doubt he had enthusiasms and blind spots. His sense of audience acceptance failed him, according to Cecil DeMille, when he complained about rising costs for *The Ten Commandments*. Shortly afterward, Zukor refused to renew DeMille's contract. Yet he seems to have delegated a good deal of freedom to Lasky as production head in earlier years. When Lasky wanted to expand the concept and the budget for *The Covered Wagon*, Zukor went along with the idea and the profits were substantial.

Other executives have been more notable for their artistic daring. A few instances can show us why such men deserve their own place in the history of American motion pictures.
Harry Aitken said "yes" to D. W. Griffith in 1914 when he wanted to make feature-length films, and his financial backing made possible *The Birth of a Nation*.
Carl Laemmle said "yes" in 1918 to Erich von Stroheim, and *Blind Husbands*, the first feature Stroheim directed, turned out to be a money-maker as well as a landmark in critical controversy.
William Fox said "yes" to the German director, F. W. Murnau, at a time when he judged his own biggest need was prestige. *Sunrise* (1927) was a gamble for attention, and he won that gamble while losing some money he had made from other films. *Sunrise* has become one of the widely accepted "classics" of the screen.
Sacrifice is clearly necessary if such works are to be consciously encouraged. A gamble on a gift does not assure us of a classic, but the motivation must be there somewhere, together with the room to act within the kind of subsidy that surplus profits can provide.
Irving Thalberg said "yes" to King Vidor, at a time when he felt M-G-M could afford a small-budget film with limited profit prospects. *The Crowd* was a gift from a man and a company to society, because Vidor's *The Big Parade* had made crucial profits after the company almost went in the red on *Ben-Hur*. *The Crowd* has be-

come one of the classics of the screen, partly because Vidor was personally ready to make a statement about ordinary people and their confused awareness of the tyranny of the American dream. Thalberg was evidently the kind of producer who knew when an artist is ready in this way, and for a moment he had the power to say "yes." But his story really belongs in the era of sound.

It was Thalberg who provided the model for F.Scott Fitzgerald's unfinished novel about Hollywood. He called it *The Last Tycoon*.

Is one form of organization better than another? Will it bring us better movies?

If we are wise we will not make hasty assumptions about the historical effects of economic structure on the artistic qualities of the films produced. It was fashionable in the 1950s to assume that breakup of the studio system into various independent forms of production (following the precedent of United Artists) was a sure way to get "fewer and better" movies. Then when the old system of production was effectively wiped out, it began to be fashionable to bewail the passing of the studio assembly line because it permitted so many memorable little films to be made while nobody was looking.

Systems do not guarantee art. On the one hand, it seems clear that any form of secure and limited corporate competition tends to provide little in the way of variety for the consumer. When focused on profits and stability, all such companies tend to offer limited programs which look very much alike across the board, from the time of the Edison trust to the heyday of network television in the 1970s. Competition breeds similarity instead of variety or uniqueness.

Yet even under such circumstances, individuals with upsetting ideas do interfere from time to time. The role of the creative executive is unpredictable and sometimes healthy in terms of support for ideas, art, and artists.

Certainly one of the untold stories, apart from his own engaging autobiography, is Lasky's actual role in the formative years of Paramount. For fifteen years he was the executive in charge of studio production. Zukor liked Lasky from the beginning and made use of his coordinating talent. This may have been one of the best artistic decisions of his long and busy life.

But of course business always came first. Audiences were supporting frequent changes of program in the theaters. A distribution office had to sell more than a handful of such films in order to have enough margin to pay for the films and the staffs. "So we decided," Zukor reports casually, "to make thirty pictures a year." By 1917, Lasky would find the yearly demand on him, as chief of production, raised to more than a hundred.

Thus, with big distribution the primary goal, the industrialization of movie entertainment was under way.

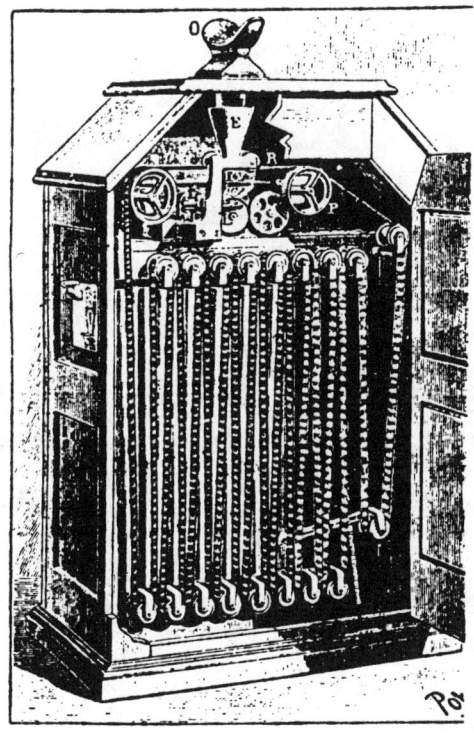

An early kinetoscope. From *Scientific American*, November 10, 1984, originally in the *London Times*, reprinted in *Image*, March 1952.

The Great Train Robbery (1903)

Chapter 1

The First Exhibitors

The nickel place of amusement . . . is multiplying faster than guinea pigs. – Moving Picture World.

Kinetoscope parlors were the first movie houses in America. The kinetoscope was a machine which ran a strip of silent film continuously past a little window fitting around the viewer's face like a mask. The big box was about the size of the customer and whirled and rattled as the strip of celluloid went round and round inside. The show lasted about a minute and served only one person at a time.

For a year or two after 1894, Thomas A. Edison was well enough satisfied with the income from his invention. But Edison was soon persuaded (mostly by the speedy arrival of competitors) that a projection machine was the logical next step. With a little help from Thomas Armat's indispensable contribution of a claw that pulled each frame into place for a fraction of a second and held it, the famous inventor was able to put on a show in Koster and Bial's Music Hall on April 23, 1896.

This has become (despite prior claims by inventors here and abroad) the traditional date for the beginning of projected theatrical motion pictures in the United States.

After that, the movies found a home for a while as one of the regular acts in vaudeville houses. Another home was the penny arcade, a place for mechanical games and all sorts of intriguing peepshow and popgun events. Here kinetoscopes, Mutoscopes (another form of moving picture peep show for which a series of picture cards flapped past a light), and the earliest projected movies all vied for the customer's attention.

Penny arcades were still money-makers in 1903, when an eleven-minute film called *The Great Train Robbery* began its long career of making exhibitors rich. This was also the year, according to Bosley Crowther, when Morris Kohn and Adolph Zukor opened a new arcade on 14th Street in New York City. Marcus Loew decided to join them. This mild-mannered man was eventually to become the owner of a chain of theaters and of the complex of companies known as Metro-Goldwyn-Mayer.

By 1903, however, it was already beginning to be clear that people would pay just to sit and watch a screen. Who opened the first nickelodeon? Was it Thomas Tally who "invented" the storefront theater in Los Angeles in 1902? He charged ten cents. John P. Harris may have been the one to make a success of the idea when he started charging five cents in Pittsburgh in 1905. All over the country nickelodeons appeared and customers came for 15 minutes or half an hour or more and the profits rolled in.

In his account of the 14th Street arcade, Crowther says that Kohn "rigged up a little electric railway with a train of open cars which ran around under the machines at regular intervals and caught the pennies as they were automatically dumped." This "ingenious electric train, groaning under carloads of pennies," helped to persuade Loew to give up selling furs and undertake full time promotion of popular entertainment and the exhibition of movies.

And why not? It was a graphic demonstration that foreshadowed the millions of dollars Americans would soon be willing to spend on visual images of stories.

It was also evidence of the financial reliability and primary importance of the real estate side, the exhibition side, of the film business. It is a curious fact that the movie industry did not begin with movie making. Of course there had to be strips of film to show. But there was no real production system until it was clear that people would come into theaters and watch.

Movies began as a business. And the first part of that business was exhibition.

TINO BALIO
The Kinetoscope

Tino Balio, a historian and librarian at the University of Wisconsin, has given us a useful anthology called The American Film Industry *(Madison, University of Wisconsin Press, 1976). His introduction to the earliest period of movie showings in America ("A Novelty Spawns Small Businesses, 1894-1908," pages 3 to 7) is a summary of the brief career of the kinetoscope and of the people in and out of the Edison shop who brought on the era of movie projection.*

On April 14, 1894, the world's first Kinetoscope parlor opened its doors at 1155 Broadway in New York City . . . No one knows who the customers were on that day, or exactly how many of them parted with some change to satisfy their curiosity about the new picture machine—but we can be sure that they had no idea of their place in history as they gazed into the peepholes in amazement. They were the first paying customers for the motion pictures, a handful of unwitting pioneers, destined to be followed by countless millions in America's long and exciting romance with the movies. That day and that place marked the commercial beginnings of the motion picture industry in the United States.

The Kinetoscope which amused Broadway strollers was a peephole machine which showed a short filmstrip. It had been perfected by William Kennedy Laurie Dickson at Thomas Edison's laboratory in nearby West Orange, New Jersey. A syndicate headed by A. O. Tate, Thomas R. Lombard, and Erastus A. Benson was the first to see the moneymaking possibilities of the machine, and so it acquired a concession from Edison to market it.

The trial balloon, launched on Broadway, was soon followed by a veritable skyful. Within the year, the syndicate (which by then had added three new partners—Andrew M. Holland, Norman C. Raff, and Frank R. Gammon) installed Kinetoscopes in department stores, hotels, saloons, and phonograph parlors in major cities throughout the country, always with the same gratifying results—curiosity, amusement, patronage, and profits. Noting the machine's domestic success, another firm, headed by Frank Z. Maguire and Joseph D. Baucus, acquired the foreign rights and marketed America's new plaything abroad.

14   THE FIRST TYCOONS

The enthusiastic reception of the Kinetoscope ensured its multiplication and success—and inevitably was the cause of its decline and supplantation. The Kinetoscope, after all, had a major limitation: it could be seen by only one viewer at a time. What if the picture image could be projected onto a screen, so that the small change of a large audience could be collected all at one time? No sooner had entrepreneurs dreamed of such an advance than technicians turned the dream into reality. Through the work of Robert W. Paul in England, the Lumière brothers in France, and, in America, the Lathams, Thomas Armat, Herman Casler, Albert E. Smith, and Dickson, the motion picture projector became a commercial reality only two years after the unveiling of the first Kinetoscope.

Edison introduced a projector to the public on April 23, 1896, at Koster & Bial's Music Hall, Herald Square, New York City. . . . Its appearance came just in time, perhaps, because by then the novelty of the Kinetoscope was wearing off. Kinetoscope business, in fact, began to decline in 1895 and showed no signs of resurgence by the time the first projector appeared. Edison himself, it appears, had limited faith in the durability of the Kinetoscope idea, since he had not even bothered to take out foreign patents on it.

Edison's projector was called the Vitascope, the invention of Thomas Armat. Edison did not wait to develop a projector of his own, since other inventors and developers were already anticipating public demand. One projector, in fact, had already been introduced, this by the Latham brothers, Otway and Gray, and their father Woodville. They had devised a projection machine based on the principle of the Kinetoscope. It was an imperfect machine, but marketable, and others were swiftly on the way. Edison, faced with the possibility of being shut out of the market he himself had created, decided to get into the swim without delay by purchasing the manufacturing and marketing rights to Armat's projector.

That same summer, on June 29, 1896, Edison received some serious competition. Another New York vaudeville house, B. F. Keith's Union Square Theatre, exhibited a Lumière Cinématographe. This was an event of major importance in the motion picture business. Since J. Austin Fynes, manager of the Keith theater, was highly respected by vaudeville managers, his acceptance of motion pictures and of the Lumière projector was a clear signal to other vaudeville houses. The Proctor circuit and other houses soon began to include motion pictures on their cards, along with dog acts, lyric tenors, and slapstick comics. Movies had come to the stage.

Less than four months later, both the Vitascope and the Lumière Cinématographe were challenged for primacy in the field. Appearing on the scene was the Biograph projector, which was capable of showing pictures significantly larger than its precursors, and much clearer and sharper, too. It was the invention of Dickson, then a partner in the American Mutoscope Company (soon to be called the American Mutoscope and Biograph Company). Dickson's Biograph made its "regular" debut on October 12, 1896, at Hammerstein's Opera House in New York. It was an instant success, making its competitors obsolete in short order. The Biograph moved to the Union Square Theater on January 18, 1897, and, with only a four-month hiatus, closed on July 15, 1905, after eight and a half years – "an incomparably long run in the history of the American theatre to that date," in the words of Gordon Hendricks.[1]

In introducing motion pictures to vaudeville, it was only natural for managers to include them as one turn in the series of acts. A vaudeville turn lasted approximately fifteen minutes, and since the early films were around fifty feet in length, it was necessary to string a minimum of ten subjects together to fill a time slot. At Koster & Bial's, for example, the Vitascope program consisted of twelve subjects and was one of eight acts given before the first intermission. The films were no doubt accompanied by music – in the large houses by the versatile pit orchestras, and in the smaller ones by a piano.

Until 1896, theater owners who wanted to book a projector could do so with a certain measure of protection, which came in the form of exclusive exhibition rights to carefully defined geographical areas.[2] But in 1896, Edison brought out a projector of his own devising, the Edison Projecting Kinetoscope, and placed it on the open market with no geographical restrictions attached. Anyone could buy the Edison and use it for commercial showings wherever the traffic would allow. Edison's bold marketing move probably made more than a few theater operators uncomfortable, but its success soon forced other companies to adopt similar policies. Sales of the projectors thus unbridled, increased dramatically, giving a significant stimulus to the entire motion picture industry in the United States.

While films were finding a ready place in metropolitan vaudeville houses, they had also taken to the road. . . . Lumière showmen began the first of their long tours in the summer of 1895. That same summer, LeRoy Latham (nephew of Woodville) purchased the territorial rights to the Latham Pantopticon for the state of Virginia. Latham's venture was short-lived, largely because of the inferior quality of the projector itself, but he obviously had the right idea. Where the pioneer Latham failed, other entrepreneurs succeeded, among them William T. Rock, who took the Raff & Gammon projector to Louisiana, a state that the Kinetoscope Company was happy to relinquish for $1,500. Rock opened a motion picture "store" in New Orleans on June 28, 1896. After three months, his meager supply of films exhausted the market, forcing him to take the show into smaller cities.

Soon after, in August 1896, Thomas L. Tally opened a "Phonograph and Vitascope Parlor" in Los Angeles. Although he, too, was plagued by a scarcity of films, he survived by making the broadest possible use of the various machines on the market: he offered customers not only the Kinetoscope, but also the Vitascope, the phonograph, and the Mutoscope, a peephole machine which flipped printed cards before the viewer's eyes, giving the illusion of motion.

Other traveling showmen brought the movies to small-town America, wherever there were enough people in one place with money in their pockets and adventure in their hearts. In New England, audiences packed amusement parks, club halls, and vacant storefronts on Sundays when legitimate theaters were closed. Harry and Herbert Miles lugged a projector all the way to Juneau, Alaska, where they played the gold camps on the outskirts of town. All of these showmen traversed rural America for reasons of their own: the promise of financial reward, the lure of the open road, the excitement of "show business." But together they performed an invaluable service for the future of the entire industry, for they helped to create a public taste for motion pictures on a national level, and by doing so they laid the broad foundation for the modern movie theater. The creation of such a theater, however, had to wait until large and efficient production and distribution companies could provide a regular supply of films at low cost.

NOTES

1. Gordon Hendricks, *Beginnings of the Biograph* (New York, 1964), p. 51.
2. Vitascope sales were handled by Raff and Gammon's Kinetoscope Company; the Cinématographe by Lumière's American representative, W. B. Hurd; and the Biograph directly by the American Mutoscope Company.

TERRY RAMSAYE
First Night on Broadway

Terry Ramsaye was commissioned by James Quirk, the editor and publisher of Photoplay Magazine, *to do a history of the movies. It went on for 36 installments, appearing from 1922 to 1925, and after a rewrite, became a remarkable book,* A Million and One Nights *(N.Y., Simon and Schuster, 1926). On pages 231-234 he tries to recapture, thirty years afterward, what it was like to view projected movies in 1896 and what people said about it at the time.*

The advertising of Koster & Bials' Music Hall, Thirty-fourth street, Herald Square, for the week commencing Monday evening, April 20, 1896, announced the coming of "Thomas A. Edison's latest marvel, the Vitascope." The music hall was on the site now occupied by the Macy department store.

Thomas Armat came up from Washington to supervise the installation of the Vitascope on the balcony of the music hall.

The opening was delayed because of the time required for the installation of the machinery. The sensation was sprung on the night of April 23. Armat was in the projection booth at the machines while the crowd, thrilled with the dancing of Annabelle, life size on the screen, acclaimed Edison. Edison in a box at the show did not respond in person.

The pictures were thrown upon a twenty-foot screen, set in an overwhelming gilded frame. The program included pictures of a bit of the finale number of Hoyt's *The Milk White Flag*, a dash of prize fight, several dancing girls who displayed their versatility to the camera, and one of Robert W. Paul's pictures, the surf at Dover, in England. The Dover picture was accepted by the audience as something from down the New Jersey coast.

The Vitascope used at Koster & Bials' was equipped with a spool bank and endless loops of film, so that subjects might be repeated indefinitely without rewinding the pictures. The machine was capable of handling film on reels, but the idea of subjects that should occupy the length of a modern reel of a thousand feet was remote indeed from the picture makers of '96.

The audience was deeply puzzled at this magic of the screen. When the waves at Dover came rolling in to crash in jets of spume

18   THE FIRST TYCOONS

and spray there was a flurry of panic in the front seats.

In public attention on Broadway that week, honors were about equally divided between the new wonder of the screen and Albert Chevalier, the famous singer of coster songs, who was then appearing at Koster & Bials' in the glory of his first engagement, introducing to the eager American ear *My Old Dutch, The Nipper's Lullaby* and *Our Court Ball.*

Koster & Bials' audiences were as full of silk hats as an undertakers' convention. The amusement world was agog with speculation about the invention.

Charles Frohman, the rising star of theatrical magnates, was in that first night audience. He gave the *New York Times* an interview.

"That settles scenery," said Frohman. "Painted trees that do not move, waves that get up a few feet and stay there, everything in scenery wc simulate on our stages will have to go. Now that art can make us believe that we see actual living nature the dead things of the stage must go.

"And think what can be done with this invention! For instance, Chevalier comes on the screen. The audience would get all the pantomime of his coster songs. The singing, words fitted to gestures and movements, could be done from the wings or behind the curtain. And so we could have on the stage at any time any artist, dead or alive, who ever faced Mr. Edison's invention.

"That in itself is great enough, but the possibilities of the Vitascope as the successor of painted scenery are illimitable."

Charles Frohman died before the screen had attained its greater triumphs of the modern period, but his prophecies have been translated into terms of practice. In a large sense the living shadows of the Vitascope have supplanted what he called the "dead things of the stage." Even the name that he left, Charles Frohman, Inc., to-day is the incidental property of Famous Players-Lasky, a motion picture corporation.

That showing of the Vitascope on the night of April 23, 1896, at Koster & Bials' Music Hall was the true introduction of the motion picture to Broadway. Herald Square, the scene of that premiere, was the heart of that gilded thoroughfare then. In thirty years the *Herald* has become a memory and ten blocks up Broadway, Times Square rules as the capital of the amusement world, while on above in the northward path of Manhattan's march is the Capitol, the world's greatest theatre, with a weekly turnover of more money than the first years of the whole motion picture industry saw.

To place this entry of the motion picture screen in a sense of time, note that the Greater New York consolidation bill, creating the city of to-day, had just been passed by the state legislature, and that this was the last year of the administration of Grover Cleveland, Democrat, statesman and fisherman of honored memory.

The same Monday newspapers which reviewed the offerings of the Vitascope at Koster & Bials' carried a story of a Sunday sermon by the Reverend D. Asa Blackburn, pastor of the Church of the Strangers, on the theme of "You can not serve God and skylark on a bicycle." That was indeed a dim long ago. The bicycle as the outstanding diversion of the public before the movie era was then the orthodox subject of attack by the church. The fundamental sin of the bicycle was in its involvement of the use of legs, the existence of which was not admitted by any proper female person. Worse yet, the bicycle led to bloomers, just as inevitably as, the Maine Puritans say, "oysters lead to dancing." The Reverend Mr. Blackburn lost the great opportunity to have been the first to denounce the movies, which daily reveal more and better legs than the entire world's output of bicycles from the reign of Queen Victoria to date.

BOSLEY CROWTHER
Marcus Loew Is Willing

Bosley Crowther was the motion picture reviewer for the New York Times *from 1940 to 1967. His history of Metro-Goldwyn-Mayer was the first important "biography" of a Hollywood studio. Referring to the famous trademark lion of M-G-M, he called it* The Lion's Share *(N.Y., E. P. Dutton, 1957). On pages 22 to 24, he tries to recreate the mood and interests of Marcus Loew, a fur salesman and real estate investor, as he began to become involved in buying and operating movie theaters.*

Loew's Incorporated eventually became a very prosperous firm, with many of the biggest and best downtown theaters in the major eastern cities. This prosperity was based on a conservative policy of cooperation with the Edison patents combine. Loew did not add production facilities to his assets until he bought the Metro studio in 1920 and Goldwyn in 1924.

. . . it was actually a modest investment, one of several that he and Baehr made, in a New York apartment building, on West 111th Street, that brought Loew into the orbit of the entertainment world. This is the way it happened: the fur salesman was standing one Sunday morning in front of his 111th Street building, looking it over with the appraising eye of an efficient landlord, when he noticed another gentleman looking at a building down the street. Instinctively, he approached his neighbor, began to converse with him and discovered that he, too, was an investor in the adjoining real estate.

The two compared notes. The stranger was frankly dissatisfied. He soon sensed, however, that he was talking to a man who knew whereof he spoke, so far as the business of managing real estate was concerned. It is also likely that Loew saw *he* was talking to a man who was pitifully inadequate in that ability but was doing all right otherwise. Indeed, it is safe to imagine that Loew clearly recognized his man and tactfully arranged the chance encounter, for Loew was an avid theatre fan and the stranger was an up-and-coming actor. He was David Warfield, who had recently made a moderate hit as a shabby Jewish character in a revue called *The Merry Whirl*.

As a consequence of their sidewalk meeting and the acquaintanceship that developed between the two men, Loew was asked by Warfield if he would help with his real estate. Graciously, Loew accepted and the two soon became firm friends. Warfield often said later that he was struck by Loew's talent for finance and by his ability to make the property pay. Loew, in turn, was no doubt flattered to be the friend and adviser of a rising theatrical star. Warfield was yet to reach his zenith, but he was on the way.

The year of this fortunate encounter was 1899. For some time thereafter, Loew continued as a successful salesman of furs. But already another close friendship was drawing him toward his destiny.

On his selling trips West, the hustling Marcus had met Adolph Zukor and Morris Kohn, a pair of Chicago fur merchants anxious to move to New York. Loew helpfully gave them suggestions and found an apartment for the Zukor family when they moved. The amiable Loews and Zukors became block neighbors and intimate friends.

Now, Zukor and Kohn were also looking for something other than furs in which to make an investment. An opportunity came when a relative of Kohn invited them to put some money into a penny arcade. The principal promoter of this venture was a former Buffalo merchant, Mitchell Mark, who had attempted the new arcade business in Buffalo and in uptown New York City. Prospering in these locations, he wanted to try downtown New York and had his eye on a vacant dairy kitchen on Fourteenth Street, near thriving Union Square. But the holders of the property weren't eager to rent it to a hustler of arcades. They wanted a more reliable tenant. So Zukor and Kohn were invited to invest and sign the lease, which would be assurance, of a sort, that the rent would be paid.

The venture was readily attractive, for the novelty of penny arcades was rapidly gaining popularity under the label of "electric vaudeville." These bright little open-front "parlors," crowded with assorted machines that vended a variety of amusements and peephole motion pictures for a penny a vend, were especially appropriate and alluring to the curiosity-seeking sidewalk trade. Zukor and Kohn liked the prospect, so they joined with Mark and his group to form the Automatic Vaudeville Company, which opened its Fourteenth Street arcade in 1903.

Inevitably the venture intrigued Zukor's good friend, Marcus Loew. He closely watched the operation with a more than objective eye. He noted the easy luring of patrons and the clattering cascade of coins. Soon he took his resolution. When the company decided to expand and open other arcades in Philadelphia, Boston and Newark, Loew asked to be let in. Zukor and Kohn, needing capital, readily agreed.

Since this was the entertainment business, Loew had talked it over with his friend, David Warfield, who was now starring grandly in David Belasco's *The Auctioneer.* Warfield was all for the venture and wanted to invest in it, too. Loew, parlaying his friendships, arranged it with Zukor and Kohn. Warfield got $15,000 worth of securities out of his safe deposit box and added that to Loew's lesser investment. They were in Automatic Vaudeville.

Through the winter and spring of 1904, Loew followed the fortunes of the arcades. Baehr, his conservative partner, was disapproving and aloof. Impressed by their parlors' prosperity, Loew thought of full-time occupation with them. But there wasn't room for him in the company. Besides, as he once explained, "Adolph didn't think I was worth $2,500 a year, and I had the same opinion of him."

About this time, Kohn concocted an ingenious device for performing the happy function of collecting the pennies from the machines. He rigged up a little electric railway with a train of open cars which ran around under the machines at regular intervals and caught the pennies as they were automatically dumped. The display became an added free attraction for the crowds. It was a literal and captivating spectacle of money rolling in.

Friends of Loew later insisted it was that ingenious electric train, groaning under carloads of pennies, that finally decided him. Any business that offered such immediate and obvious cash returns was irresistible to the fur merchant who had been battling with credits for years. He talked to Baehr and Warfield. Would they go along with him if he pulled his money out of the Zukor arcade and put it into one of his own? Baehr was not enthusiastic. He didn't want to lose his "outside" man, who he realized was largely responsible for the moderate prosperity of their firm. But Warfield again was agreeable. Loew looked around for a place. Soon he found one—a vacant store at 172 West Twenty-third Street, off the southeast corner of Seventh Avenue. He and Warfield removed their investments from Automatic Vaudeville. With a little more money raised from Loew's mother-in-law, from a merchant friend, Morris Drucker, and, indeed, with a small amount from Baehr, they dumped it together and started the

People's Vaudeville Company on Nov. 14, 1904.

A lease was taken on the Twenty-third Street property, Loew fixed it up as an arcade, and it was opened for business in January, 1905. Loew was employed as general manager at $100 a week, plus profits, receivable in stock.

Thus the little furrier was started in the entertainment business—on his own.

Marcus Loew

TERRY RAMSAYE
The Screen Theatre Arrives

Terry Ramsaye cannot precisely pinpoint the elusive history of the nickelodeon, giving us only some of the instances of it in Los Angeles, San Francisco, and even in Newcastle, Pennsylvania (the Warner brothers). But he is quite certain that the motion picture exchange—that is, the precedent for the whole process of distribution—occurred in Oakland in 1902. He reports this in A Million and One Nights, *op.cit. pages 425 to 427.*

*Robert Grau (*The Theatre of Science, *1914, pages 28-35) gives considerable credit to a man named Archie L. Shepard for building popular audiences for hour-long runs of short films in the midwest, New England, and finally in New York City in 1904-1905. Even with a careful selection of European, American, and specially made subjects and providing his own publicity staff, he had great difficulty in securing bookings in the large halls he wanted. Grau never met Shepard and lost track of him after the nickelodeons became the accepted form of exhibition.*

All the way down through screen history the art of the motion picture and the industry of the motion picture have run a relay of alternate steps of progress. Each advance in the art has brought a resulting advance in the business. It was therefore inevitable that the period of the birth of the story picture should be marked by important commercial departures and developments.

The morning of April 16, 1902, a reader of the theater advertising column on page one of the *Los Angeles Times* would have discovered a modest announcement:

ELECTRIC THEATER, 262 S. Main, opp. 3rd St.
New Place of Amusement
Up to date high class moving picture entertainment, especially for ladies and children. See the *Capture of the Biddle Bros., New York, in a Blizzard,* and many other interesting and exciting scenes. An hour's amusement and genuine fun for
                10 CENTS ADMISSION
                Evenings: 7:30 to 10:30

This was the way that Thomas L. Tally informed Los Angeles that the motion picture was making its début as an independent entertainer. He saw that its destiny was not locked up in the peep show machines in his phonograph parlor.

The advertisement of the next day indicates that the business of the opening night was so encouraging that Mr. Tally had decided to open his house in the afternoon with "matinees for children, five cents admission."

By April 27, Tally had discovered an improvement in nomenclature calculated to make the public understand better what it was all about. He called the Electric Theatre's program "A vaudeville of motion pictures lasting one hour." The bill had also been improved by adding pictures of Prince Henry of Prussia who was then visiting the United States. This show continued through May, and on June 1 there was a complete change of program to make room for *A Great Bullfight, fought before President Diaz and his entire Cabinet in the City of Mexico, Feb. 2, 1902*. Melies' *Trip to the Moon, Gulliver's Travels, The Kingdom of the Fairies*, and similar subjects appeared on the Electric's screen.

When Edison's *The Great Train Robbery* arrived, Tally was so filled with enthusiasm at its success that he sold his theatre and took the road, showing the exciting one reel super feature of 1903 all over the West. He later returned to Los Angeles and resumed the operation of motion picture theatres. He has been an exhibitor continuously for more than twenty years.

Closely contemporary with Tally were David Grauman of San Francisco, father of Sid Grauman, who now exhibits pictures in Los Angeles, and Anthony Lubelski of Oakland. Also Fred Lincoln in Seattle and Charles Peckham in Spokane conducted motion picture shows in the same period. They appear on the old accounts of George Kleine's Chicago concern with standing orders for films as early as 1901.

Early in 1903 Harry Warner and his brothers, now engaged in the motion picture on a large and international scale, opened a ninety-nine seat store show called the Cascade Theatre in their home town of Newcastle, Pa. The chairs were hired by the day from the town undertaker and on days when there was a funeral the audiences at the theatre had to take their amusement standing up.

All of the first theatres alike had to purchase their films outright from the makers in the East or their agents, concerns like the Kleine Optical Company of Chicago, or Richard Nehls' film department at Montgomery Ward's. The standard price for motion pictures then was ten or eleven cents a foot, making a reel cost approximately a hundred dollars. This was a heavy burden of expense upon such modest enterprises as the first screen theaters. The film exhausted its entertainment value in any community long before it was worn out. The remaining value in it was a dead asset on the hands of the theatre man. A change in the system of distribution had to come before any considerable growth of the industry was possible.

Harry J. Miles, who had returned from his adventures with the motion picture camera in Alaska, was struck with an idea. The idea had more gold in it than was ever taken out of Alaska. There was Grauman buying a reel a week for a hundred dollars to show it in San Francisco and there was Lubelski doing the same thing in Oakland across the bay. It was the summer of 1902. Herbert Miles, Harry's brother and partner on the Alaskan expedition, had gone to New York to sell their films to Biograph and had connected with that concern as an independent sales agent.

"If you will send me some films," Harry J. wrote to Herbert Miles, "I can rent a reel to Grauman for a week for $50 and then get another $50 from Lubelski. After that whatever we get is profit."

So the motion picture exchange was born.

This first exchange was the parlor floor of the boarding house where Harry Miles was stopping, at 116 Turk street in San Francisco.

It seemed an interesting but unimportant venture then. But it was the most important development in the motion picture since the invention of the projection machine.

From that point onward distribution developed until it became the controlling element of the film institution.

MOVING PICTURE WORLD
The Nickelodeon

An unknown writer in The Moving Picture World and View Photographer *(Vol. 1, No. 9, May 4, 1907, p. 140) gives us a graphic description of what it was like to own and operate a nickelodeon, a store-front theater devoted entirely to the presentation of motion pictures. This article was reprinted in George Pratt's anthology,* Spellbound in Darkness *(Rochester, N.Y., University of Rochester, 1966). Its language links the five cent theaters with side shows at the circus.*

There is a new thing under the sun – at least new within a short period of time – and entirely new in the sense that the public is waking up to what it means.

It is the 5-cent theater.

The nickel place of amusement made its appearance with no greater blare of trumpets than the noise of its phonograph horn and the throaty persuasions of its barker. It came unobtrusively, in the still of the night. It is multiplying faster than guinea pigs, and within a few months has attained to that importance where we may no longer snub it as one of the catch-pennies of the street.

One day a Pittsburg man hit on the 5-cent theater idea. He equipped a building at a cost of $40,000, brought a phonograph with a big horn, hired a leather-lunged barker and threw his doors open.

The theater was such an unqualified go in Pittsburg that the men who started in competition with the originator of the scheme decided that a new popular chord had been struck in the amusement line. They hiked to Chicago and opened a theater near State and Van Buren streets. The theater prospered from the moment the barker first opened his mobile face to extol the wonders of the show "upon the inside." That was the beginning in Chicago.

Of course, they were opened in other cities, until now it is estimated there are from 2,500 to 3,000 5-cent theaters in the United States.

One of its chief attractions is the knowledge that if you are stung it is for "only a nickel, five pennies, a half a dime," as the barker says, and that if you don't like the show they can inflict only fifteen minutes of it on you.

Here are the ingredients of a 5-cent theater:

One storeroom, seating from 200 to 500 persons.
One phonograph with extra large horn.
One young woman cashier.
One electric sign.
One cinematograph, with operator.
One canvas on which to throw the pictures.
One piano.
One barker.
One manager.
As many chairs as the store will hold.
A few brains and a little tact. Mix pepper and salt to taste.

After that all you have to do is to open the doors, start the phonograph and carry the money to the bank. The public does the rest.

It makes little difference what time of day you go to a 5-cent theater. The doors are opened as early in the forenoon as there is a chance of gathering in a few nickels, the downtown theaters opening earlier than those in the outlying districts to accommodate the visitors. Each "performance" lasts fifteen minutes. At the end of each a sign is thrown from the cinematograph on the canvas announcing that those who came late may stay for the next "performance."

Often they stay for several. After they find out that nobody cares and that they can stay all day and far into the night and bring their lunch if they want to, they leave, disappointed because nobody tried to get the best of them.

They are great places for the foot-sore shopper, who is not used to cement sidewalks, to rest: and it took the aforesaid foot-sore shoppers about one minute to find this out. It is much more comfortable than to take street-car rides to rest, and they don't have to pay the return nickel.

The name of the play is flashed on the canvas, so that it may be identified if ever seen again. Understand that the young men who sing the "illustrated songs" are the only live performers in these theaters. The rest is moving pictures: and that is the startling part of the great favor with which these theaters have been received by the public.

The plays that are put on at the 5-cent theaters are for the most part manufactured abroad. Paris is a great producing center. London has numerous factories that grind them out. They are bought by the foot.

This system of buying drama and comedy by the foot has its distinct advantages. If the piece grows dull at any point the manager can take a pair of shears and cut out a few yards or rods, thereby enlivening the whole performance.

The worst charge that has been made against the 5-cent theaters is that some of them put on pieces of the blood-and-thunder type, depicting murders, hold-ups, train robberies and other crimes. This charge has led the managers of the new style theaters into a hot discussion with the uplifters of the public morals.

Few people realize the important part these theaters are beginning to play in city life. They have been looked upon largely as places of trivial amusement, not calling for any serious consideration. They seem, however, to be something that may become one of the greatest forces for good or for evil in the city.

On the other hand, in the congested districts the 5-cent theaters are proving a source of much innocent entertainment. The mothers do not have to "dress" to attend them, and they take the children and spend many restful hours in them at very small expense.

The possibilities of them in an educational way are unlimited. The tuberculosis society already has seen this and has under way a plan for having the cinematograph theaters show pictures which will instruct the public about precautions to be taken against consumption. A great many educational lines might be developed among the people in this way.

Albert Einstein visiting Carl Laemmle at Universal

Chapter 2

Earliest Production Companies

> *This was an industry that deserved the same kind of attention as any other legitimate industry.*
> —A. H. Giannini

Thomas A. Edison, precursor and prototype for future movie tycoons, was keenly aware of the money-making potential of most of his patented inventions. In none of his enterprises, however, did he reveal more acumen and acquisitiveness than in his film production operations. He did not limit himself to equipment sales but went immediately into the production (as we say nowadays) of "software." He built the first movie studio, a sensible, ugly, light-controlled contraption that turned with the sun. It looked like a huge police wagon and was shortly dubbed "the black Maria." And he set up a company under his own name which continued for years as one of the major producers.

Edison had been accustomed, of course, to selling or leasing his kinetoscope machines together with a batch of the films he made that were designed to be put through them. As soon as movies began to be projected on screens, he faced the prospect of selling pictures to strange people in store-front situations who owned projectors and could just as easily buy product from other sources, some of whom claimed they had patents, too. Edison's thoughts naturally turned to the ways in which he might keep control of any income attributable directly or indirectly to any of his patents.

32   THE FIRST TYCOONS

It took a while to bring everyone in line, especially Biograph, but it was the superdeal of all time while it lasted (1908-1915). Edison's "trust" in its two corporate forms (the Motion Picture Patents Company and the General Film Company) first signed up all the major producers, then tried to buy out all the distributors of the day, and finally told all the theater owners they would be charged a fee for the use of projectors and a footage fee for all films.

The "trust" was a crabbed and accounting-minded bunch. They were determined never to allow films to be longer than about twelve or fifteen minutes (one reel) and never to let performers become "stars" and therefore expensive.

Of course this couldn't last long in the land of the free and the home of the brave, especially when there were people whose livelihoods were threatened. Carl Laemmle and William Fox were the most notable of the independents who resisted the trust. Between the volatile world of show business and the surviving political progressivism of the antitrust laws, the whole monopoly arrangement finally crumbled. But it established in the beginning a model of vertical control which film tycoons—including Laemmle, Fox, and Zukor—admired and copied, more or less, for 40 years.

Today it is a mildly interesting scholarly controversy whether the Trust was enough of a monopoly to work its will on the whole industry even in the beginning. Another issue is whether the independent producers and distributors outside the Trust would have been able to do as much on their own if there had not been divided counsels and occasional support within the Trust membership. Still, it took courage to be independent. Carl Laemmle was the subject of 289 lawsuits and even went to Cuba for a while to escape the Edison investigators.

The Laemmle story is an especially appealing one. An immigrant from Germany, he had tried many kinds of jobs, from bookkeeping and selling newspapers to farming. He later managed a retail dry goods store in Milwaukee and had begun to set up shop in Chicago when the steady income of the nickelodeons caught his attention and he took a plunge into movies. When the crisis came, he could have sold out to the Patents Company, but he saw their proposition as basically unfair not only to him but to everyone. He chose to fight in the advertising columns for freedom of access to the screen.

Earliest Production Companies 33

In later years, Universal was known as a home for Laemmle relatives, but "Uncle Carl" was also an innovator. He gets credit for (1) discovering and training Irving Thalberg, later head of production at M-G-M (2) persuading Florence Lawrence to leave Biograph and come to his Independent Motion Picture Company, thereby starting off the "star system" and (3) agreeing to a production proposal by a young unknown director who had worked with Griffith, thereby unleashing Erich von Stroheim on the industry.

ROBERT M. HENDERSON
Biograph

Robert Henderson's careful study of documents and memoirs at the Museum of Modern Art Film Library, D. W. Griffith: The Years at Biograph (N.Y., Farrar, Straus, Giroux, 1970) includes a description on pages 5-8 of the conflict between Edison and Biograph before the Trust was finally formed in 1908. We are also treated to a brief tour of the building at 11 East 14th in New York City, where Griffith began his career as a director.

The principal movie companies in 1908 were Edison, Kalem, Vitagraph, Lubin, Selig, Essanay, Méliés, and Pathé. A bitter patent war had been fought by the Edison Company against the others for several years prior to 1907, but in the fall of 1907 an agreement had been reached. These eight companies were licensed to use the Edison equipment, especially the Edison camera, and the group became known as the Edison Licensees. Remaining outside this group was The American Mutoscope and Biograph Company.

This company, formed in 1895, had been an outgrowth of the friendship between Edison's assistant, William Laurie Dickson, and Henry Norton Marvin, a partner in the machinery firm of Marvin and Casler, located in Canastota, New York. Dickson, one of the principal developers of the motion picture, having become disaffected with Edison, suggested to Marvin a new device for competing with the Kinetoscope that would depend upon a series of flipped still photographs viewed by reflected light and producing the effect of motion, rather than upon the strip of film used in the Edison patented machine. After successful demonstrations of the new device, Marvin proceeded to form a company for the manufacture of this new peep-show machine, called a Mutoscope. Backing for the new company came from various sources, including Abner McKinley (brother of the 1896 Presidential candidate, William McKinley) and a bank, the New York Security and Trust Company.[1]

Marvin had gone to Edison to secure the use of the Edison camera for making the still photographs to be used in the Mutoscope, but Edison had refused. The new company therefore undertook to invent a camera for their own use which would not infringe on the Edison patents. This they were able to do, using the advice and knowledge of Dickson concerning the patented features of the Edison camera that had to be avoided. The actual design of the new camera was credited to Marvin's original partner, Herman Casler, since it was not desirable to have Dickson too closely associated with the project because of his former connection with Edison. The new camera was patented by the new film company, christened the American Mutoscope Company. The name "Biograph" was added when the company began making films for projection on screens. To distinguish these films from those made for the Mutoscopes, they were named "Biographs." Before the end of the period covered in this book, the company changed its name to The Biograph Company, having dropped the production of pictures for the Mutoscopes in the spring of 1908.

At the very start of the new firm's history, one specific event in New York successfully launched Biograph on its future course of presenting motion pictures projected on large screens. On October 12, 1896, they presented at Hammerstein's Olympia Music Hall short films of William McKinley in the midst of his campaign for the Presidency. As the New York *Tribune* reported the next day:

> The biggest part of the enthusiasm began when a view of a McKinley and Hobart parade in Canton was shown. The cheering was incessant as long as the line was passing across the screen, and it grew much greater when the title of the next picture appeared: "Major McKinley at Home."
> ... Seven boxes were occupied by members of the National Republican Committee and their friends, who came to see Major McKinley walk across his lawn.

Biograph had been invited to join the Edison Licensees but refused, claiming that the patents it held on its own camera were equal to those of the Edison Company. This refusal to join prevented the Edison interests from exercising a monopoly.

Now, in 1908, Biograph's financial fortunes were declining. The Empire Trust Company, another of their backers, became worried about an outstanding Biograph loan of $200,000 and sent Jeremiah J. Kennedy to look into their affairs. His instructions were to liquidate the company, if necessary, to protect the bank's investment. Kennedy, instead, decided to attempt a revival of the fading company, becoming the president and retaining Henry

Marvin as vice-president and general manager. Kennedy remained the company president throughout Griffith's association with Biograph.[2]

Throughout 1908 Kennedy and Marvin were involved in negotiations designed to maneuver the Edison group into recognition of the Biograph patents and to accord Biograph a favored position among the licensees. During the period of the negotiations, the Biograph camera was kept from use. The battle was not resolved until December 18, 1908, when the Edison Company capitulated after Kennedy threatened to place the Biograph camera on the open market, licensing its use to all comers. Terry Ramsaye[3] has recorded J. J. Kennedy's final threat, which turned the tide of the negotiations:

> "Say!" Kennedy exploded, "if that agreement does not go through, just the way it is, without the change of one word in it, Biograph is going to bust this business wide open. We will put our cameras on the market and license everybody! If we can't get together and control this business, we will make a first-class wreck of it – and we'll have it now."

The new combine, including The American Mutoscope and Biograph Company, was renamed the Motion Picture Patents Company, although popular parlance dubbed it the Film Trust, and its new chief executive officer was Jeremiah J. Kennedy.

By 1908 Biograph was located in studios and offices at 11 East Fourteenth Street in New York City. The building was a typical New York brownstone with four stories, and a commercial basement opening on the street. Entrance to the stores was gained by descending a half flight from the street level. Entrance to the Biograph offices was made by ascending through a set of double doors and then up another short flight to the main floor. The building had originally been a private home, and in terms of physical layout very little above the basement level had changed from its former private status. The tenant before Biograph had been the Steck Piano Company.[4] Biograph leased the property for $5,000 a year, rerenting the basement stores. A center hallway ran almost the length of the building, terminating in a large room at the rear that had once been the ballroom. It was this room that Biograph had converted into an indoor studio. On either side of the hallway were the business offices, quite literally the "front offices." The projection facilities where film was viewed, edited, and prepared for shipment were located on the floors above.[5] A building in Hoboken, New Jersey – renamed by J. J. Kennedy a "film laboratory"—was used to process film. The exterior of the building was similar to hundreds of others in New York. A large sign advertising a Singer Sewing Center next door was reflected in the first-floor windows. There were no large signs proclaiming the nature of the business within. The building has long since vanished and the site is presently (1970) occupied by a modern apartment building.

NOTES

1. Gordon Hendricks: *Beginnings of the Biograph* (New York, 1964), p. 30.
2. G. W. Bitzer: Unpublished notes about Biograph, in the possession of the Museum of Modern Art Film Library, New York City.
3. Terry Ramsaye: *A Million and One Nights* (New York, 1927), p. 472.
4. Linda Arvidson Griffith: *When the Movies Were Young* (New York, 1925). Mrs. Griffith noted that the successor to the Biograph Company on Fourteenth Street was a sculptor named Calder, the father of the creator of the mobile, Alexander Calder.
5. Blanche Sweet, in a taped interview with the author, June 17, 1965, New York City.

PAUL C. SPEHR
Pathé Frères

Paul C. Spehr, motion picture specialist at the U.S. Library of Congress, wrote a history of movie production in New Jersey for a special exhibition at the Newark Museum, published by Morgan Press in 1977. On pages 70, 72, and 74 of this book, The Movies Begin, *he reports on the history and activities of the leading foreign film company represented in the U.S., one of the members of the Edison Patents Company.*

The French began an invasion of New Jersey in 1910 when Pathé Frères, the largest filmmaking company in the world, converted a warehouse in Bound Brook, N.J., into a movie studio.

From 1896 until 1910 French movie companies had been most aggressive and had captured a large part of the world market. Pathé Frères was looked upon as a world leader in the infant film industry. Their move to the United States was a recognition that the American market had grown to a point where it required a product tailored to American audiences. Even more important, it recognized that there was an American film product that was of increasing significance on the international market. The French company was meeting its growing competition on its own grounds.

The decision to make this move was that of J.A. Berst who had been sent earlier to manage Pathé's interests in the United States. He recommended that specialized production, made in the United States, was the logical course for the company.

It is significant that the first film released, *The Girl From Arizona,* was not an American-made version of French film, but another New Jersey-made western. If imitation is the sincerest form of flattery, Pathé clearly recognized that the growing American trade in adventure and action pictures represented a challenge to its leadership. The films that followed continued to be "American" in style, shunning imitation of the French product.

J.A. Berst's recommendation also included the establishment of an American version of the newsreel release which Pathé had pioneered in France. The newsreel was established early at the Bound Brook studio and remained there for several decades. It proved to be a consistently popular base for the American operation, with an estimated circulation to 13,000 American movie houses at its peak of popularity.

Pathé's release program prior to World War I consisted primarily of French-made films, with the American product scattered among them for variety.

To staff its new operation, Pathé sent a basic crew of experienced French filmmakers, led by director general Louis Gasnier. A supplementary staff of Americans was hired to fill other necessary production roles and the staffing became increasingly like that of its American competitors. However, Pathé and the other French companies which also opened American branches — Méliés, Gaumont and Éclair — infused a sufficient number of French filmmakers into the American production system to make France a major contributor to the growth of the American film industry.

By 1912, Pathé had completed modern studios in Jersey City, at 1 Congress Street, a site overlooking the Hudson and the towers of Manhattan. These studios were to be the major center of Pathé production for the next eight years. It was here that Pearl White, already an experienced movie player, arrived to become an authentic movie legend as Pauline in *The Perils of Pauline*.

The popularity of this serial and several that followed it, *The Exploits of Elaine, Pearl of the Army* and *The House of Hate*, has rather obscured the fact that Pathé was the source of a wide variety of motion picture productions. Its studios made short films of all types and ventured cautiously into feature film production.

Although Jersey City and Bound Brook remained the basic centers of production, studios were built in Long Beach, Cal. (producing under the name "Balboa"), and an affiliated company operated at Ithaca, N.Y., run by the Whartons, who regularly produced films under the Pathé name as well as their own.

In 1914 the French parent company sold its American facilities to Merrill, Lynch and Co. which gradually changed the management and the pattern of production and distribution. Several subproduction companies were formed with names like Eclectic (producer of *The Perils of Pauline*), Balboa, Astra and Arrow Film Co. Pathé became primarily a releasing organization and the name was eventually changed to Pathé Exchange, a firm prominent on the American film scene until the late 1920's.

Diversity remained a hallmark of the Pathé operation. In addition to the many films shot at New Jersey studios, it released the popular animated cartoons of J.R. Bray and the west coast company made a comedy series featuring "Lonesome Luke," played by a youthful Harold Lloyd.

The Jersey City studios also spawned talent. In addition to Pearl White, players as diverse as Henry B. Walthall, Billy Quirk, Ernest Truex, Creighton Hale, Fannie Ward, Frank Crane and Irene Castle appeared in Pathé pictures. Two men who were later prominent directors, Raoul Walsh and Henry King, began their movie careers as actors with Pathé. Cameraman Arthur Miller, later to win three Academy Awards for cinematography, worked for much of the decade of the teens as a newsreel and studio cameraman, learning most of the basic skills of his profession there.

Later in the decade, as production shifted more to feature filmmaking, Pathé began to stress its role as a movie distributor and its production activities became more diverse. In 1919 the company headquarters, which had been in Jersey City, were moved to New York City. The production facilities in Jersey City were phased out, although the newsreel company continued to be based in Bound Brook.

ROBERT GRAU
Help from Overseas

Robert Grau was a publicity writer who collected some of his articles in a book called The Theatre of Science *(N.Y., Broadway Publishing Co., 1914). On pages 42–46 he honors the memory of John J. Murdock, who chose to protect his interests in vaudeville and at the same time promote the success of the independents who stayed out of the Trust. He seems to have acted as a kind of benevolent agent for them, getting films and film stock from abroad and lobbying in Congress to forestall tariffs which would benefit Edison's group.*

One of the film pioneers to make his impress first in the West was John J. Murdock, whose achievements in vaudeville have already been recorded in this series of volumes. Murdock exerted the main influence in the organization of the "independents."

It must be understood that in the period from 1896 to 1902 the manufacturers of film in this country were the Vitagraph, Edison and Biograph companies, later augmented by W. N. Selig and George K. Spoor, the last two operating from Chicago. Mr. Spoor afterward was joined by Gilbert M. Anderson, the company being called the S and A (Essanay). Murdock being in Chicago in practical control of vaudeville and affiliated with the Keith and Kohl interests which operated the majority of the best vaudeville theatres, was looked to by his associates for some remedy to existing conditions. These were the days of guerilla warfare, and the duper was in his glory. Subjects were no sooner filmed than they were immediately duplicated. The vaudeville managers having learned the lesson of discipline and organization, authorized Murdock to go as far as he liked with a view to establishing an impregnable competition; but it was 1906 before it became apparent to thinking minds that something should be undertaken seriously. It was from this state of affairs and the gradual decline of public interest in the period from 1902–1906 that created the organization of what is now known as the Motion Picture Patents Company.

On June 10, 1908, this company was formed with the combined American manufacturers, namely, the Edison, Vitagraph and Biograph, of New York and Orange, N. J.; Lubin, of Philadelphia;

Essanay and Selig, of Chicago; Kalem and Melies, of New York, and George Kleine, of Chicago, who controlled then the Gaumont and Urban Eclipse output for this country. The Pathé Frères were already strongly entrenched in the American market, and of course were included in the combination, which as an entity was about as formidable an amalgamation as this country had known up to that time, and the vaudeville managers concluded that one of the objects of the amalgamation was to prevent the use of its product in the theatres where vaudeville was the basic attraction. It was commonly reported that a measure was to be adopted forbidding the service of film in cooperation with vaudeville acts. Also it was claimed that the so-called "trust" had so fixed things that foreign manufacturers of film could obtain no footing in this country.

Such was the state of affairs in 1908, when a contract was placed before the members of the so-called Film Rental Association. This contract, duly signed, placed the Motion Picture Patents Company in the position of controlling 98 per cent of the film output, a condition that caused the United Vaudeville interests of the country to look after their welfare. Murdock immediately formed the International Projecting and Producing Company. This was within forty-eight hours after the formation of the Patents company.

Before the ink was dry on the signatures of the Film Rental Association the cables under the ocean were carrying messages from Murdock that resulted in the formation of an organization comprising the best film manufacturers abroad. In a few days either the principals or the representatives of this large body of motion picture experts were on the seas with film, bound for this country. Like a bolt from a clear sky came the announcement in a Chicago trade publication—"The Show World"—that the International Projecting and Producing Company was ready to release 20 reels or more, if demand warranted it, each week. As far as quantity of film was concerned, the new-born independents were on a par with the amalgamated American manufacturers.

Though this was something of a surprise to the Patents company, its officers figured that it still held the trump card up its sleeve, and at the next session of Congress they brought to bear all their political influence to have a prohibitive duty placed on film in the Aldrich tariff bill. Had they succeeded, the deathknell to Independent moving pictures would have been rung. Murdock went to Washington, and remained there during the entire summer, while Congress was in session on the Payne-Aldrich tariff bill. There was a continuous fight during the entire summer, between the so-called trust faction and Murdock, representing the Independents, which he had formed. But when the war at Washington was over, instead of the duty having been raised, Murdock succeeded in getting the duty lowered on all imported moving pictures, both raw and manufactured film.

Soon after this, Murdock's International Company began to release the foreign-manufactured film, but soon learned they were handicapped to some extent by not having American-manufactured goods, to have their program compare favorably with the trust. It was then that he succeeded in getting men to start manufacturing American product. Messrs. Baumann and Kessel, the first independent producers, started the Bison; Mr. Carl Laemmle started the Imp Manufacturing Company; Messrs. Thanhouser, P. A. Powers, and about ten or twelve others immediately set to work to manufacture American films, under the direction of Murdock, as he had agreed to protect them against the trust claim of infringements. He organized a strong force of lawyers in New York and Chicago to protect all these people. Working night and day, he broke down in health, and had to take a trip to Europe. When it was announced that he was going to leave, it was joyous news to the trust, and the Independents felt for the moment like a ship without a captain; but they soon found there was still the strong law force to protect them during his absence. Murdock remained in Europe a short time, and, after returning, made smooth sailing for the Independents, so they could supply a bill combining European and American manufactured goods equal to the Patents company output.

This completed, Murdock then retired to take a rest and regain his health, later returning to the vaudeville field, and allied himself with the United Booking Offices, where he is still active. However, even after retiring from the film interests, he was the advisor, and all the American manufacturers sought his advice. The Independents continued to succeed and build up, although handicapped and harassed by the opposition. The only great drawback they seemed to have was securing the raw material for the productions. The Patents company had a contract with Eastman whereby the Eastman Company would supply no one but the amalgamated manufacturers with the raw material, which made it necessary for the Independent manufacturers to depend upon Europe for their raw material. While some of it was up to the standard, at least fifty per cent was of an inferior grade, so that the losses were tremendous. The Independent manufacturers then sought Murdock's aid to secure for them the Eastman stock. This he succeeded in doing after a time, with the aid of two of his very close friends, E. F. Albee and Colonel T. C. Marceau.

The fact remains, had it not been for Murdock in the very beginning, it is doubtful whether there would have been any Independent moving-picture concerns aside from the Bison output in America to-day. Since the birth of the Independents, hundreds of new concerns have sprung up, and it is a question whether any of them ever stopped to think of the man who claims he made it possible for them to do business in the moving-picture field.

RICHARD GRIFFITH & ARTHUR MAYER
The Men Who Owned the Business

Richard Griffith, film critic and curator of the film collection at the Museum of Modern Art, collaborated on a picture book called The Movies *(N.Y., Simon and Schuster, 1957) with Arthur Mayer, an independent theater owner who had earlier worked in the Paramount offices in New York City. Pages 20-21 are a lively summary of the "trust fight," and we also get an introduction to Carl Laemmle.*

. . . the leading American companies of the day, Vitagraph, Selig, Essanay, Kalem, Biograph, Lubin, and Kleine, together with two important French concerns, Pathé and Melies, joined Edison in forming the Motion Picture Patents Company. In January 1909, the ten partners announced that they alone owned the right to photograph, develop, and print motion pictures, that they alone could do so under the patent laws of the U.S., Great Britain, France, Germany, and Italy, and that no license to do so would ever be issued to anyone else.

Having declared a monopoly on production, the combine speedily sought to extend its stranglehold to distribution and exhibition. It formed the General Film Company, which was to be its instrument of control over the wholesaling and retailing of pictures. The leading film exchanges were acquired and the exhibitors were informed that they could continue to operate only at the pleasure of General Film. Since the manufacturers controlled production, exhibitors could book only films made by the members of Motion Picture Patents; since they controlled the manufacture of projectors, exhibitors needed a license from General Film in order even to show the motion pictures of General Film itself. And that license cost each of them two dollars a week fifty-two weeks a year. This license fee was to net the General Film Company an income of $1,250,000 per year.

The nine producers whom Edison had so generously taken to his bosom could not believe their good luck. Their lawyers advised them that Motion Picture Patents and General Film constituted between them an "airtight trust," but that the beauty of it was that they could not be prosecuted under the Sherman Act because their monopoly was firmly based on patent protection. Their competitors were eliminated, their business standardized, and, best of all, the "riff-raff" of exhibitors far below them in the industry structure would have to pay them to continue to exist. The license fee was the hallmark of their impregnable position, or so they thought.

It proved, however, the rock on which the trust broke. The nickelodeon operators reacted to it much as the colonists of 1760 reacted to the Stamp Act. Legal it might or might not be, but it was taxation without representation, and they needed only leadership to declare their independence.

The nickelodeon operators found leadership in William Fox and Carl Laemmle, two exhibitors who had climbed into the distributing end of the business by operating "exchanges." Exchanges were at first literally just that: offices where exhibitors met to barter prints of films they had already used for others their patrons had not yet seen. When renting instead of buying films became the rule, the exchanges developed into wholesaling outlets, buying films in job lots from producers and renting them individually to nickelodeons. They were the middlemen between manufacturers and consumers, and as such had to be brought into the closed system General Film was creating. But when General Film announced that it was buying the leading independent exchanges and that those it did not condescend to buy out must get out, Laemmle and Fox refused either to sell or to quit. They proclaimed the right to run their businesses as they pleased, and to hell with the patent laws.

Their position seemed hopeless. Lately risen from obscurity, they lacked the capital which General Film with its vast resources could array against them in the form of lawsuits, injunctions, and boycotts. All they had on their side was the resentment of exhibitors against the trust and their willingness to flout its requirements whenever they could get away with it. But that turned out to be all they needed.

Fox at first contented himself with ignoring the Patents Company, although eventually he fought and won a lawsuit against the trust. But Laemmle declared open war. He created the character of "General Flimco," and in a series of cartoons contrasted the trust's wealth and greed with the plight of the small exhibitor. When the trust threatened to boycott exhibitors who dealt with him, Laemmle printed the threatening letters as evidence that General Film was a coercive monopoly. When the trust, as a precaution against exhibitors' "going independent," added to its exhibition contract a "3rd Condition" requiring the payment of the hated weekly license fee in advance and on a yearly basis, Laemmle declaimed, "Read that '3rd Condition' again. Take it home and play it on your pianola. Play it upside down, sidewise, before and behind. Tell, when you're all through, tell me what you think of it!!!" When the trust cut off his exchanges' supply of films, he began to make them himself, significantly calling his producing firm The Independent Motion-Picture Company. And all the time he harped on the frustration of exhibitors, horse-traders all, at the trust's rule that all films, good and bad, should be paid for at ten cents a foot.

"'Ten cents a foot" was indeed as good a war cry for Laemmle as "two dollars a week," and this the moguls completely failed to understand. The corporation lawyers, big-business executives, and financiers who controlled the trust believed that their films as well as everybody else's were shoddy stuff fit only for illiterates, and what was the use of trying to improve them? They were too far removed from their audiences to sense what exhibitors and exchange men knew at first hand—that this motley rabble of "immigrants, children, chambermaids, and streetcar conductors" wanted better films. As more and better independent films came on the market, more and more exhibitors were willing to pay high for them and unwilling to abide by the trust's ten cents a foot and two dollars a week. Long before General Film was abolished by judicial decision in 1915, it had become a hollow shell.

JOHN DRINKWATER
The Trust Fight

John Drinkwater, who had written a well-regarded biography of Abraham Lincoln, looked around for a more contemporary kind of hero to write about and accepted an offer from Carl Laemmle, so prominent publicly in the cause of independent film making. In The Life and Adventures of Carl Laemmle *(N.Y., G. P. Putnam's Sons, 1931) some of the flavor of the Laemmle personality in this crisis comes across (condensed from pages 65-74, 80-86, 110, 128-129).*

. . . It was not that Laemmle's personal interests were assailed. He was not a big enough man for the Trust to fear as an antagonist, but he was big enough to be welcomed as a confederate. Had he chosen at this time to comply with the Trust's demands, the accommodation would have been very richly rewarded. His refusal was inspired by genuine hatred for what he conceived to be abominable trade morals.

He considered the position. On reflection it became clear that the only hope lay in communicating his own sense of injustice to the rank and file of consumers throughout the country. . . .

He began to formulate a plan that in its daring and in its brilliant execution affords, I think, one of the most stirring episodes of modern industrial history.

It was based on no less formidable a realisation than that somehow in spite of the Trust he must produce pictures of his own, and somehow induce the exhibitors to defy the Trust by buying them. It was a gigantic undertaking, and Laemmle spent three months bracing himself to it. By April, 1909, his mind was made up, and on the 18th of that month *The Sunday Telegram* contained the following statement:

> The monotony of absolute quietness in film circles, both among Independents and the Patents people, was broken last week when it was announced that the Laemmle Film Service, with nine branches, had gone independent. . . .

He rented prominent advertising space in *The Show World* and *The Moving Picture News* on long contracts, and week after week he deluged the Trust with invective . . .

A company of players who shared Laemmle's dislike for the Trust had been engaged, and cameras had been secured from a producing firm that had recently gone out of business. The celluloid film, known as raw stock, was another matter. It was almost entirely in the control of Eastman, who was under agreement with the Trust to supply no independent producer. But the French firm Lumiere had recently opened an American office in New York, managed by Jules Brulatour. To him Laemmle turned, and finding the French Company unsympathetic to Trust authority, he was allowed a small ration of raw stock. The last obstacle to production was removed. He incorporated as "The Yankee Films Company." Dissatisfied with the name, he offered a prize for a better. "The Independent Moving Pictures Company of America" was suggested. Mr. Mapes of New York, who took the twenty-five dollars, was run close by Mr. Bradlet, also of New York, who, however, was awarded only a consolation prize for the same suggestion, since Mr. Mapes ingeniously adorned his entry with a trade-mark design bearing the legend "IMP." The name was to be famous in the film history of the following years. The first advertisement of the company, with Carl Laemmle as President, appeared in the early autumn:

First Release of IMP Films
Almost Ready.

There's no use pretending we are not excited about it, for we are. After weeks and months of terribly hard work and lavish outlay of coin, we are about to throw the product of our new factory upon the market. Watch! Listen! Wait! We're not going to make any rash claims, but we do promise you the grandest American-made moving pictures you ever saw.

And on October 23rd, this was followed by:

At last! At last!
With a soul full of hope and a heart full of pride and enthusiasm, I now announce the
First Release of "IMP" Films
Monday, October 25th!

Film exchanges and exhibitors by the hundred have been urging me to hurry up with this first release, but to all alike I have said: "None of the going-off-half-cocked business for mine!" I have held back week after week to be absolutely certain that everything is in ship shape. And I now present

"HIAWATHA"

Length 988 feet. Taken at the Falls of Minnehaha in the Land of the Dacotahs. And you can bet it is classy or I wouldn't make it my first release. The title explains the nature of the picture. It is taken from Longfellow's masterpiece of poesy and it is a gem of photography and acting. Following this I will release some more pictorial corkers and some screamingly funny stuff, bearing the true stamp of American humour. Get "Hiawatha" and see if you don't agree that it starts a brand new era in American moving pictures.

Carl Laemmle, President

My Motto will be: The best films that man's ingenuity can devise and the best films man's skill can execute. And no cheating on measurements.

All genuine "IMP" films bear this little trade mark which is fully protected by law. Address all IMP mail to

111, East 14th Street,
New York, N. Y.

Laemmle held the release back until the 25th, because that was his father's birthday.

"Hiawatha" was followed by eleven more releases by the end of the year; in 1910 there were a hundred, three companies of players being in operation, and the directors were allowed a week for the making of each picture; in 1911 the number rose to a hundred and twenty, and twenty-four were released in the first five weeks of 1912, at the end of which time the company was merged in the new Sales Company, an association of Laemmle with other independent producers who by then had followed his example.

Laemmle had been a man to disregard, then one to fear, and now he was a man to break. In spite of difficulties, both of time and equipment, IMP pictures soon began to reach a surprisingly high level of production. In February, 1912, that is to say little more than two years after the release of "Hiawatha," Laemmle could announce that west of Chicago he and his fellow independents were providing no less than fifty percent of the entire moving picture consumption.

Don't let old Gen. Flimco shake you down for two bones a week or anything else! He is laughing openly and brazenly at every exhibitor who is enough of a soft mark to stand for such a hold-up and shakedown. If you got anything for the money it would be all right. But what do you get? Protection? Don't be absurd! You are *less* protected in his hands than anywhere else on God's green footstool. Better films? If you think so it is because you probably have not seen any Independent films for the past few months. Or else you have been up against the *fake Independent* exchanges run for the purpose of hurting the independent game. No, dear old top, *you're not getting a blooming thing for your two dollars* and the sooner you admit it, the sooner you'll assert your independence. But, for the love of Profit, when you go independent, *go independent RIGHT!* Connect with the *biggest* and *best* film renter in the world – the one man who has fought to keep you from being gouged, plucked, skinned, pickled and parboiled while you were snoring at the switch! . . .

To be involved in a law-suit is generally acknowledged to be a debilitating experience. What it may be like to be involved in law-suits over three years at the rate of a hundred or so a year is, I suppose, the peculiar privilege of Carl Laemmle among living men to know. As the record cannot have been approached before, and is not likely to be equalled in the future, we may take it as a classic. All remarkable feats of endurance are apt to follow natural law by dwindling in perspective, and it needs some effort even dimly to reconstruct the strain endured by Laemmle under an offensive of unexampled ferocity in its kind. The figures are worth repeating: two hundred and eighty-nine actions in less than three years. . . .

At length the long deferred deliverance came, and it was unconditional. On October 15th, 1915, the United States government ordered the Film Trust to discontinue all unlawful practices. Since the entire organisation was founded on activities that were themselves defined as unlawful, the order in effect meant the dissolution of the Trust into its constituent units, each one of which, if it remained in operation, must do so without privilege in a free and open market. The monopolistic power of the Trust was broken, and without it the Trust ceased to be. Anticipating this end, the monopolists had made prudent use of the law's delay. In abolishing the Trust as such, the Court ordered among other things that all the two dollar fees paid under duress should be returned to the defrauded exhibitors. The government, with a view to making the order effective, sought to attach the bank account of the combine. But the Patents Company and Gen. Filmco had gone silently away, leaving behind them closed doors and empty offices. The fortunes that had been made by exploiting an industry slid furtively into the backwaters of sundry private accounts. No compensation for wrongs done was recoverable. The Trust had to be written off as a bad debtor, bad to the core. But it was exterminated. When at an earlier date the Trust had begun to suffer serious inroads on its business through Independent competition, one of its lawyers had said—"Laemmle is the man to whom, more than any other, is due the large damage inflicted on the Motion Pictures Patents Company."

ROBERT SKLAR
New Producing Companies

Robert Sklar, in Movie-Made America *(N.Y., Random House, 1975), is especially helpful in detailing the multifarious activities of independents, large and small, who attempted to band together in opposition to the Trust. Before long, they began to fight with one another, especially at Universal. According to some accounts of the time there were physical encounters in the best western tradition between Laemmle's forces and his erstwhile partners, Bauman and Kessel, both in New York and Hollywood, in order to gain control of studio facilities.*

At the end of this selection (which is taken from a section called "Edison's Trust and How It Got Busted," pages 29–41) Sklar also introduces us to William Fox.

Sklar has taught American studies at the University of Michigan and at Yale, has written extensively on TV programming for American Film *magazine, and was for several years head of cinema studies at New York University.*

. . . within a year perhaps a dozen new producing companies entered the field, knowing they had an open market in independent exchanges and nonlicensed theaters. The New York Motion Picture Company was the first new firm, founded early in 1909 by the independent distributors Adam Kessel and Charles O. Baumann and the producer-director Fred Balshofer. They made Western films under the Bison trademark. Then Edwin S. Porter left Edison and joined a new company, Defender; later he established the Rex Film Company with the same partners. David Horsley, a pre-Trust independent producer, reorganized as the Nestor Company. Patrick Powers, a former distributor, began a production company bearing his own name. Kessel and Baumann's New York Company, Laemmle's Imp, and Powers became the big three of the independents.

Using Lumière film stock, the independent producers tried to work with noninfringing European cameras, but since the results were unsatisfactory, they began using Edison machines surreptitiously. The Trust retaliated by hiring spies to gather evidence of patent infringement and even tried forcibly to disrupt independent production activities. The independents camouflaged their cameras, engaged bodyguards to protect their cameramen and eventually scattered to locations in Cuba, Florida, Arizona and California, where they had the advantages of year-round sunshine and distance from the Trust.

The Trust, well versed in Edison's tactics, harried the independents into court. Laemmle himself, according to his biographer, was the target of 289 separate legal actions, which cost him more than $300,000 in defense expenses. The Trust, like Edison before it, had more losses than victories in the courts, and this time the defendants had the resources and stamina to hold out; unlike Edison's earlier opponents, they had no alternative except to go out of business. In 1910 the Trust lobbied in Congress to have duties raised on imported film stock. It lost. J. J. Murdock, president of the International Projecting and Producing Company, persuaded the legislators to lower duties on both raw and manufactured film in the otherwise infamous Payne-Aldrich tariff bill.

Year by year the independents grew stronger. In 1910, with Laemmle and Kessel and Baumann taking the lead, they organized the Motion Picture Distributing and Sales Company, designed to consolidate the movement of films from producers to exchanges. At first a number of the small companies refused to join, but a compromise was arranged, and the Sales Company became the sole outlet for independent films. By mid-1910 the Sales Company and its affiliated exchanges could offer theaters a choice of twenty-seven films a week. Building on their solid base of storefront nickelodeon customers, the independents began to lure licensed exhibitors away from the Trust. Laemmle's associate, Robert C. Cochrane, waged a devastating campaign of ridicule against the Trust in trade-paper ads, attacking its strong-arm tactics and especially the $2 weekly royalty.

In 1912, the year the independents nearly equaled the Trust in total film production, they split into two rival camps. Harry E.

Aitken, a Wisconsin distributor, organized the Mutual Film Corporation, with the intention of buying exchanges and becoming sole national distributor of several production companies. Ten independent producers went with Aitken, and seven others formed their own corporation, the Universal Film Manufacturing Company, to succeed the Sales Company and continue supplying films to independent exchanges.

Laemmle, Kessel and Baumann, and Powers were again the central figures in Universal, but they soon quarreled over who was first among equals, and Kessel and Baumann quit. Laemmle and Powers then demonstrated what they had learned in their struggle with the Trust: they claimed that the assets of the New York Motion Picture Company had been signed over to Universal in exchange for stock, and tried to seize its property in New York and Los Angeles by force. Eventually Universal lost the battle in court, gaining only the Bison trademark. By the time the Justice Department filed suit against the Trust in 1912, the independents may have deserved scrutiny just as much.

But the independents were on the ascendancy. They consistently demonstrated the initiative and innovative energy that the Trust producers lacked, most particularly in their swift adoption of a "star" system, similar to the traditional billing in the theater and vaudeville. The actresses, hoping some day to achieve "legitimate" success in the theater, were glad of the anonymity. But the growing movie public picked their favorites anyway and wrote fan letters to "The Biograph Girl" or "The Lone Indian" of the Bison company. Laemmle decided to capitalize on this audience desire for stars.

In 1909 he hired "The Biograph Girl," Florence Lawrence, away from Biograph and gave her star billing by name in Imp films. The next year he lured Mary Pickford from the same company by nearly doubling her salary. And he discovered that stars sold pictures as nothing else could. So long as theaters changed their programs daily—and the practice persisted in neighborhood theaters and small towns until the early 1920s—building up audience recognition of star names was almost the only effective form of advance publicity.

When word got out that the independents offered opportunities to build a career, talent came to them from the Trust producers, from vaudeville and from other trades, and by the mid-1910s they had the three leading filmmakers. Thomas H. Ince left vaudeville in 1910 to join Imp and was hired away by

Kessel and Baumann's company, where he became one of the first important producer-directors. Kessel and Baumann also lured Mack Sennett from Biograph to Keystone. When Biograph refused to let D. W. Griffith make films longer than two reels, he resigned to work for Harry E. Aitken's Mutual company.

The defeat of the Trust was, however, above all a victory for the men who ran and supplied the storefront nickel theaters. Among them were a considerable number of East European Jews who had come to the United States as youths and struggled up the economic ladder, specializing in businesses like clothing and expensive accessories such as furs and jewelry, where skill in meeting and pleasing the public and a flair for fashion were essential to success. Some entered the amusement business as a sideline, others in escape from a dead end, but both groups quickly learned that providing inexpensive commercial entertainment was a necessary service, and far more profitable than selling apparel. The Trust threat led the most ambitious and talented among them to seek power over their own destiny. Laemmle was their pathfinder and prototype. More than any other man he had established the independents and kept alive the neighborhood theaters in the ghettos. But Laemmle's triumph, important as it was, was only a stepping stone. Waiting in the wings were others who had stood aloof from the independents' struggle, for their ambitions ranged far beyond the needs of nickelodeons.

The first titans to emerge were two New York showmen, William Fox and Adolph Zukor, both Hungarian Jews. Even before the Trust was formed they had raised a question of untold portent: if businessmen could make tens of thousands of dollars, even hundreds of thousands, showing movies for a nickel to the lowest classes in American society, what could they make if everyone went to the movies? The Trust took up their ideas, at least partially, and both men were content to cooperate with it until it became, in Fox's case, hostile, and in Zukor's, ineffectual. They were younger than Laemmle – Zukor by six years, Fox by twelve – and closer to other sectors of the amusement world that catered to the middle and even to the leisure class.

Fox made the first breakthrough into middle-class audiences. He had not yet turned thirty when he led New York exhibitors in opposing Mayor McClellan's 1908 order closing the nickelodeons, by which time he owned more than a dozen neighborhood theaters and had startled the New York amusement world by taking over established vaudeville houses and successfully showing movies as half the program. His nickel and dime admissions filled large houses that had been playing to small audiences and brought him greater profits despite the lower price. He not only made vaudeville accessible to the working classes, his use of larger and more comfortable theaters attracted the vaudeville-going middle classes to movies.

When Fox expanded his operations into motion-picture distribution, he came into conflict with the Trust. At first his was a licensed exchange; but as it began its efforts to take over all licensed distributors, the General Film Company tried to buy him out. He refused to sell, and his license was canceled. He took the Trust to court—a switch on the usual procedure—and won the right to keep his license. . . .

ROBERT GRAU
The Growth of Universal

Robert Grau, again, in The Theatre of Science, *pages 47–52, op. cit., has written what is obviously a promotional piece for the Universal Film Manufacturing Company, its impressive New York offices, and the new Universal City, a self-contained municipality in the San Fernando Valley with spectacular location areas. Taken over by the latter-day agency tycoons of the Music Corporation of America in the 1950s, this famous movie lot has survived and prospered on the same expansive acres along the Camino Real.*

The calm reflected in this 1914 report is deceptive. As Ramsaye wrote later, "The peace that followed the settlement of the Kessel and Bauman controversy in the Universal must have lasted almost a day." Laemmle and Powers engaged after that in a struggle for control which was so camouflaged that Lewis Selznick could come in on his own one day and set up a desk as "general manager." Laemmle had a stock majority by 1914 but didn't buy out Powers until 1920. (A Million and One Nights, op cit., pages 584–593).

Just two years ago on May 17th, four desks were successively carried from the elevator and placed in a row on the hardwood floor of the Lincoln Building, Union Square, New York. These

Earliest Production Companies 55

desks were plain and unpretentious, but of good solid oak, reflecting the solidity of their owners. These four desks were to be occupied by Carl Laemmle, W. H. Swanson, P. A. Powers and David Horsley, and it was not long before the film world realized that the new Universal Film Manufacturing Company, conceived and brought into existence by these men, was a dominant factor in the world of motion pictures. Avoiding the rocks upon which its predecessors had been wrecked, the Universal adopted as its policy the largest individuality to its constituent companies, with perfect accord of purpose in its relations to the exchangeman and the exhibitors.

The enthusiastic reception of the Universal Program by exhibitor and patron alike, and the eagerness with which its many feats and features were anticipated, caused the business to grow by leaps and bounds. The space in the Lincoln Building, which had seemed ample on May 17th, the day the new offices were opened, proved wholly inadequate before the summer of 1912 was far advanced. With their usual enterprise, the Board of Directors commissioned a real estate firm to secure new premises, and the magnificent quarters in the Mecca Building, 1600 Broadway, the Universal's present home, was the result.

When the Universal first started, it promised its patrons a program of at least twenty-one reels a week. By the introduction of some of the biggest features ever presented to the public, it has increased its original program from twenty-eight to thirty-two reels a week. It has needed no spur other than the approval of its patrons to accomplish this record-breaking achievement.

In speaking of the removal of the Universal to its new offices uptown, it is interesting to note that this move shifted the center of gravity, so to speak, of the film industry in New York City. In the wake of the Universal followed scores of allied and similar enterprises, until the vicinity of Longacre Square has now wrested from Fourteenth street the title of Film Centre.

The present home offices of the Universal occupy the entire third floor of the Mecca Building, with frontage on Broadway, Forty-eighth street and Seventh avenue, with immediate transportation by surface cars, subway and elevated railroads, making it the most accessible spot in the metropolis. The fixtures and office furniture are of massive mahogany and plate glass and the projection room is the last word in luxurious splendor. The offices of the individual officers, the room of the Board of Directors, the quarters of the Universal Weekly and the export and accounting departments occupy the Forty-eighth street and Broadway frontage, while the Seventh avenue side is devoted to the scenario department and to the Mecca branch of the Universal Film Exchange of New York. In between are located the shipping and stenographic departments, the telephone exchange and the reception room for visitors.

Not far from the Mecca Building, near the corner of Eleventh avenue and Forty-third street, are the studios of the popular Imp and Victor brands and the Animated Weekly. Up in the Borough of the Bronx, at the corner of Park and Wendover avenues, the Crystal films are made. Over in New Jersey, at Fort Lee, the studios of the American Eclair Company are located, and a little further north, at Coytesville, where the Palisades are seen in their full majesty, is another Universal studio, where Victor films are made. . . .

In the latter part of March, President Carl Laemmle, with David Horsley and others, made a trip to the Pacific Coast, and among the more important business transacted was the closing of negotiations for purchasing a new ranch. Universal City will be moved over to this new ranch. One-half million dollars it took to secure this new home—250 acres in all—located in the San Fernando Valley, about ten miles from the center of Los Angeles. The ranch lies on the El Camino Real (The King's Highway), this highway being the original road that connected the various missions from San Diego to San Francisco. It is half way between the missions of San Gabriel and San Fernando, about a mile from the connecting electric line. Immediately on purchasing the ranch, the Universal set to work and built a railroad to the main line to be used for the transportation of studio equipment, building material and passenger service. The ranch has one-mile frontage on the Los Angeles River. This river front is finely fringed with trees and shrubbery, affording excellent backgrounds for pictures.

Recently the Universal have commenced the production of big four- and six-reel features on a lavish scale which are to be released on its program as Universal Special Features. The first feature under this brand and a sensational success was "Absinthe," made in France by the European Imp Company. Others that followed were "Samson," a tremendous six-reeler; "The Merchant of Venice," "Won in the Clouds," "Washington at Valley Forge," and "The Spy," "Richelieu," and "Neptune's Daughter."

In connection with the production of these master features, the Universal have commenced a national campaign of advertising with an appropriation of a quarter of a million dollars.

The Pacific Coast studios of the Universal Film Manufacturing Company constitute, from a standpoint of film-producing capacity, the largest assembled plant of its kind in the world. The year around not less that twenty-one thousand feet of finished film a week is turned out at this establishment. Fifteen companies, each composed of a director, assistant director, cinematographer, actors, property men and stage hands, operate continually at an annual expense of over $1,000,000.

A̧TTILIO H. GIANNINI
The First Loans

A. H. Giannini was a banker. His brother, A. P. Giannini, was founder of the Bank of Italy (later the Bank of America). They were among the first in California to gamble on movie makers and their constant need for short-term loans. They evidently judged each case on character and on performance and decided the business was as good a risk as most others. This rare insight into the views of a top financier was shared at a symposium at Harvard University, presided over by Joseph Kennedy, himself then involved in financing and producing films, and published in his book, The Story of the Films *(N.Y., A. W. Shaw Co., 1927) pages 78–82, part of a chapter entitled "Financial Aspects of the Industry." The speaker was at that time president of the Bowery and East River National Bank.*

My first contact with the motion picture business dates back about fifteen years. The first man that I, as a banker, had anything to do with was the owner of a nickelodeon in San Francisco. He is today a director of one of the largest motion picture companies in the world. He also conducted an exchange; he bought and sold photoplays. These photoplays were exhibited in San Francisco and nearby cities. He had very little capital, as capital is reckoned today from a banking standpoint. I am not going to mention names nor will I mention pictures, but it became necessary for him to purchase a photoplay. He came to me as the officer of the bank. He did not have the required three C's with which you gentlemen are familiar; character, capacity, and capital. But he did possess two of the C's, character and capacity for work, and I made him a small loan, which was paid at maturity.

He then wished to improve his theatre and install a new projecting machine and new chairs. He again sought credit and, for the same personal considerations *alone,* he was given that credit and again paid me off at maturity.

Then came a second man, who is today engaged in the industry as a highly successful producer. He likewise was conducting a small exchange, buying and selling photoplays. He informed me that there was a photoplay in New York for which he could get the California and western rights and that he desired a loan. At that time I considered the sum requested a great amount of money. No statements were presented. None of the usual standards whereby credits were and are measured were before me. The same personal considerations permitted me to extend that loan – character and capacity. The loan was quickly liquidated, as the picture sold rapidly and the proceeds came in fast. Similar propositions were submitted to me from up and down the state, and all loans were satisfactorily met.

A year or two elapsed. Only a few producing companies were operating. The star system was not yet in vogue. There were men and women who were featured, but not in the sense in which they are featured today. Then more companies began to be organized, executives appointed, departments created, interdependence and coordination of those departments established, stories purchased, scenarios written, directors selected, photography studied and developed, special locations chosen. All those factors which make for a perfect and efficient producing organization were gradually developed, and the officers and directors functioned like those of any other legitimate business.

The executives of these companies came into the bank for credit – this was about ten years ago – and we then began to insist on financial statements before granting credit. We required the three C's – character, capacity and capital. These statements had to show the usual items of capital, merchandise, accounts and bills receivable, accounts and bills payable, amount of sales, dividends, if any, loans to partners or friends, contingent liability, and so forth.

Much of the financing at this time was done by certain individuals. They either loaned money at excessive rates of interest or participated in the profits. These were the so-called bonus sharks. I speak feelingly on this point because it was the one menace that struck at the very vitals of the industry and it was a deadly menace up to two years ago. I have attacked it repeatedly, and we have pretty nearly succeeded in eliminating it entirely. These bonus sharks saw tremendous profits in the business and sought opportunities to invest their money, as they stated. They also charged a usurious rate of interest. We stepped in and made loans to deserving companies, thereby eliminating some of these so-called money lenders. Our loans were at the current rate of interest, with no charges for service or attorney's fee.

The men that were being attracted to the industry were of a finer type; they were employing executives who had had business training. We took into consideration the element of experience, the element of judgment in the production of pictures.

The banks at this time were indifferent to this kind of credit. They were, indeed, very indifferent. There was an occasional loan made by a bank, but most infrequently. But my observation of the growth of the industry, even as far back as ten years ago, the hold that it had upon the public, the construction of theatres, the increase in seating capacity, the increase in comfort for the theatre-goer, induced me to believe that this was an industry that deserved the same kind of attention as any other legitimate industry.

I then came east about eight years ago and I also found the banks in New York City exceedingly indifferent to this business. I was a newcomer; I was in a new pasture; there were many grazing herds and the grass was short, and I was obliged to turn to a business that the other bankers did not particularly wish to finance. My California connections naturally introduced me into the moving picture offices of New York City, for here were located the executive heads.

I commenced to make loans as I did in California, and in a short time these loans ran into high figures. As ours is a national bank and a member of the New York Clearing House, it was subjected to examination by both the Clearing House of New York City and the National Banking Department. At each examination the examiners found upon our books large sums of money loaned to the industry, and I was criticised in the written reports to my board of directors. The criticisms were kind; the criticisms were well meant and as such considered by me. These criticisms all invited caution. Being a novice in a great city, it was probably thought that I might be easily victimized. In each instance, however, I was able to show that the loans were liquidated just as promptly as the loans made to any other company or any other individual. A clean record impressed the examiners.

BENJAMIN B. HAMPTON
J. Stuart Blackton

From Benjamin Hampton's A History of the Movies *(N.Y., Covici-Friede, 1931) reprinted in paperback as* History of the American Film Industry *(N.Y., Dover Publications, 1970) we include pages 22–23 to introduce J. Stuart Blackton, founder along with Albert Smith and William Rock of Vitagraph, a member company of the Trust. Blackton was usually entrusted with the actual directing of the films, and Smith was the business partner.*

James Stuart Blackton, a clever but none too prosperous painter, had two ways of adding to his income: one, which he called "chalk talks," consisted of a lecture and pictures rapidly drawn in view of the audience; and, when business was dull in lecture halls and on variety stages, and he was at home in New York waiting for engagements, he wrote special articles for newspapers and illustrated them with his own drawings. Tall, handsome, magnetic, with a rich, melodious baritone voice, Blackton always managed to keep busy at one or another of his occupations.

In lyceum and variety theater work he became acquainted with a youth named Albert Edward Smith, who followed the profession of public entertainer, usually as a magician; when stage engagements were not available, he fell back on his trade of bookbinding. Smith was a quiet chap who liked to stay in his room at night, reading and thinking. After he and Blackton became friends they did a lot of reading and walking and thinking and talking together. The earliest screen shows, coming at a time when they had no stage engagements, received their earnest attention, and, soon convinced that this form of entertainment possessed almost unlimited possibilities, they searched for ways and means of engaging in the alluring new business.

One day in 1897, Blackton went over to the Edison laboratory in New Jersey to do a newspaper story, with pictures, about the inventor, and before the interview ended Edison had agreed to sell him a projector and an outfit of films for eight hundred dollars. This was a huge sum of money for the two young men – each was about twenty years old – to raise, and they had to beg and borrow to get it; but they got it, and gave living-picture exhibitions in theaters and halls in neighborhoods and cities in which screen shows had not been opened.

Merely showing pictures did not satisfy them very long. Their heads were full of ideas of pictures they would like to photograph, but no cameras were for sale or for rent. They talked and thought, and thought and talked, and one day Albert Smith made the discovery that the projection machine could be transformed into a camera – if he could invent several devices to make it work properly. He invented the devices, the projector became a camera, and Smith and Blackton were able to photograph film.

Under the title of "Vitagraph," they became producers of motion pictures, photographing street parades, news incidents, prize fights, dramatic episodes – any subject that would interest screen patrons without involving the film-makers in too much expense of production. Albert Smith's inventive mind kept at work and evolved various improvements of the projecting machine as well as the camera. Vitagraph had abundant energy and imagination, but it needed more capital to permit expansion.

In these years, Harlem was "way uptown," a district of quiet, home-loving German and American families. One Hundred and Twenty-fifth Street was its business center, and on this street was a billiard and pool hall operated by William Rock, a cheerful soul generally known as "Pop." Pop Rock was a showman himself, traveling summers and autumns with side-shows to country fairs, street carnivals and the like. He had been one of the first to sense the public interest in living pictures and had been showing them around the country in tents, halls, and small theaters. Smith,

Blackton, and Rock merged their films and film machinery and cash in Vitagraph, as equal partners, their consolidated assets totaling perhaps three thousand dollars. This modest capital was enough to permit them to push their producing and trading activities vigorously.

ALBERT E. SMITH
Vitagraph

Albert E. Smith, in his autobiography, Two Reels and a Crank (N.Y., Doubleday, 1952), pages 250–260, provides us with a unique entrepreneur's memoir, dollar by dollar, of the way a struggling young capitalist saw his company grow. The title of his book refers to his chief partner and himself plus "Pop" Rock, who evidently put in some money but mostly sat on the sidelines. He also recalls the decline of the General Film Company, his own venture into theater ownership, and his determination not to go too far toward some kind of real estate empire which would compete with his first love, production. But the future of the industry was moving toward that very top-to-bottom control which he was trying to avoid, and he could not escape the consequences, as we shall see.

Vitagraph had progressed in big healthy jumps. As early as 1896 I kept a modest set of books. I always say, when speaking of the start of Vitagraph, that our initial capital was $936 – used in the building of our first machines and purchase of the first films.

The following figures represent net profit after expenses and suffice to show its growth from the struggles in a ten-dollar-a-month attic room to a million-dollar operation:

In 1896 and 1897 – all income went toward building up of the company, including the making of new Vitagraph projection machines, purchase of office furniture, etc. The fees of our Lyceum engagements paid living expenses.

In 1898 – $4,750. In that year we began to draw fifty dollars a week.

Earliest Production Companies 63

In 1899 – $7,975 – derived from theaters furnished a Vitagraph machine, operator, and weekly program of films.

In 1900 – $6,742. This year Vitagraph was incorporated. William T. (Pop) Rock became an associate and one-third owner. My traveling expenses of the trip to South Africa were charged on this year's books, accounting for the reduced figure.

In 1901 – $8,449. This year we sent out three traveling film companies, exhibiting mainly the Boer War films. Each company carried an illustrated song singer and a pianist. The program lasted about two hours. One company traveled through Pennsylvania and adjacent states, another in Canada, and the third in New England. All three did very well, although the New England states appeared to appreciate pictures the least, and after a while we called in that company, but kept the others going for several years.

In 1902 – $10,778 – largely from film sales. Tent shows and nickelodeons were commencing to start up, and they bought films outright at the beginning.

In 1903 – $15,860. In this year we built our first studio, in Flatbush. It marked a change in operations – decline of our projector rental business and growth of sales of film.

In 1904 – $25,750. An addition built to the first studio buildings. Nickelodeons were mushrooming so swiftly this year that many film rental bureaus started up, particularly west of the Mississippi.

In 1905 – $38,860. Opened a Chicago office which sold pictures as fast as we produced them. A third addition to our studio. Also arranged for an agency in London to handle sale of our films.

In 1906 – $120,749. Canceled the London agency and opened Vitagraph sales offices in London, Paris, and Berlin. This reflected in profits. Number of nickelodeons was now tremendous.

In 1907 – $248,764. Set up a laboratory near Paris for printing of films for our European customers. At Flatbush studio we now used cameras which accommodated two negatives at one time; the second negative was sent to the Paris laboratory.

In 1908 – $279,814. European offices now going full blast. Paris laboratory turned out four times the footage printed in Flatbush plant, but the prices received in Europe were much lower.

In 1909 – 308,849. The General Film Company was formed in the United States. Fourth addition erected at Flatbush.

In 1910 – $665,372 – due partly to share of business received from General Film. Also we were turning out films in greater number. A new laboratory building for the processing of films constructed this year.

In 1911–$695,969. In February of this year we started Vitagraph's California studio. Expense of new plant accounts for the fact this year's earnings only slightly higher than 1910's.

In 1912–$924,782. Constructed the fifth studio building at Flatbush, as large as the other four put together. Now releasing six films a week. Length of the films had grown gradually from fifty to one thousand feet in length. Now no picture was less than a thousand feet. Also this year Vitagraph produced a three-reel picture each week. Amount of negative footage tremendous.

In 1913–$1,116,349. This year an entirely new laboratory building replaced the one built in 1910, and twice its size. Our biggest year. Business booming here and abroad.

In 1914–$997,321. World War I soon eliminated foreign receipts, with grave effect on company for several years. Opened Vitagraph Theatre.

The influenza epidemic of 1918, which closed down Vitagraph, reduced our gross earnings to $19,297, but the earnings rose swiftly. Vitagraph's peak year was 1920. Its gross receipts: $6,193,519.

The first ten years of this century was the heyday of the one-reeler. By 1912 nickelodeons were dying. Public apathy toward "galloping tintypes" daily became more marked.

Some sort of move had to be made. A new era was in the offing, held back by the old order. Producers were willing to film two- and three-reel movies but were fiercely opposed to anything longer. Against this view, Vitagraph took the position that the future rested on long features, and backed it up.

Three super productions rolled out of Flatbush—*The Juggernaut, The Christian,* and *A Million Bid*—and we were in trouble. The exhibitors told us the public wouldn't sit through a film lasting more than a full hour. We sent them reams of material telling our idea of how to put a feature picture over, how to bring patrons into their houses in greater number than ever before. Some exhibited *The Juggernaut,* but their theaters were small, seating a few hundred persons. The returns did not justify the rental they paid Vitagraph for the picture.

We decided the only way to test our faith in big pictures was to lease a large legitimate theater and convert it into a motion-picture house.

We took over the Criterion on Broadway and renamed it the Vitagraph Theatre.

As the first movie house devoted to feature films, the Vitagraph was a landmark in motion pictures. It signaled the emergence of motion pictures on a grand scale and in the grand manner.

Blackton and I could not decide which of the two films should open the new Vitagraph. Blackton had produced *The Christian* and I *A Million Bid*. Each championed the other, Jim voting for my film and I for his. Finally we decided to let Vitagraph players and workers make the choice. After a showing of the pictures, they voted in *A Million Bid*. As an additional feature Blackton wrote a fascinating pantomime called *The Honeymooners*, performed in person from the stage by John Bunny, Mary Charleson, and James Morrison.

After weeks of details and minor crises, the theater was ready. Among the additions was a mammoth pipe organ. I did not want the patrons to see merely a screen when the curtain went up, so I searched for a new proscenium design. The view of the Hudson from the study window of my home gave me the idea. For the theater we reproduced a segment of New York Bay with the Statue of Liberty, complete with torch, boats, and water-reflected lights. It was arranged so that as night came on lights twinkled and a Liberty torch shed an orange flame. Local pride plus the patriotic appeal brought cheers from every audience and put them in excellent spirits.

We scaled our admissions—one dollar for the best seats and as little as twenty cents for those farthest back.

The formal-dress opening drew recognition from Alan Dale, the urbane dramatic critic of the New York *American*.

Dale was what the present literary fraternity might call a slick writer, a sort of modified Wolcott Gibbs, whose essays titillated the tea crowd and set each day into motion with, "Well, what did Alan Dale have to say this morning?" The sharp pen of this darling of the literati angered its victims, but delighted all others. He was more shockingly flippant to that era than, say, *The New Yorker* is to this. Flashes of unholy wrath would leap from his typewriter, and we feared the introduction of flickers to the Broadway scene might stir his literary bile. The lowly film had taken over a temple of legitimate drama!

The orphan of the arts had been soundly thrashed before, and another beating, even from Alan Dale, could not lower its estate much. Dale's approval, however, would be a considerable boost.

No one could believe it when, on the following day, Dale's column contained a ringing salute to the Vitagraph Theatre opening. His followers were shocked, assuming either that the columnist had lost his grip or had been bought off by the movie interests. Vitagraph breathed a sigh of relief and let it be known that the cantankerous Mr. Dale was indeed a man of rare vision.

Here is what he wrote in The New York *American's* Sunday issue of February 8, 1914:

> No swaggerer or more "bung-tung" gathering than that which graced the opening of the new Vitagraph Theatre (formerly the Criterion) has been seen at any "legitimate" opening this season. The famous almost-old theater of Hammerstein's brand, was crowded with a most un-"movie"-looking audience, and the house, itself, has been spruced and brightened up for the Silent Actors as it had never been for the Chatty Ones. Boxes were added, filled with pure white chairs, and the entire appearance of the Vitagraph Theatre was cozy, ornate, and chic.
>
> "Movie" actors were a great deal in evidence—just as critical as un-"movie"-ones. They knew all those that appeared in the pictures last night. They gossiped about them, commented on them, scrutinized their make-up and made the filmers seem real and vitalized.
>
> A very admirable organ was used during the performance, and a more elaborate one will be ready in a week. In the meantime, the music was so good and such a delightful relief from ragtime and pestiferous commonplace that the promised "Hope-Jones masterpiece" need not hurry to materialize. Chopin, Rubinstein, Paderewski and other classical composers snatchily accompanied the films, and the effect was charming, refined, and intelligent.
>
> I'm bound to admit that I love a good picture. Last night, after pictures of famous "movie" actors had been shown—they bowed, they smiled, they stared at us with their film-y eyes, and they magnetized us, vitagraphically—the programme began with a modern drama in four acts by George Cameron (Mrs. Sidney Drew), called *A Million Bid*.
>
> This was "picturized" (isn't that a lovely new vitagraphic word?) from the play I once saw, called *Agnes,* and very thrilling it turned out to be. In fact, it was undoubtedly the very finest picture I have ever seen. I don't speak of the "plot," or the story, but of this particular episode showing the wreck of Geoffrey Marshe's yacht. Not since I saw *S.O.S.* at the Grand Guignol in Paris had I such cold chills down the spine.
>
> The little yacht's cabin is smashed into smithereens. The millionaire is seen dead, floating in the water. The evil mother-in-law is shown in her cabin, the water gradually rising—to her knees, to her waist, until she is submerged. They are revealed floundering in the dismal waters, a hopeless and awe-struck lot, until rescue, in the

shape of an ocean steamer, arrives. No "drama" could give one such an idea of the terrors of a wreck. The agony and anguish of it were rushed home to us. We palpitated at the silence of it—that seemed part of the tragedy. Not a word—not a sound—as the terrible catastrophe was pictured for us. We realized every newspaper description of shipwreck's misery as these films greeted us.

But, of course, there was a long story to *A Million Bid*. I'm always awfully nervous at "movie" shows for fear I shall miss the words flashed on the screen. You see a woman talking silently in apparent stress and storm and then comes a long tirade on the screen. If you nap for a moment—you have lost it all! It is dreadfully perplexing. Letters also embarrass me. I'm so afraid they are going to be written in handwriting as bad as mine. Fortunately, they rarely are. "Movie" handwritings are usually uniform.

Last night *A Million Bid* was not so permeated with reading matter and I was thankful for that. I love to drink in the pictures and imagine! Stereotyped words worry me. The beauty of pictures is that you can imagine if you have anything to imagine with!

Charles Kent, Julia Swayne Gordon, Anita Stewart, E. K. Lincoln, Harry T. Morey and Gladdin James were the actors in this particular film.

Then came John Bunny, Mary Charleson, and James Morrison in person in a select drama called *The Honeymooners*, by J. Stuart Blackton. Bunny is the Edwin Booth, the Henry Irving, and the E. H. Sothern of the "movies." He was a good actor out of movies. I can remember him. In *The Honeymooners*, which told a very simple story, he had just to be his fat, unctuous self.

The last picture last night was a burlesque in three parts, called *Movies As They Shouldn't Be*, with Sidney Drew, Clara Kimball Young, and Etienne Girardot as stars; also Ned Finley, Kate Price, and James Lackaye. Altogether, it was an exceedingly interesting affair in its vivacious silence. Nothing missed fire. Drama concentrated into silence, farce that got there without music, comedy that told without rampage—all got in their fine work. . . .

A shudder ran through the ranks of the owners of little theaters—some forty thousand of them—throughout America. Was the Vitagraph Theatre the first shadow of an inevitable doom? Large theaters snuffing out the life of little ones? Big features being shown only in ornate film palaces?

Vitagraph heard from these little exhibitors almost immediately. They sent wires and letters. One day they came to my office, nearly two hundred of them. They were old customers of ours. They had bought and shown Vitagraph pictures for years.

As many as were able crowded into my office that day, expressing their one worry:

"Is Vitagraph going to buy or build new theaters?"

I said the only thing I could say. "We have no such plan."

They said:

"If Vitagraph goes into the theater business it will become our competitor. We have no objection to your own theater in New York, but if you buy more theaters in New York and other cities you leave us only one course—to stop buying Vitagraph pictures immediately."

That, I said, was a matter of personal decision. I told them that our plan from this moment forward was to make big pictures and release them through our old customers.

From one standpoint the opening of the Vitagraph was a mistake; it provided for Vitagraph pictures exclusively, and at the same time gave rival producers the opportunity to view our pictures, one right after another, and thus benefit from our experience. Too, they were able to see which Vitagraph artists and workers were involved in the successful pictures. There began numerous raids on our staff—directors, cameramen, and scene painters, lured away with larger wage offers.

Then in August 1914, we suffered a blow from an unexpected quarter—the first World War. It killed our foreign market overnight, a tremendous loss.

The success of the Vitagraph Theatre touched off another trigger—a rash of theater building. Most of these were founded on borrowed money which, until the success of the Vitagraph Theatre was apparent, was not available for so speculative a venture. Now loans were made freely and hundreds of large theaters went up all over the country.

Other film companies started producing special features. They had no way to distribute them, so they arranged with the General Film Company for their handling.

They met our fate.

We released eight feature pictures through General Film. Some were very good, but none made any money. General Film's method of handling was the reason for the loss in almost every instance.

General Film was foundering. Its golden days were over. Its ideas were old-fashioned.

So now, in 1914, Vitagraph decided to form a special organization to sell its feature films. But we knew we did not have enough features to give a continuous supply to the large theaters now rapidly going into operation. We needed other studios to join with us. I discussed the need for a new sales group with producer members of General Film, but we did not see eye to eye. Some did not believe in the future of feature productions; a few did.

In May, 1915, Vitagraph, the Selig Company, Essanay, and the Lubin Company – all pioneers – agreed to make one special five-reeler feature each month to be released through a new organization to be known as "Vitagraph, Lubin, Selig, and Essanay." For business reasons we shortened it to VLSE.

The results were not satisfactory. Vitagraph had had some experience in producing features, but the others did not. Ours made money, but the films of our partners failed.

In 1916 we bought out VLSE. For their stock we paid twenty-five thousand dollars each to Selig and Essanay, and fifty thousand to Lubin.

We also bought the Kalem Company for a hundred thousand dollars. Kalem had no studio, but we got his negatives. One was quite valuable, *The Life of Christ,* which the Kalem Company had produced in Egypt in 1912.

We stepped up our production program, releasing four pictures a month.

Above: *Queen Elizabeth* (1912). Below: *The Squaw Man* (1913)

Chapter 3

Enter Lasky and Zukor

> *A distributor could not maintain an office and do business on six or eight pictures a year because the overhead would not permit it. So we decided to make thirty pictures a year.* — Adolph Zukor.

Adolph Zukor, like Laemmle and Fox, came up against Edison's Patents Company. By 1912 the trust was weaker but adamant against "long" pictures. Two-reelers were still profitable enough. Why rock the boat?

Zukor was a newcomer, a successful fur salesman and owner of a partial interest, along with Marcus Loew and Morris Kohn, in the 14th Street penny arcade. He had taken time off to do some research on movie theaters and audiences in the United States and Europe, and he was convinced that feature films were the next big development to come. He was so sure that he gambled some of his hard-earned profits on an imported movie, *Queen Elizabeth,* three reels long.

Benjamin Hampton says that Zukor had to cool his heels for hours in the waiting room of the high and mighty Patents Company before he was finally turned down for a license. What could he do? He rented a legitimate theater in Chicago and New York, and with the help of Daniel Frohman, the theatrical producer, he finally managed to get a one-time license from the trust. He makes no big claims about *Queen Elizabeth's* boxoffice, but there was apparently enough of a response to the famous name of Sarah Bernhardt to pay the expenses.

Zukor was not the first to try to make feature films (as Kenneth Macgowan explains for us from a later historical vantage point) but he got into the business of making them at just the right time. He was not the first to promote the idea of star personalities, nor the first to hire Mary Pickford. But by the time he did these things, they were the pattern that worked. He was not the first to try to bring together all three levels of the industry: production, distribution, and theaters. Edison had tried that already. But he made his moves with such care that he managed to survive longer than anybody else.

He pulled away from his friend Marcus Loew and went into film production. Soon he decided to ally himself with the early Hollywood operations of Jesse Lasky, Samuel Goldwyn, and Cecil B. DeMille. On the distribution side, he accepted for a while a subordinate relationship to the leadership of W. W. Hodkinson and his partners, who called their company "Paramount."

One by one all these men left the company. Their modest expectations extended only to one level of the grand vertical structure of the business Zukor was building. All of them tried thereafter to work on their own. Goldwyn was dropped almost at once; eventually he built, with great success, an independent company. DeMille departed in 1925, and after an interval of independence, went back under the roof of Paramount again. Lasky, eased out when Zukor himself was demoted in a financial reorganization in 1932, worked at various studios after that and never achieved real independence.

Hodkinson's name, however, disappears into history, remembered only as a stubborn supporter of the idea of a free and easy three-level business system Zukor was systematically making obsolete. Consolidation was the order of the day, and Lasky's account of the sudden blowing-away of Hodkinson gives no hint that he doubted the path his boss was taking.

For Lasky, who gives us the best inside view of these early days, it was a time of excitement, fears, doubts, and heady achievements. He was evidently a first-rate day-to-day problem solver, and could not be expected to foresee troubles at higher levels. His story of the technical blooper that threatened *The Squaw Man* with disaster, his generous recollection of the meetings with Zukor, his pride in multitudinous tasks of production, his satisfaction in personal intervention which changed *The Covered Wagon* from an ordinary picture to an "epic,"—these are among the most revealing and attractive of all the memoirs we have of the period.

ADOLPH ZUKOR
I Felt the Freedom in the Air

In this engaging reminiscence, Adolph Zukor tells one of the more famous stories of American immigration. It is part of an autobiography he wrote in 1953, with the editorial assistance of Dale Kramer, long before his career was over. When he died in 1976 (at the age of 103), Zukor was still chairman emeritus of the board at Paramount.
In The Public Is Never Wrong *(N.Y., G. P. Putnam's Sons, 1953) pages 30–39, he describes his coming to the United States as a teen-ager, his first jobs, his marriage, his early encounters with show business. On his first day in New York City, staying with friends of his parents, he took a bath in a tub in the kitchen: "The water running out of the taps did not amaze me, for I was prepared for miracles."*

My school marks were not exceptional, and I had no passion for a profession. Consequently, at twelve I was apprenticed for three years to Herman Blau, who had a store in the hamlet of Szanto, a wine-growing center about ten miles from Ricse. My duties were to sweep, run errands, and perform other chores while learning to be a clerk. Two evenings of each week I went to night school.

In Hungary there was little individual freedom or opportunity of rising in life, but an effort was made to look out for orphans. The Government took a part of the estate of the parents and set it aside for the use of the children. Thus, after my father died, a little of the revenue from the store and fields was put into a fund for my brother and me. After my mother died, my stepfather was called upon to contribute her share to us.

The store apprenticeship paid nothing beyond board, but twice each year my father's brother, who was trustee of the fund, certified to the Orphans' Bureau my clothing needs. In the spring, around Easter, I would be given a light suit and a pair of shoes. In the fall I would receive a heavier suit, boots, an overcoat if the old one was threadbare, and a few other essentials. None of these clothes were of good quality.

My lot was not a terrible one, for Herman Blau and his family were kindly people and I did not balk at hard work. But I soon looked about me and was able to see no future. After finishing the apprenticeship I would become a clerk at an equivalent of perhaps two dollars in American money a month, plus board and lodging. Many clerks with whom I was acquainted had worked for a long time for little more. And once a clerk, always a clerk. You might have far better qualifications as a tailor or a carpenter, but to switch from one trade to another was impossible. Even to move from town to town required a certificate from the employer. I could see nothing but darkness in Hungary for me.

All the while, letters were coming to the village from emigrants to America. These, speaking glowingly of freedom and opportunities, were passed from hand to hand. I read them along with such books about America as were available. Whenever someone returned for a visit I was quick with questions about that faraway and promising land. At fourteen I had definitely made up my mind to go. My problem was to figure out how in the world I could make it, for a great deal of money was required to travel to Bremen or Hamburg and take passage on a boat.

My apprenticeship was over in the fall of 1888, when I was fifteen, and I sat down and wrote a letter to the trustee of my orphan's fund. I poured my heart into it, telling of the things I had heard and read of America and begging to be allowed funds to go there.

It made a good impression and I was called before the superintendent of the Orphans' Bureau in a town some distance away. There I poured my heart out again. The superintendent questioned me closely and I could see that he suspected I had done some wrong and wished to escape to America.

He checked up by writing to my boss. But Herman Blau replied that I had done no wrong and he wished me good luck. I had already told him of my ambitions.

The Orphans' Bureau did not give the money directly to me, but to my brother, who was attending the University of Berlin. I was given only a ticket to Berlin and a little money to keep in my pocket for food on the way. After my brother had bought a steamship ticket he made an exchange of the balance into United States money. There was forty dollars and a few pieces of change. We sewed the forty dollars into my vest and he warned me not to take the vest off or touch the money until I had arrived in America.

These instructions I religiously observed, and the vest was still on me when I arrived at Castle Garden, the point at which immigrants then debarked. No sooner did I put my foot on American soil than I was a newborn person. The reader will understand from my background that I am not using an empty phrase in saying that I felt the freedom in the air.

There must have been fifty or more express wagons waiting to take the immigrants to destinations. In my notebook was the address of friends of my parents. On the boat, and long before, I had been trying to learn English. But at Castle Garden no one understood what I said, and I don't blame them.

Finally I showed the address to an expressman and he motioned for me to hoist my suitcase and myself in the wagon. He delivered me to East Second Street for twenty-five cents, which I was able to pay out of the silver in my pocket.

The family had not known that I was coming and did not recognize me. Nevertheless, I was welcomed with open arms. At last my vest and the rest of my clothing came off and I took a bath in a tub in the kitchen. The water running out of the taps did not amaze me, for I was prepared for miracles.

A few days later I was working in an upholstery shop at two dollars a week. Not long afterward I ran into a boy about my own age whom I had known in Hungary. His brother got me a job as an apprentice in a fur shop. I began at a salary of four dollars a week — more than I needed, since board and lodging was only two and a half dollars a week. A kid like myself slept on the sofa in the home of a family whose head earned only ten or twelve dollars a week, and the additional income was welcome.

I was very happy, earning big money, living among hundreds of boys of my own age and interests. We boxed, played baseball, and sang Hungarian songs. Having been to night school in Szanto, it was natural for me to ask right away, "Do you have night school here?" The answer was affirmative and I enrolled.

After learning the fur trade, it occurred to me to go into business for myself. With that thought in mind I went to Chicago, though another reason was that I wanted to see the World's Fair. The shop in which I had worked specialized in fur neckpieces made from a single animal, with the head left on. The style was now catching on in Chicago, and since I knew the methods of preparation there was no trouble finding small contracts to fill. Gradually I went into business for myself.

Each fur scarf had a hook and eye or some other clasp to hold the ends together around the shoulders. I invented a spring that allowed the mouth to open and close, making the mouth itself a clasp. I had never heard of patents, but doubtless a patent would have made little difference, since the method could be changed enough to get by. Nevertheless I was off to a head start and sold my scarves at a good profit.

And so here I was at nineteen, swimming in money. In the next couple of years I accumulated seven or eight thousand dollars, a large sum in those days. Many times I congratulated myself on having composed the letter to my trustee. Even so, I was occasionally homesick, and just before reaching twenty-one I returned for a visit and incidentally saw a number of the sights of Europe.

I gave little thoughts to marriage, except to make a mental note that such an event was unlikely to transpire for many years to come. I did not miss family life, never having had much of it. While not exactly a man about town, I lived well and comfortably in a hotel and often took a girl to the theater or for dining and dancing.

I was to learn that it is one thing to plan bachelorhood, another to carry out the plan.

One dealer in raw furs with whom I did business was Morris Kohn, a fellow Hungarian some ten years older than myself. He had entered the fur trade in a rather curious way. With his sister and brother-in-law, Mr. and Mrs. Herman Kaufman, he had taken up homesteading in the Devil's Lake section of North Dakota. To supplement the farm income, Morris had traded with the Sioux Indians for raw pelts. In that way he learned about furs, and after returning to Chicago he stayed in the business.

The Kaufmans had stayed on for a few years in their sod house, but finally they too returned to Chicago, partly because the region was thinly settled and they wanted their daughters to have a chance to meet eligible men.

One Sunday afternoon I called at Morris Kohn's home to keep a business appointment. When the maid told me he had not yet returned from a drive with a niece, I seized the opportunity to join a game of baseball in a vacant lot nearby. A broken finger which remained stiff had finished me as a catcher, and now I valued myself as a second baseman. I am told that it was while I was fielding a grounder—without an error, I hope—that my future wife laid eyes on me for the first time.

Morris Kohn had returned with his niece Lottie Kaufman, second of the four daughters of that pioneer North Dakota sod house. Lottie was unimpressed by my baseball skill, or, at first, by me. But I was not long acquainted with the slender Lottie, with her beautiful dark eyes and exquisite skin, before my notions about marriage began to change.

The courtship was nevertheless rather slow in getting under way. There were many suitors and I was required to play a vast number of hands of cards at the homes of Morris Kohn and Herman Kaufman before my presence was felt. Gradually Lottie and I became better acquainted. She had been born in Hungary too, in a rural area like my own. She was quiet, yet full of warm laughter, and very discerning – a natural homemaker. We were married on January 10, 1897, a week after my twenty-fourth birthday.

About this time Morris Kohn and I went into partnership as Kohn & Company, manufacturing furriers. Morris was a genial man, easy to meet, with a wide acquaintanceship in the trade, and at first he handled most of the outside business. It was while on the road that he first met Marcus Loew, then also a furrier, a dandy in a high hat and fur-lined coat. Marcus was a retiring fellow but he said the high hat and coat impressed the trade. The showman was there all the time. After Kohn & Company moved to New York, in 1900, we lived across from the Loews at 111th Street and Seventh Avenue and were soon warm friends.

It was two years later that I first began to think about going into the motion picture business, or a phase of it. This was before the term Nickelodeon had been invented. In Los Angeles, Tom Tally had converted his arcade into The Electric Theater, "For Up-to-Date Motion Picture Entertainment Especially for Ladies and Children." But the peep machines were still the main outlets for such films as were being made.

My first interest in the show business came through the conversation of a cousin, Max Goldstein, an importer, who had gone to the Exposition in Buffalo to introduce Puerto Rican cigars. While there he had become acquainted with Mitchell Mark and a friend of his named Wagner, who were operating a penny arcade at the Exposition. Mitchell Mark was to make a large name for himself with construction of the Strand Theater on Broadway, the first of the big houses devoted exclusively to pictures. And he was a founder along with Tom Tally and other exhibitors of First National.

Mark and Wagner came down to New York and with Max

Goldstein opened a small arcade on 125th Street. Out of curiosity, Morris Kohn and I accompanied Max on a visit to it. We peeped into the movie machines and listened to the phonographs—which were still the main part of the business—and stood about observing the interest of the customers. This was my first experience in studying audiences, and I have been doing it ever since. After becoming more interested in the operation, I studied the "box-office" figures, another vital thing to do.

At that time the center of show business in New York was Fourteenth Street. In time the conversation got around to the possibilities of a penny arcade in that section. Such a venture would cost a lot of money. It would require a certain amount of glamor, the rent would be high, and expensive kinetoscope and phonograph machines and special cabinets would have to be purchased from Edison. The total cost, the three partners estimated, would run to $75,000—a sum far beyond their reach.

After a dozen conferences and much figuring, Morris Kohn and I agreed to provide the necessary cash and credit. Neither of us expected to leave the fur trade, but it was agreed that one ought to spend a reasonably large share of his time keeping an eye on the arcade, especially since Mark and Wagner remained in Buffalo and Goldstein continued with his import business. The assignment went first to Kohn.

We leased a building on East Fourteenth Street at Broadway, where Ohrbach's department store now stands. A restaurant occupied the first floor, which ran through to Thirteenth Street. It was ripped out and the long room redecorated with bright colors and flashing lights. A hundred or more peep machines were installed, about 60 per cent of them phonographs and the rest motion pictures. The phonographs were the more popular because changes of record were available. Sufficient film was hard to get.

Other slot machines delivered peanuts, candy, and the like. Everything cost a penny, a penny to get in and a penny a look, a listen, or a handful of food. Morris Kohn, in an inventive turn of mind, rigged up a small locomotive which ran around a track and released the coins into itself.

The basement contained a shooting gallery and various athletic devices—punching bags, stationary bicycles, hobbyhorses. Everything was a penny here too, including the shooting. The gallery was operated something like the electric-eye galleries of today. One dropped a penny in a slot, aimed a gun, and pulled the trigger. I don't know the exact science of it, but somehow the target registered the hit.

Enter Lasky and Zukor 79

From the beginning the enterprise was a success, the daily take ranging from five hundred to seven hundred dollars. Our fur offices were nearby on Twelfth Street, and, though handling the main end there, I couldn't keep away from the arcade.

By the end of 1903 we were expanding to Newark, Philadelphia, and Boston, with the result that Kohn and I decided to close out our fur business to devote full energies to the arcades. The liquidation was time consuming, and, since neither of us wanted to be tied down, we brought in Emil Shauer, a buyer for Mandel Brothers' store in Chicago and a brother-in-law of Kohn's, as manager of the arcades.

Marcus Loew, hearing us talk about the arcades, wanted in. So did David Warfield. We could make only a little room for them, since the enterprise was already crowded with partners. But Loew got his feet wet and soon began looking for a place to open an arcade of his own.

Our next step was to convert the floor over the Fourteenth Street Arcade to a motion picture theater. Workmen ripped and hammered, and in 1904 the Crystal Hall, as we named the theater, was ready. To reach it, Morris had devised a glass staircase; inside it water cascaded over lights of changing colors.

While not the first theater devoted to motion pictures, it was perhaps the most attractive of its time.

ADOLPH ZUKOR
Nobody Would Make Big Pictures

"They did not believe that people would sit through pictures that ran three, four, or five reels." Thus Adolph Zukor, the daring young business man with a vision, explained to Joseph Kennedy's Harvard symposium in 1927 how he worked and waited to make bigger movies. The Sarah Bernhardt gamble was just successful enough to encourage him to risk going into feature production for himself.

"Famous Players in Famous Plays" was the idea, and Famous Players became the name of his company. His most successful star, however, had something more than fame on Broadway, something the audience knew was right for movies. It was all right there in the personality of Mary Pickford.

Zukor's talk to the business students, entitled "Origin and Growth of the Industry," was reprinted in Joseph P. Kennedy (ed.) The Story of the Films (N.Y., A. W. Shaw Co., 1927). This selection is from pages 55–67. Note that he makes some claims about his first two feature productions which are corrected later by Kenneth Macgowan.

It is indeed a privilege to have the opportunity to address a class in Harvard College. You gentlemen living here and developing your ideals and ambitions here are so close to the institution that I do not believe you can appreciate the opportunities you have. To a man like myself who never had the chance of a college education, this is a great opportunity, and if I am a bit nervous it is not because I am not glad to be here. Even if it should be an ordeal to talk to you I do it with pleasure and I hope that it may do some good.

I may begin by referring to my early experiences in the business. About twenty-two years ago we had "Hale's Touring Car," which was a Pullman car constructed with the rear end open. A picture was thrown some twenty feet from the rear, and one would turn around, as if in an observation car, and watch the scenery. These pictures were taken in Switzerland, Italy, and all parts of the world. That was the first moving picture that attracted my attention seriously. I thought it was very interesting and I knew that it would appeal to most of the people. William A. Brady, a theatrical manager in New York, who had bought the rights for that state, asked me to join him in exploiting this form of entertainment.

We started out by taking a store on Fourteenth Street and put this Pullman car in. We made the front of the store look like a depot and we were able to get films for about six different tours. The first day was a big success. It was very interesting. We also had a lecturer who pointed out the interesting points, such as mountains, rivers, and buildings, and I felt sure we were on the road to success. But it did not last long because there were not enough subjects to make changes. We found that after about two weeks we had to repeat the subjects and, of course, when they were once seen people were no longer interested. Pretty soon we found ourselves with no business.

We approached all of the people who had made pictures in this country – Edison, Biograph, Lubin, and Selig, and the Belasco Company – and tried to get them to supply these travelogues, but they did not think we could dispose of enough to warrant their spending money for the negatives. So we had to shut down.

In the meantime they had been making a lot of short subjects that ran about 150 to 200 feet in length. By putting together several of these, they made up 1,000 feet of what they called "chase pictures." Many of you will remember that every picture finished with a man who was painting, or washing a window, using a ladder. Then he ran away, and the man who was painting ran after him and the police chased him, and the dogs and the cats and the children ran after him. That was the climax of every picture; it seemed they could not think of any other.

We were compelled to remove the cars and put seats in our stores and show these chase pictures. That lasted about three years. All the subjects were of much the same type, though occasionally some director hit upon the idea of making a picture with a story to it that had some heart interest. Each time we were lucky enough to have a subject of that kind our business felt it. The response to that kind of picture was surprising. It was really a foretaste and a prophecy of what we have now.

At this time the men who made these pictures earned most of their money on the projection machines. The main business of the Edison Company, as well as of Lubin and Selig, was to make these machines. Naturally, they all concentrated on the mechanical end of the business. That was very necessary and very important for this reason: In those days you could buy a projection machine for $75 or $95. People with money or with a substantial business would never think of opening a little store show, but as long as it did not take more than $300 or $400 to open up a theatre, a good many small investors took a chance, and that helped to develop the business. The making of these low-priced projection machines made it possible for a number of store shows to come into existence, without which I believe there would be no moving picture industry today. The great number of these store shows created a market for the moving picture producers and gave them an opportunity to develop.

The novelty of the chase pictures began to wear out, too, and about 1907 or 1908 we found ourselves where we could not carry on the business profitably. There were plenty of pictures made but they were so much alike that there was no more public interest in them.

In those days when anybody wanted a lease he had to put up a good deposit and take the lease in his own name. I had taken about fourteen leases and found myself where I had to go through bankruptcy to get out of the leases or else continue in business. I chose to continue in business. So I made every effort in this country as well as in Europe to obtain pictures. They were making the best pictures in Europe then, in France and Italy. We did not make very good pictures in this country. As luck would have it, the Pathé Company in Paris made a picture, "The Passion Play," which was in three reels and hand-colored. That was really the first picture of any consequence that I can recall. When I saw that picture I made up my mind to bring it to America.

We arranged for an organ and a quartet to play and sing appropriate music. I did not dare open in New York. So we tried it first in Newark. We were on a street adjoining a big department store and opened up Monday morning. A great many of the bargain hunters—I mean the ladies—dropped in early to see and hear the performance. As they walked out, I stood at the door eager and anxious to hear the comments. People with tears in their eyes came over to me and said, "What a beautiful thing this is." I felt instinctively that this was the turning point, that my rent would be paid from now on.

About eleven o'clock, a priest who was in the audience came over and said he thought that showing a picture like that in a theatre was sacrilegious and he would have to report it to the city authorities. I could see that rent staring me in the face again, so I had a talk with him and asked him what objection he had and why he objected. He said he did not object to the picture itself, that everything in it was fine, but that the subject belonged to the church and not the theatre. He did not think the church and the theatre had the same mission. I told him the plight I was in; I told him my circumstances; I told him all about it, and I said, "If you have this place closed you see what will happen to me." He looked at me and sympathized and he thought he would let it go, and so the picture stayed on. We stayed on with that picture for months and did a land office business.

That gave me courage to go into New York and wherever else I had theatres, and we showed that picture with the same success everywhere. Then it occurred to me that if we could take a novel or a play and put it on the screen, the people would be interested. We should get not only the casual passers-by but people leaving their homes, going out in search of amusement. However, I had no experience in making pictures and nothing was farther from my mind. I did approach all the producers then in the business and tried to sell the idea of making big pictures.

At that time the producers numbered ten, and so many store shows had jumped up—thousands throughout the country—that there developed a great demand for the one-reel and two-reel pictures that were being made. They were so busy turning out these pictures that they would not undertake anything else. In fact, they did not believe that people would sit through pictures that ran three, four, or five reels. I tried for a number of years to convince them, but nobody would undertake to make big pictures.

I had no faith in the pictures as they were then. There were other managers who had been very successful in vaudeville theatres and used these one-reel and two-reel pictures for "chasers." I then took a few houses and ran vaudeville and pictures jointly, and the combination was a success. Yet I never gave up the idea that finally developed in later years.

As a vaudeville operator, I was in partnership with others, including Mr. Loew, who had had a great number of vaudeville theatres. One day in 1909, someone made the suggestion that we all join and make one corporation out of these theatres. Mr. Loew had the greater number of theatres, so we adopted the name of Loew Enterprises and all my vaudeville interests were melted in the Loew Enterprises. I made a condition that I would put my interest in but that I would not take any active part in the business, because it was not the thing I had in mind. My mind was made up on these pictures.

Turning my interests into the Loew Enterprises gave me an opportunity to be foot-loose. I was well taken care of; the corporation paid good dividends, and from 1909 to 1912 I made a study of moving pictures. I traveled all through Europe and this country, watched the audiences, and was interested in any picture that had a subject that I felt would appeal to the public. In my own mind I wanted to verify whether my judgment was right. I would go to a theatre, take the first row or sit in a box and there study the audience and see what effect the picture had on them. So I was pretty certain in my mind after the experience I had had in watching audiences that I could use a subject and not go very far wrong.

In 1911 I made up my mind definitely to take big plays and celebrities of the stage and put them on the screen. While I was looking around to get an organization together, word came to me that Sarah Bernhardt was appearing in Paris in a play called "Queen Elizabeth" and that she would be willing to put that play into motion pictures for $35,000. Of course that was an awful lot of money. There was a Mr. Porter at the head of Rex, which was the trade name of a one-reel picture released weekly. They knew I was interested in going into this big picture making. Sarah Bernhardt's agent cabled to Mr. Porter, and he came to me with the proposition and said, "I merely mention it to you, because the price is prohibitive." I asked him what it was, and he said she wanted $35,000. I said, "All right; I will take it," and we cabled $5,000 that very day.

That was in November, 1911, and in March, 1912, we released the picture in this country. By the time that picture was finished there had been formed what was called the General Film Company and the Patents Company. They had everything in their control. The Patents Company controlled the patents not only of the camera but of the projection machine, and they made it a condition in leasing a machine that only their pictures could be shown on the screen. So I found myself with "Queen Elizabeth" and no place to go. There was only one thing I could do and that was to take the legitimate theatres. I went to Klaw and Erlanger and got bookings. It was in the spring, and there were not many shows on the road. I booked Daly's in New York and the Powers Theatre in Chicago.

We found that our matinees were fine. I remember in Chicago I stood in the lobby and I was very proud. We had almost a full house at the matinee. The show went off well and everything was lovely. A great many thought Sarah Bernhardt was there in person. I may mention that this was the first time lithographs were made of the pictures. We had used lithographs before, but they had nothing to do with the pictures shown. We also advertised in the newspapers.

Just about that time I interested Mr. Daniel Frohman in the enterprise and told him what I thought could be accomplished. He used his influence with the Patents Company to have this Bernhardt picture licensed, and that opened the doors and I was able to distribute the picture. I believe we had to gross about $60,000 to cover expenses, but we took in enough so that our first experiment was not costly. We did gain the knowledge that made us absolutely certain that pictures of the right type had a great future.

At that time Mr. Frohman had the late James K. Hackett under contract. He was on the road with "The Prisoner of Zenda." I asked Mr. Frohman to see Mr. Hackett, who was then playing in St. Louis, and explain that we wanted him to go into pictures and assure him that it would not hurt his reputation or affect his popularity. Mr. Frohman prevailed on Mr. Hackett to appear in a picture, though it was a very hard job. At that time it was beneath the dignity of a well-known star to appear on the screen. But Mr. Hackett was a good business man as well as a good actor. He realized that this was an art that was going to amount to something and thought he might as well have the honor of being its first American star.

The first long picture made in this country was "The Prisoner of Zenda," with Mr. Hackett as star. We had all sorts of handicaps to overcome but finally, after a great deal of trouble, the picture was made. Of course, everybody who heard about it in the theatrical world thought I was crazy. Nobody believed that people would sit through a picture for hours as they would a play. There were all sorts of reasons why the thing would not succeed. However, when we finished the picture and had a showing at the Lyceum Theatre to invited guests and critics, the thing was pronounced a great success. The characters were recognized and called by name. People said, "See who is playing Black Michael! Look at so and so! Isn't that so and so?" The effect was tremendous. I was sure then that personalities plus a good story were all that we needed in pictures. . . .

Following that we made a picture of "The Count of Monte Cristo," with James O'Neill. By this time the Patents Company had almost come to the realization that perhaps I was right, and yet they did not feel like changing their method or their line of business. But when they heard that I was going to make this picture, "The Count of Monte Cristo," with O'Neill, they made another on the same subject in a hurry. By the time my picture was finished they had theirs in circulation, and, although it was so inferior to the one we made that it would not be in the same class at all, nevertheless the damage was done. I could not release mine because they would not license it as long as they had their own, and we had to put "The Count of Monte Cristo" on the shelf. That was our first financial setback.

Just about this time Belasco had a little girl in a play called "The Good Little Devil." She played a blind girl's part and her name was Mary Pickford. I knew Mary Pickford had had picture experience, because she had been with Biograph a couple of years before and knew the camera. We had already discovered in making these pictures that the makeup and action required were entirely different from those of the regular stage. The regular actors did not have screen experience and they did not seem to want to learn. We tried people who were well advanced on the stage, but the director could not make them do things to suit the camera.

I felt, if we could get people who had experience on the stage and also had some camera experience, the results would be much better. It appeared to me that Mary Pickford would be a good choice, so I made Mr. Belasco a proposition to produce "The Good Little Devil" on the screen. While the play was going on we would take the picture during the day. As soon as she came into the studio we recognized her ability, and I induced her to stay in the motion pictures permanently. Her salary with Belasco was $175 a week. I offered her $500. Of course, that was a great deal of money and she could not resist it. So she joined the Famous Players. About the same time we contracted for several other stars of Broadway, such as Mrs. Fiske, John Barrymore, and many others, and prepared to do about six pictures that year.

As that plan worked along I found that we could not release the pictures through the General Film Company. We had to work out some other method of distribution. The only method we could think of at that time was to sell our pictures through state rights, meaning that to take care of a section like this we would organize the Famous Players' Company of New England; in Michigan we would have the Famous Players' Company of Michigan; and so on. We divided the country into fifteen units, and each unit would buy and distribute the pictures in a certain territory. One unit had no connection financially or otherwise with the others. When we got to that point we realized that a distributor could not maintain an office and do business on six or eight pictures a year because the overhead would not permit it. So we decided to make thirty pictures a year. We felt that that number of pictures would give an office about two and one-half pictures a month, and on that they could maintain an organization and run their business. So we made thirty pictures a year.

WILL IRWIN
Waiting at the Theater

Adolph Zukor told his Harvard audience that Daniel Frohman "used his influence" with the Patents Company to get a license for Queen Elizabeth. But it was not all clear sailing after that. Will Irwin's authorized biography of Zukor, The House That Shadows Built, *(N.Y., Doubleday Doran, 1928) gives us on pages 170-173 of his chapter, "Edison Writes a Letter," a further suspenseful sidelight on these latter days of the still powerful patents trust.*

When he planned his revolution in the business of making motion pictures, Zukor had faced and acknowledged one cardinal trick. The Trust stood in his way, as in that of every independent with a new idea. "If you can't bust a trust, join it; if you can't join it, bust it," said business men in those days. Zukor cherished no moral abhorrence to trusts. Indeed he preferred that the lords of industry should take him into their circle of nine or ten approved companies. Otherwise, he might expect both a nasty fight involving heavy legal expenses and an artificially restricted market among distributors and exhibitors. To insure himself against this contingency, he had engaged as attorney for his new company the shrewd and theatre-wise Elek J. Ludvigh.

However, he faced the battle with considerable hope. The Trust had of late appealed more and more to public opinion. "We present the best films, and clean films," said its publicity agents.

He proposed to offer more ambitious films than the Trust dreamed of. If it refused them licence, it put itself in an illogical position. The enemy might command the heavier battalions, but he had most of the ammunition. Working sixteen hours a day at his complex task of organization, Zukor stored this worry in the cellar of his mind. He would cross the bridge when he came to it.

As he prepared to exploit and exhibit *Zenda*, the bridge began to look more and more like a barrier. Following its precedent, the Trust had licenced *Queen Elizabeth* as a foreign film. *Zenda*, made by an upstart company on American soil, stood in a different category. Ludvigh and Frohman put out feelers, and got no satisfaction either of approval or disapproval. But that incident of a rival *Monte Cristo* gave a sinister indication. The day of *Zenda's* promotional showing arrived; and still the Trust had not spoken. The personnel of the Famous Players entered the Lyceum Theatre that afternoon in a state of tense anxiety. Zukor, looking over the assembling audience, imagined that every male spectator was a process server waiting to tag him with an injunction.

However, the Trust was not holding its peace merely by way of dangling Famous Players on the string. There were divided counsels in its directorate. One minority faction believed with Zukor that refusal of a licence would alienate public opinion. Another had itself been urging longer and better films; it saw in *Zenda*, as in *Queen Elizabeth*, a stimulus from the outside. The Trust, with the inertia of a business grown soggy through prosperity, characteristically delayed action until the last moment. As the doorkeepers unlocked the Lyceum Theatre for that vital matinee performance, its directors were considering the problem at luncheon. And the two minorities, acting together, won the day. They resolved to licence *Zenda*, with the canny reservation that this action must not be considered a precedent.

One of the directors, appreciating the anxiety at the Lyceum Theatre, had promised to telephone news of the final decision. At half-past two the audience was assembled, but the telephone rang not. At a quarter of three the house began to grow impatient.

"What shall we do?" whispered Frohman.

"Run it, licence or no licence," responded Zukor.

Then, just as the operator lit up his booth, came the good news.

So far, so good. But the Famous Players, which intended to produce films continuously, could not go on through the fogs of such uncertainty. Ludvigh, Frohman, and Zukor began pressure for a continuous licencing arrangement. The Trust refused to commit itself. Then Frohman thought of Thomas A. Edison. He it was who, taking many ideas from many sources and adding a few of his own, harmonized them to make the practical moving-picture camera. The American public, indeed, credited him with the entire invention. So far as he was still involved in the motion picture, his interests lay with the Trust. I need not dwell on his personal prestige. A word from him might melt all opposition. If that failed, and they had to draw the public into the game, his support would be the ace of trumps.

DANIEL FROHMAN
Edison Is Agreeable

Call it personal diplomacy, an end run, intuitive business acumen, or luck—this little known meeting between Thomas Edison and Adolph Zukor's friend and associate, Daniel Frohman, is a remarkable example of the search for peaceful methods of adjustment in business. It is reported in a chapter called "Famous Players," on pages 277 to 280 of Daniel Frohman Presents *(N.Y., Lee Furman Inc., 1935).*

So an engagement was made for me to call upon "The Wizard of Menlo Park." My visit to him was booked about two weeks in advance. Arriving at Menlo Park, I asked his secretary whether Mr. Edison expected me. He said, "Yes, he has asked several times whether you had arrived."

I thought this sounded promising. Shortly afterward he came out and greeted me cordially.

"Mr. Frohman," said he, "what can I do for you?"

I explained the situation fully to him. He seemed to doubt his ability to help us, stating that he had only certain interests in the company, and that he could be out-voted. I then stuck to my point and explained how important this new movement was in behalf of elevating the standards of moving pictures that the Famous

Players' was conducting. It would improve the character of the entire industry, and its activities would not be confined alone to Famous Players'. Others would follow in our footsteps in bringing great plays and great stage stars to the screen.

Whereupon Mr. Edison gave me a letter which, upon reading, I found was a courteous and well-intended note to an important official, but not quite of the direct value I intended.

I saw that Mr. Edison was highly interested in the plans and purposes of our company. He had listened attentively and was thoroughly sympathetic, for there were certain elements in this new enterprise that appealed to him as a public-spirited citizen, aside from his interest as a business partner associated with the opposing company. But I wanted a stronger letter. But how to secure it was a delicate problem.

As he seemed to be having a bit of leisure and began to chat genially about matters concerning the theatre, I said to him, "Mr. Edison, I remember the day that you were married."

"You do?" said he, surprised.

"Yes," I answered. "I was a boy in the business department of the New York *Tribune* and I remember what struck me as a most remarkable incident of that event, because the remembrance of it has lasted so long; for there was printed in the newspapers at the time an account of this wedding. You were then, I believe, a telegraph operator in Nashville, and you had a laboratory on the side, in which you worked during your spare time. After the ceremony you repaired to your den to work upon some inventions. The hours passed. You had evidently forgotten entirely about the wedding. Then one of your friends came to you and said that everybody was awaiting your arrival for dinner. You jumped up in alarm. In consternation, you remembered that you had been married and rushed back to the assembled guests."

The story of this incident was at the time printed in all the newspapers.

Mr. Edison seemed greatly amused, and said, "Did you know Whitelaw Reid and John Russell Young, or George Ripley, the Literary Editor?"

"Yes," I replied. "At that time Bronson Howard, who afterwards became the leading dramatist of America, was the Political Editor. Mark Twain was associated with the editorial department, where he was then occupied with writing his letters from the Sandwich Islands. John Hay, afterwards Minister to England, was then a young man associated with the paper."

Enter Lasky and Zukor 91

I went on to name a number of other big men connected with the editorial department, for it was then my business to supply each one every day with one or more copies of the paper. And I also mentioned to him my peculiar association as part office boy to Horace Greeley. This little recital interested Mr. Edison greatly and he began to tell me glowingly of his early efforts as an inventor in those days. He spoke warmly of some invention which he had just then created and which he felt would be of great service to the business community; but his progress was opposed by a certain firm that felt, wrongly of course, that the success of these inventions would jeopardize their business interests. He was confronting a stone wall. He tried to explain that his invention would be an aid to them rather than a hindrance.

"Mr. Edison," I said, "I am in the same position now that you were in then, and you are the only man who can help me."

"By Jingo, I will," he said sympathetically, and thereupon he wrote me two letters somewhat mandatory in their character, directed to the two chief officers of the company. When I read these notes I found that at last I had secured just what I was out to obtain.

I expressed the warmest gratitude to Mr. Edison and was about to depart, feeling like the youth in the play of "Richelieu" who had also accomplished an important mission, when Mr. Edison asked me to stay, as he wished to show me his latest invention, which was then the talking moving pictures. He requested me not to hurry away and I spent a most delightful hour with this grand old man. Then, eager to go, I departed gleefully and returned to our offices.

I might add here that the talking motion pictures referred to here were not the present style of talkies as exhibited in the theatres. It was talking pictures in association with the phonograph, and was displayed in many vaudeville houses years before the new vogue of talkies swept the country like a broom.

Some time later, when I delivered the letters to Mr. Zukor, he found them of such inestimable value that he had them photographed in our studio.

Thus the object he sought was obtained.

KENNETH MACGOWAN
The Coming of the Feature Film

Now we step back and look at the general scene of picture-making, to ask the question, with Kenneth Macgowan, "Who made the first feature film?" While Zukor's adventure with Sarah Bernhardt caused quite a splash in the news and the trade papers, Italy had sent over a five-reeler the year before, in 1911, and other American and foreign companies were into production with long movies in 1912. Macgowan pulls these strands together as best he can, and meanwhile explains how hard it is to sort out the facts in recent history. The cost of the rights for Queen Elizabeth, *for instance, varies in different accounts, and the delay in releasing* The Count of Monte Cristo *was not as long as Zukor seems to imply in his own report. Zukor was certainly not correct in claiming that* The Prisoner of Zenda *(1913) was "the first long picture made in this country."*

Kenneth Macgowan deserves a special note as scholar and participant in Hollywood history. Harvard graduate, drama critic for newspapers in Boston, Philadelphia, and New York, editor of Theatre Arts Magazine *for six years, he came to Hollywood as story editor and producer at RKO-Radio Pictures, 1932–35, moved to 20th Century-Fox for six years and was at Paramount as a producer when he was appointed chairman of theater arts at UCLA in 1947 and given responsibility for the new motion picture division there. This selection is from a book he completed just before his death in 1963,* Behind the Screen *(N.Y., Delacorte Press, 1965) pages 155–161.*

What was the first feature film? Who made it? And when? Most moviegoers of today would probably pick Griffith's *The Birth of a Nation* of 1915. Because I was a motion picture critic on a newspaper around that time, I happen to know that the idea of the feature film was born some three years earlier. Griffith himself had finished at least four features before he started his epic. And prior to 1915 more than fifty features had been made in Europe and America.

I think we had better begin by defining the feature film. In the first place, it doesn't have to last two or three hours like the blockbusters of the sixties. On the other hand, the French picture *Queen Elizabeth*, which launched Adolph Zukor and Famous Players in 1912, cannot qualify as a feature; it was only three reels long, though the distributor later advertised it as four. Zukor himself was rather slow in accepting the trade dictum that a feature ought to fill at least five cans, each can holding about 1,000 feet of film. He made at least two five-reelers in 1913, but among his movies of that year and the next were a dozen shorter films, three of which were only three reels long. Zukor—and some other producers of such short features—could hardly plead that the story material was scanty, for almost all were based on novels or plays. Though five reels got thoroughly established by 1914 as the rock-bottom minimum for the kind of feature that was called a "program picture," there were more and more "specials" that ranged from 6,000 to 12,000 feet.

It may seem absurd to add to the definition of a feature film that all of its five or more reels have to be shown, one after the other, at every performance. Yet we must recall the case of J. Stuart Blackton and *The Life of Moses*, made in 1909. So far as I know, this Vitagraph production was probably the first film of feature length, but the public never saw it as a five-reel movie. The short-sighted resistance of the "trust" and its booking office was so great, that though Vitagraph was one of the member companies, they sent it out, as I have said in the last chapter, one reel at a time for five weeks. Whatever the merits of *The Life of Moses* —and the three "stills" I have seen seem from a stage production with such things as mountains painted on a backdrop —Blackton deserves the credit for producing the first feature that could have met the test of the five-reel yardstick. Moreover, he himself intended it as a continuous show.

Except for Vitagraph, the resistance of the members of the trust to films longer than one reel was bitter and uncompromising —and suicidal. Even 2,000-foot movies upset the monopolists. In 1910, when Biograph discovered that Griffith had made a two-reeler called, ironically, *His Trust*, the company cut the film in two, and sent it out successively as one-reel shorts called *His Trust* and *His Trust Fulfilled*. The studio tried to do the same thing with his *Enoch Arden* (1911) — an expansion of his 1908 *After Many Years* — but, as more and more such dismembered films appeared, exhibitors got into the habit of holding up the first reel and showing it with the second. This quiet revolt of the exhibitors was significant. It signalled the turning of the tide. It foreshadowed the destruction of the film trust, hoist on its own petard. By 1912 some members of the trust were making three-reelers, an independent had turned out a feature, and the Continent had sent us the first of a series of spectacles.

94 THE FIRST TYCOONS

In Europe there was no patent monopoly to dictate the length of films. Italy took the lead. In 1911 a company in Milan devoted five reels to *Dante's Inferno,* and in August this film became the first feature to be road-shown in American theaters. Italian directors, turning history into screen spectacle, were as prodigal of film footage as of extras. Enrico Guazzoni's *Quo Vadis?,* made in 1912, opened at the Astor Theater on Broadway on April 21, 1913, at $1.50 top, and ran off eight or nine reels to a special orchestral accompaniment. That year Italy turned out two versions of *The Last Days of Pompeii,* Ambrosio's in six reels and Pasquali's in eight. From the rather short and quite static products of Film d'Art, France plunged ahead in 1913 to *Germinal* in eight reels and *Les Misérables* in twelve. With *Cabiria,* the same year, Italy matched *Les Misérables* in length and outdid the French film in lavish spectacle. It seemed that the Italians would dominate the film world with what one of their critics called "such solemn, terrible, and overwhelming images." Then came World War I and an end to their dreams of cinema conquest.

As the trust weakened and the independents prospered, more and more American companies were able to produce and exhibit three- and four-reel films. At last, late in May or early in June, 1912, H. A. Spanuth, a now-forgotten independent, made film history that few remember by showing New York critics the Broadway star Nat Goodwin in a true feature, *Oliver Twist.* Its five reels were shown, unsegmented, at every performance. Here was the forerunner of the program pictures that were to meet the five-reel test-gauge of the feature film.

Whether or not *Oliver Twist* was shown publicly before Zukor's *Queen Elizabeth,* the American film was overshadowed by Zukor's importation. We shall never know if the Dickens film was as stagey and unimaginative as the French movie, but Zukor's had the advantage of a great international star, Sarah Bernhardt. The actress was old and lame and shorn of her golden voice. But she was still Bernhardt, and Zukor took pains to exploit star and film to the limit of his ingenuity. Also, he planned to follow this up with the organized production of other films displaying "Famous Players in Famous Plays." . . .

Getting the facts of the film history of only fifty years ago is no easy matter. The story of how Zukor obtained the American rights to *Queen Elizabeth* in 1912 is one of many examples. In 1926, Terry Ramsaye said in his voluminous and valuable history, *A Million and One Nights*, that Zukor and two partners bought the rights for $18,000. Some twenty-five years later, Zukor himself stated in his book *The Public Is Never Wrong* that he had put up $40,000 to finance this French production by Louis Mercanton.

To launch *Queen Elizabeth* in proper style and to advise on the production work that was to follow, Zukor enlisted the stage producer Daniel Frohman. The picture was shown to the press and "a distinguished audience" at the Lyceum Theater on the afternoon of July 12, 1912, blessed by a Broadway accolade: "Daniel Frohman presents *Queen Elizabeth.*"

When Zukor organized the Famous Players Film Company, the tone of his publicity suggested that he—like the men of Film d'Art—believed he had to depend for success on stage stars and stage plays. But he knew there was an art of the film that the French had not grasped, for he offered the post of director general to Griffith at $50,000 a year, and when he refused, Zukor hired Porter of *The Great Train Robbery*. He added to his staff J. Searle Dawley, who had had experience in directing short films as well as plays, and he engaged as press agent B. P. Schulberg, who was later to head Paramount production on the Coast.

At first Zukor concentrated on actors with stage reputations. His initial production, made late in 1912, starred James O'Neill—the father of Eugene O'Neill—in *The Count of Monte Cristo*, which the actor had played for almost twenty years up and down the country. Selig was first in the field, however, with a version starring Hobart Bosworth. In *A Million and One Nights* Terry Ramsaye states that the Famous Players film had to be shelved until "the Selig version should have been forgotten by the exhibitors." Their memories must have been short, for the O'Neill film was in release within a year. The first Famous Players production to reach the screen was *The Prisoner of Zenda* (1913) with James K. Hackett, who had made a hit in the play. Then, in 1913 and 1914, came a procession of stage stars in films made from stage plays and a novel or two. Among the actors were Mrs. Minnie Maddern Fiske, Henrietta Crosman, and young John Barrymore, all from the American stage, and Lily Langtry and Cecilia Loftus from the British.

In Zukor's first year of production he discovered that a screen actress could be more effective and more popular than the best player the stage could offer. The actress was Mary Pickford. On

Broadway she had played a child in two of David Belasco's productions, but she was essentially a silent screen actress, well trained by Griffith in her Biograph days. Beginning with *A Good Little Devil* (1913), her first Famous Players production, Mary Pickford was to prove more successful than any of Zukor's stage stars. Through *Tess of the Storm Country* (1914), *Rebecca of Sunnybrook Farm* (1917), *Pollyanna* (1920), and a number of other films, she had a series of successes that vindicated Zukor's belief in the feature film – and Miss Pickford.

Of course there were other producers making features besides Zukor – and some before him. Late in 1912, the Kalem company released a six-reel film, *From the Manger to the Cross*, which Sidney Olcott had directed in Palestine. During the next year *Traffic in Souls,* directed by George Loane Tucker, in six reels, opened in a rather small theater, Joe Weber's, but it was soon playing in nearly thirty New York houses. In 1914 Colin Campbell finished *The Spoilers,* at least two hours long. By the end of 1913, so many features had been made – even England had a 7,500-foot version of *David Copperfield* – that producers and distributors could take over Broadway theaters and even think of building new and bigger houses.

Early in 1914, the Blackton-Smith-Rock company had enough long films to lease the Criterion Theater on Broadway, a legitimate house of modest capacity, and rename it the Vitagraph. Much more important, the supply of features was now so abundant that Mitchell L. Mark, who started with penny arcades, had no qualms about building the 3,300-seat Strand. This first of American's big new theaters opened in April, 1914, with Selig's nine-reel production of *The Spoilers,* still remembered by some because of the super-colossal fight between William Farnum and Tom Santschi. The success of the Strand, which charged from ten cents to fifty cents a seat, had much to do with the building, during the next three years, of many new theaters that seated more than 1,200 moviegoers.

GEORGE PRATT
Multiple Reel Films

George Pratt, editor of Image *and chief research associate for many years at Eastman House in Rochester, N.Y., has also tried to pin down the "first" feature and he seems to have turned up a bit of evidence not known to MacGowan.* The Life of Moses, *a Vitagraph series of five reels (1909-1910) was actually shown all together in New Orleans for eight days. He gives his own list of 1912-1913 long films in this extract from an article in* Image, *November 1957, pages 208-211. The article was originally titled, "A Myth Is as Good as a Milestone."*

... take the myth that D. W. Griffith's early costume spectacle *Judith of Bethulia*, completed in the fall of 1913, was "the first American four-reel picture,"[9] and thus, by implication, the longest film made in America up to that time.

It was nothing of the sort.

The whole question of the increase in length of the American film is one which never seems to have been examined closely, although almost everyone has something to say about it. First, of course, were the early brevities of film production. Then came the occasional "long" film of one thousand feet (one reel), or even more, but despite this innovation, shorter lengths still predominated throughout the industry. Frequently two, three or even four separate subjects were wound on the same thousand-foot reel.

Our fragmentary knowledge of American film production before 1907 prevents us from speaking with authority about that period. But thanks to release records, detailed reviews and synopses, we are on certain ground from 1907 on, and a study of such source material tells us that *Judith of Bethulia* must bow to films as long or longer which were issued before the Griffith film was ready.

The four- and five-reel features (eventually called "multiple-reel films" to distinguish them from the shorter product) entered hesitantly—split into sections—upon the American film scene.

Afterward, it was not easy to recapture and tabulate the film past. *Motion Picture Magazine* as early as December, 1911, frankly gave up on a question about film lengths with: "We cannot state positively the 'longest film.' . . . Better call that bet off and buy an ice cream soda with it."[10] And by 1914 *The Moving Picture World* was calling for help: "We do not know the date of release of the first multiple. The change came so gradually from the four-or five-part story released part by part that it would be pretty hard to locate. The change came sometime in the last four years. Does anyone know just when?"[11]

It is true that some companies experimented by issuing a long story in separate reels strewn throughout their regular release schedules. In 1909, the Edison Company filmed the candlestick episode from *Les Miserables* in less than a reel (560'), packaged it with an unrelated comedy on the full reel, and released it on Aug. 13. They followed it up with *The Ordeal* (950'), "the second chapter in the life of Jean Valjean," released Sept. 21, and later with *A New Life* (1000'), third of the episodes, on Oct. 12.

However, the writer has found no evidence that these reels were ever shown together on one program. Nor has he discovered that this was true of the Vitagraph 1909 version of the same Hugo novel, issued in four separate reels from September to November of that year.

But Vitagraph's *The Life of Moses,* of which Reel One was issued Dec. 4, 1909, and the fifth and final reel on Feb. 19, 1910, was definitely screened later as a five-reel feature. There is proof of this in the jubilant letter of the manager of a New Orleans movie-house, printed April 30, 1901: ". . . We also ran *The Life of Moses* series for eight days to record business. We used the entire five reels in a series and used both piano and organ for musical effects . . ."[12]

There seem to have been no really lengthy films produced in this country in 1911, although the successful importation from Italy that same year of *The Crusaders; or Jerusalem Delivered* in four reels, and *Dante's Inferno* in five reels, must have set the American producers to thinking about the further potentiality of consecutive screenings of related reels, so that the entire story could be followed at one sitting. For next year there was quite an outbreak of domestic multiple reels.

To 1912 belong the following American features, presented from the outset as single units: *Ten Nights in a Bar Room* (Atlas, 4 reels, advertised in January); Nat C. Goodwin's *Oliver Twist* (General Film Publicity & Sales, 5 reels, previewed in May); *Hiawatha* (F. E. Moore, 4 reels, reviewed in March); Blanche Walsh's *Resur-*

rection (Masko, 4 reels, reviewed in July); Helen Gardner's *Cleopatra* (Helen Gardner Picture Players, 6 reels, previewed in November); *Monte Cristo*, with James O'Neill (Famous Players, 5 reels, copyright in December); *Quincy Adams Sawyer and Mason's Corner Folks* (Puritan Special Features, 4 reels, copyright in December).

Furthermore, the following American multiple-reel films belong to the first half of 1913, before *Judith of Bethulia* was finished: *The Prisoner of Zenda* (Famous Players, 5 reels, completed in January); *The Tonopah Stampede for Gold* (Yale Feature Film, 4 reels, advertised in March); Shakespeare's *Richard III*, with Frederick Warde (Shakespeare Film, 5 reels, advertised in April); *A Good Little Devil*, with Mary Pickford (Famous Players, 5 reels, completed in June) and Thomas H. Ince's *The Battle of Gettysburg* (New York Motion Picture, 5 reels, New York City premiere June 1).

NOTES

9. Lewis Jacobs, *The Rise of the American Film* (Harcourt, Brace and Company, New York, 1939), p. 116; also see *Life* magazine, Aug. 2, 1948, p. 31: "Movies Lose Their Great Pioneer. D. W. Griffith, Who Made The First Four-Reeler and *The Birth of a Nation*, Dies at 73."
10. p. 134.
11. May 16, 1914, p. 963.
12. *The Moving Picture World*, p. 697.

BEN M. HALL
The Strand Theatre

Ben M. Hall, in a chapter entitled "A Wonderful Audience in Costly Togs," describes the planning and opening of the Strand Theater on Broadway and 47th Street. Our selection is pages 37–41 from his book, The Best Remaining Seats *(N.Y., Clarkson N. Potter Inc., 1961), a celebration of the grandiose movie houses like the Strand and the Vitagraph which were built during the late teens and twenties. Note that the opening bill offered two hours and a quarter of* The Spoilers *in April of 1914, eleven months before the New York showing of* The Birth of a Nation. A Million Bid, *a four-reeler, had been shown in February by Vitagraph.*

The Mark brothers, Mitchell and Moe—late of Buffalo and a lucrative nickelodeon business—had leased the site of the old Brewster carriage factory on the corner of Broadway and Forty-seventh Street, to erect a giant "million-dollar" theatre. Their original plan, as announced in the papers, had been to build a fifty-cent vaudeville house, seating 2,800. But they lost interest in this idea when William Morris beat them to it with his Wonderland Theatre at Broadway and Forty-fifth Street—a Longacre Square Luna Park that combined bazaar and indoor fair, amusement rides for children on the roof, with continuous movies and music-hall acts in the theatre proper....

Movies, of course, were not new to Broadway. Marcus Loew had made a mint with them since his days on Herald Square; the old Broadway Theatre, at Forty-first Street, was showing them. The Astor, one of the city's most elegant legitimate theatres, had gone over to films with *Quo Vadis* on April 19, 1913, for a twenty-two-week run. And the stately Criterion, it had just been revealed, would become a movie theatre after the first of the year, when the Vitagraph Company would reopen it, boasting one of New York's first Mighty Wurlitzer organs (then known as the "Hope-Jones Unit Orchestra") to accompany the pictures, and a stage setting that would reproduce the New York Harbor complete with Statue of Liberty.

The more the Marks thought about it the better the idea seemed. They would attract "high class" crowds to their new theatre (now officially named The Strand) and they would show the wiseacres of Longacre Square a thing or two. Most of the stigma of the storefront peepshow had melted away, as bigger and more respectable theatres were being converted to the showing of films. New York, in 1913, could count 986 movie houses—of all kinds—though even the largest and finest of these suffered from all the architectural ills of the day: tiers of avalanching galleries supported by view-killing columns, hard wooden "opera chairs," and becalmed ventilation systems. They were ill-suited to showing films, and the Marks knew that the new Strand would be perfect.

They had already made free with their hoard of Buffalo nickels, so carefully saved during all the nickelodeon years in upstate New York, to insure that the Strand—to whatever purpose it might eventually be put—was going to be the most beautiful, comfortable and up-to-date theatre in the world.

"From the first moment we conceived of erecting the Strand," stated Mitchell in a newspaper interview, "we made studies of all the best theatres in Europe and America, and we selected Mr. Thomas W. Lamb for the task of putting all their best features into making the Strand a 'National Institution' which would stand for all time as the model of Moving Picture Palaces."

The die was cast. It would be movies for the Strand. But not *just* movies. To expand on this sudden and daring new concept, they started searching for an impresario who would do justice to their ambitions. They didn't have to search long or far; everyone was talking about the sensational accomplishments of young Sam Rothapfel up in Harlem at the Regent. He was obviously the man for the job. On this point, Rothapfel readily agreed, and allowed himself to be lured away from the Regent in spite of the fact that he and a group of associates calling themselves The Photoplay Theatres Company, had just taken a five-year lease on the 116th Street house. When Roxy saw the chance to do his stuff on Broadway, he left the Regent with scarcely a backward look.

When he arrived on Forty-seventh Street, the Marks gave him *carte blanche* to devise the most spectacular entertainment New York had ever seen in a movie house. And Roxy, his head bursting with visions of electric-lit sugar plums, didn't let them down.

The day after the Strand opened (April 11, 1914), Victor Watson, dramatic critic of *The New York Times* wrote:

> Going to the new Strand Theatre last night was very much like going to a Presidential reception, a first night at the opera or the opening of

102   THE FIRST TYCOONS

the horse show. It seemed like everyone in town had simultaneously arrived at the conclusion that a visit to the magnificent new movie playhouse was necessary.

I have always tried to keep abreast of the times and be able to look ahead a little way, but I must confess that when I saw the wonderful audience last night in all its costly togs, the one thought that came to mind was that if anyone had told me two years ago that the time would come when the finest-looking people in town would be going to the biggest and newest theatre on Broadway for the purpose of seeing motion pictures I would have sent them down to visit my friend, Dr. Minas Gregory at Bellevue Hospital. The doctor runs the city's bughouse, you know.

Among the costly-togged that night were Vincent Astor and his fiancee, Helen Dinsmore Huntington; John Bunny, the beloved fat man of the comedies; George M. Cohan, Sam Harris, Daniel Frohman, Al Erlanger—delegates from Forty-second Street; and William Farnum, who had come to see himself on the Strand's Radium Gold Fibre screen in the opening feature, the first of many productions of Rex Beach's *The Spoilers*.

Roxy had mustered a little army of ushers, doormen and ticket takers, had drilled them in a curious blend of Marine discipline and Chesterfieldian courtesy. The Strand's sumptuous foyer was the scene of much heel-clicking, saluting and bowing from the waist as Old Sergeant Rothapfel's elite guard overwhelmed Broadwayites who had never gotten such attention in a theatre in their lives.

The auditorium, done as a sort of neo-Corinthian temple topped by a vast cove-lit dome, was a revelation. The single balcony swept back in a gentle slope from the loges (fitted out with wicker armchairs) to a broad promenade at the top of the auditorium. The seats both downstairs and up were upholstered in the coziest of Pullman-car plush. Music from a hidden orchestra completed the dream-come-true atmosphere, as the first-nighters took their places for the opening performance in Broadway's first genuine movie palace.

Suddenly three shots of heavy artillery shattered the mood, and the abrupt dousing of the house lights brought on near-panic. But panic was averted in the traditional way as Carl Edouarde led the fifty-piece Strand Concert Orchestra into "The Star Spangled Banner." In a moment the audience sheepishly realized that the whole thing had been part of the program.

The Moving Picture World reported it this way:

A second afterward we saw in lightning rapidity the scenes which inspired the deathless hymn of glory. In the roar and sweat of battle the starry flag still breezed in eloquent triumph over the brave hearts of the country's defenders. With the swiftness of thought the audience recognized the happy inspiration of sending the new theatre on its career to the strains of patriotic music with this rare glimpse of American glory visualized and, as we all stood up in loving homage, no one failed to congratulate the management on its inspiration. At the same time Rothapfel unmasked his artillery, the darkness in and about the screen was converted into a flood of light and the splendid decorations, the flowers, the hedges of green, the graceful fountains of changing color, and the pretty effects in the wings stood revealed as if by magic.

This horticultural setting for the National Anthem (trade history does not reveal if Rothapfel opened the Family, the Milwaukee Alhambra, the Minneapolis Lyric, or the Regent with similar patriotic fanfare; but it is certain that he launched all his theatre openings for the rest of his career this way) was followed by the *Hungarian Rhapsody No. 2*. Next came The Strand Topical Review, showing baseball scenes made at the Brooklyn Federal League that morning and rushed through the developing fluid to stun the Strand audience that very evening. This was followed by a "scenic" one-reeler made in Italy called *A Neapolitan Incident* and accompanied by a tenor singing "O Sole Mio" behind the screen, then a Keystone comedy which featured the Mutual Girl (public darling of the Mutual Film Corporation) paying a visit to the Strand and being entertained by Roxy himself. Next came the Strand Quartet singing the quartette from *Rigoletto*, which, as Mr. Watson of *The Times* put it, "couldn't have been rendered more perfectly in the great temple of music further down the street."

At last the feature picture, *The Spoilers*, came on the screen — and stayed on for an unprecedented nine reels, each reel lasting fifteen minutes. Not only was Rothapfel's special musical setting much admired; he also was applauded for the happy idea of putting the picture on without any break whatever. "*The Spoilers* is one of those novels we like to read right to the end, if possible," wrote one critic, "and where we cannot indulge in our impulse, we lay the volume down with regret. Breaks and pauses in a running visualization of the novel would be even less welcome than interruptions in the reading. That the audience was well pleased with this new wrinkle was plain. It absorbed the story without an effort and its interest never lagged — at 11:30 we were more interested in the fate of Glenister and all the rest than at 9:15 though we had been looking intently at the screen for more than two hours." Roxy won hearts when he threw out the "One Moment While The Operator Changes Reels" slide and installed four projectors instead.

TERRY RAMSAYE
Lasky Rents a Barn

> *Now we are back with Terry Ramsaye again and taking up the story of Jesse Lasky (A Million and One Nights, N.Y., Simon and Schuster, 1926, pages 620–625). The sequence of events here may be as Lasky remembered it later or as other participants in the conversations told it to Ramsaye. But the drama of Lasky, broke from his adventures trying to introduce the Folies Bergere, listening with the utmost gloom and incredulity to the proposition of investing in movies, is given special flavor by our realization that within a few years Lasky would be presiding over a major studio in Hollywood.*

The brightening dawn of the feature drama illuminated promises of opportunity to more and more adventurers in the realm of the new art as the months went by.

Among these interested observers of the new trend in pictures was Arthur Friend, a lawyer with some theatrical experience and connections in Milwaukee and New York. By the spring of 1913 Friend was enthusiastically telling everyone that there were great things ahead in the motion pictures and urging some sort of a venture. Among his friends were Jesse L. Lasky and Lasky's brother-in-law, Samuel Goldfish, now Goldwyn—which is yet another motion picture story.

The Laskys, the Goldfishes and the Friends gathered at Naples, Maine, a summer resort, in the season of '13. There Arthur Friend had a practically unlimited opportunity to pour out his excited anticipations concerning the motion picture business.

Samuel Goldfish was then a salesman for a glove manufacturing concern in New York. He had some other business projects in view, but he listened with a tolerant patience and a growing interest. Jesse Lasky listened, too, perhaps not so much interested.

Enter Lasky and Zukor   105

Lasky had an eventful background of ups and downs. He had had experiences calculated to make him careful of the new and untried. He had started his working life as a cornet player in a San Francisco theatre and, for a time, enjoyed the distinction of being the only white man in the Royal Hawaiian band. Then came a few months of newspaper reporting and a try at prospecting in the gold rush at Nome. Back home and broke in San José, Lasky and his sister Blanche went in for music as a juvenile team, appearing at benefits and club performances. An offer from a vaudeville agent brought them east, where they took an engagement to play with Leon Hermann's show of magic. Leon was a nephew of Alexander Hermann, and on his uncle's death assumed the title of *Hermann the Great, Napoleon of Necromancers*. Lasky became his manager.

With the rise of the vaudeville boom Lasky booked Hermann at a thousand dollars a week, an amazing salary for the time, and set looking about for more wonders to book. In Utica, N.Y., he found B. A. Rolfe, a cornetist, whom he promoted in vaudeville. The partnership of Lasky & Rolfe, producers of vaudeville acts, followed, with such numbers as *Colonial Septette* and the *Military Octette*. Soon Henry B. Harris, then a theatre manager, became Lasky's associate. Their vaudeville enterprises prospered and Lasky found himself the master of a fortune of $150,000. He went to Europe looking for ideas and found one—the cabaret.

The Folies Bergère, the Lasky-Harris introduction of the cabaret idea to America, burst on New York like a rocket the night of Monday, April 24, 1911. It was a sensation for a minute. Its admission price, $2.50, was the highest in New York outside of the Metropolitan Opera House. A hot wave came early in the season and New York left for the seashore. The Folies Bergère brilliantly and completely failed.

Lasky was broke. He thought of California and home again. Then he caught afire with a new idea, an operetta inspired by California. Looking for some one to write the libretto he consulted Mrs. H. C. DeMille, who then conducted a dramatic agency. Lasky wanted William DeMille, but William was busy with *Strongheart* and various Belasco affairs. Mrs. DeMille vigorously suggested her younger son Cecil, who was not so busy. Lasky was dubious. He did not know Cecil, but out of courtesy he had to talk to him. Cecil had winning ways. He talked Lasky into the deal and a one hundred dollar advance. The operetta succeeded and the Lasky-DeMille association was cemented.

Lasky was now beginning to recover from the shock of the grand collapse of the Folies Bergère. It was hardly to be expected that he would have an enthusiastic ear for another new project. He had bought about a half a million dollars' worth of pioneering experience in the cabaret. While Friend talked feature pictures, Lasky went fishing in Lake Sebago.

When the vacation was over and the Friends, Laskys and Goldfishes were again in New York, Friend was still talking pictures. He convinced Blanche Lasky Goldfish.

Finally at the luncheon table at the old Hoffman House, Goldfish surrendered to Friend's everlasting campaign. They would go into the motion picture business.

Jesse Lasky was still wary. He could be committed no farther than to participate by permitting the use of his name. So the Lasky Feature Play Company was born, with $26,500 capital.

At the Lambs club, Cecil DeMille and Jesse Lasky overtook Dustin Farnum and sought to decoy him into the motion pictures. They suggested that he might have a substantial interest in the concern for his services. They intended to make *The Squaw Man*, a stage success, purchased for $5,000, a thousand down and the rest on terms. Farnum was cautious. He opined that he would rather have $5,000 in cash. Farnum on this occasion missed a bet, but on the grand average of such propositions he was correct.

The Squaw Man was Indian and western. Cecil DeMille was to make the picture. The Lasky Feature Play Company looked over the map and elected to go to Flagstaff, Arizona, to make the first production. The name seemed majestic, lone, dignified as a cactus and sufficiently romantic to inspire a great picture.

When Cecil DeMille and Dustin Farnum got off the train at Flagstaff they looked about and saw absolutely nothing. There was nothing to see.

When the train was iced and watered to resume the long haul across the desert, the engineer whistled and the conductor highballed for a departure. Dustin Farnum and Cecil DeMille got on right behind the conductor, bound for Hollywood. They had heard that it was a good place to make films.

Shortly the New York office of the Jesse Lasky Feature Play Company, established in the Longacre Theatre building, was petrified with a wire reading

"We have rented a barn in Hollywood for two hundred dollars a week."

The barn stood, and still stands, at Vine and Selma streets, now a shipping room for the output of the adjacent acres of the Famous Players Lasky studios.

JESSE L. LASKY
The Squaw Man

Jesse Lasky's own recollection of some of the events told by Ramsaye conflicts in details—the amount of capital they had to start with, the rental price for that barn in Hollywood, the contents of the telegram Cecil DeMille sent to the partners in New York. But there is a richness of detail in his account and an occasional confessional honesty ("I had no great personal faith in the project") which keeps us going as readers and makes us realize that small bits of financial and transactional data are not nearly as important as gaining a sense of how it was to be there trying to make a go of it. The possibility that The Squaw Man *had been ruined beyond repair—what a harsh blow to have to carry and hold in doubt for more than a week!*

This is the first of several extracts from Jesse Lasky's autobiography, I Blow My Own Horn *(Garden City, N.Y., Doubleday, 1957) pages 92-101.*

The Jesse L. Lasky Feature Play Company was organized with myself president, Sam general manager, and Cecil director-general. We each held a quarter of the stock and Farnum agreed to accept the other quarter in lieu of salary for his acting stint. We had only $20,000 capital and had agreed to pay $15,000 for the play.

At first we planned to make the picture across the Hudson River at Fort Lee, New Jersey, where a good many one-reel Westerns and other short subjects were being filmed. But I didn't think a two-mile trip would satisfy Cecil's thirst for adventure, so I recklessly tossed in the suggestion that an Indian picture ought to be made in real Indian country—like Flagstaff, Arizona. I remembered seeing some Indians in Flagstaff while traveling with Hermann the Great.

Cecil was delighted with the proposal, as I had anticipated, but Dustin Farnum balked. He said he didn't mind being paid off with stock as long as he could live at home and work across the river, but he insisted on having his $5000 in spot cash before going West. The whole project threatened to collapse—until I talked Bessie's uncle and brother into buying Farnum's stock. If he had hung onto his piece of paper for eight years, he could have sold it for nearly $2,000,000. But Farnum didn't do badly, even so, as the picture put him in the vanguard of early screen heroes, where he maintained a worshipful following for many years.

We hired a cameraman who owned a crank-handled movie camera, and Oscar Apfel, a director with experience on one- and two-reelers, to help Cecil get started. When it was time to leave for Flagstaff, I backed out. I had no great personal faith in the project and I couldn't see myself wasting time in Arizona when I had business to look after in the East. So I said good-by to the rest of them at the train and promised Cecil I'd come out if he needed me.

In the meantime Salesman Sam had learned enough about how pictures were booked to start selling states' rights for our initial production. A print was sold for a flat sum to service a specified territory and could be rerun in its assigned region till it wore out. A small state got only one print, a large state two, and a block like New England, four or five. Sam sold New York state rights for several thousand dollars, New England's for much more, then Pennsylvania, Ohio, and the Pacific coast. Before long we had nearly $60,000 worth of contracts. Sam was a master merchandiser, whether he was pushing a consignment of gloves or a motion picture not yet made by men who had never made one.

While these orders and advance payments were piling up, Cecil seemed to have disappeared. We hadn't heard a word from him for two weeks and we were worried. Finally a telegram arrived—but it wasn't from Flagstaff. It said: "FLAGSTAFF NO GOOD FOR OUR PURPOSE. HAVE PROCEEDED TO CALIFORNIA. WANT AUTHORITY TO RENT BARN IN PLACE CALLED HOLLYWOOD FOR $75 A MONTH. REGARDS TO SAM. CECIL."

Sam hit the ceiling. I insisted that Cecil must know what he was doing, although I really didn't feel too sure of it. When you're president of a company you assume is located in Flagstaff, Arizona, it's very disconcerting to have it turn up in a place you've never even heard of. Sam was all for calling the company back where we could keep an eye on it. We argued for hours. At last we agreed to let them stay and wired Cecil: "AUTHORIZE YOU TO RENT BARN BUT ON MONTH-TO-MONTH BASIS. DON'T MAKE ANY LONG COMMITMENT. REGARDS. JESSE AND SAM."

The reason for that cautious proviso was that we didn't have any definite plans beyond *The Squaw Man*. Sam may have convinced the states'-rights buyers of our corporate soundness, but he himself was still hanging onto his job with the glove company, and I still had my fingers crossed.

Cecil had passed up Flagstaff as our shooting locale because the weather was bad when he stepped off the train in Arizona, and he suddenly realized there would be no facilities for processing the film there. But he knew there must be film laboratories in California, because, while no one had yet made a feature picture in the West, a few companies making one-reelers had moved there from the East to take advantage of cheaper land, labor, and materials and to benefit from the milder climate and more dependable sunlight. The latter was a potent economic factor in as much as artificial lighting was still unknown to motion pictures. (Sunlight didn't go out of style even after kliegs came in, because the early carbon-arc lamps had the intensity of an acetylene torch, making temporary blindness an occupational hazard for actors. After a scene the players would poultice their burning orbs with cooling slices of raw potatoes.)

The barn he rented at Selma and Vine streets had excellent accommodations for the cast of our horse opera, save for the *human* actors. Stalls were turned into offices, dressing rooms, and a projection room. One end of the barn was used as a storeroom. In a clearing made among the acres of orange and lemon trees that went with the barn a small wooden platform was built as an open stage. Production started on *The Squaw Man* on December 29, 1913. Before it was finished a few weeks later, Cecil had inveigled me into making a trip to the Coast, contending that my duty as president of the company was to be at my desk, which he had installed in the stall next to his.

I arrived at the old Santa Fe Depot in Los Angeles, called a taxi, and told the driver I wanted to go to Hollywood. He gave me a puzzled look but said, "Get in, boss—we'll find it."

He drove to the Alexandria, then the city's leading hotel, and had a conference with some other taxi drivers, who set his course out of the city over dirt roads, past endless orchards and an occasional farmhouse. We found Hollywood by the lone landmark that antedated even the movies, a sedate rest haven way out in the country, where city dwellers could get away from it all and relax in perfect tranquillity—the Hollywood Hotel—now the bustling site of three modern buildings. The taxi driver suggested that I make inquiries inside the hotel about where I wanted to go.

I told the clerk my name and explained that I was president of the Lasky Feature Play Company. "This is my first trip here and I'm not sure where our studio is located," I added. "Would you please direct me?"

"I'm sorry," said the clerk, "I never heard of it."

"Perhaps I should have told you that the director-general of the company is Cecil B. DeMille," I stated impressively.

"Never heard of him," the clerk said crisply.

Considerably crestfallen, I was starting toward the door when he called me back. "Tell you who might help you," he said. "Drive down this main road till you come to Vine Street. You can't miss it — it's a dirt road with a row of pepper trees right down the middle. Follow the pepper trees for about two blocks till you see an old barn. There's some movie folks working there that might know where your company is."

When I heard "barn," I knew I was on the right track. Sure enough, a sign identified the barn as the Jesse L. Lasky Feature Play Company.

My reception committee was waiting for me at the hitching posts in front of the barn — a dozen horses and a little boy stationed there to direct me inside. He led me to my stall, where I found a fresh bouquet on the desk, and then out the barn through the orange orchard to the stage, which had a clumsy arrangement of canvas diffusers over the top. These worked something like window shades to control the sunlight. It looked like a big raft with a tattered canvas canopy.

After the reluctant and conditional permission Sam and I gave for his rental of the barn Cecil had withheld an accounting of other expenditures, undoubtedly with the admirable motive of keeping our blood pressure down. Among other things he had rented a two-ton Ford truck. It was standing now in front of the stage, with "Jesse L. Lasky Feature Play Company" emblazoned prominently on its side. When he saw me coming, he ran out, grabbed my hand, summoned the company, made a speech of welcome, pushed me against the truck, and signaled the photographer. He knew I would automatically smile for a snapshot, and I think he wanted to send Sam photographic evidence of what would appear to be my happy endorsement of his extravagance in renting the truck.

I guess it was the first picture ever taken of a movie mogul's arrival in Hollywood.

I stayed that night at Cecil's very modest rented house in Cahuenga Canyon, but I don't think I slept much. I had never heard coyotes howling before. . . .

When Oscar Apfel and Cecil finished shooting scenes for *The Squaw Man* and patched them together with the help of the cameraman and a man from the lab that processed the negative and first answer print, I still hadn't seen any of it, since Cecil had wanted me to wait until it was completely assembled.

Everyone connected with the picture, from Dustin Farnum and his leading woman, Winifred Kingston, whom he later married, to the carpenters and secretaries, was invited to the first showing in the barn. It was such a proud occasion that the men put on collars and coats and brought their wives. There were about fifty of us.

Cecil gave a signal, the lights went off, and "JESSE L. LASKY PRESENTS" flashed on the screen. Then the words immediately went into convulsions, dancing and crawling to the top of the screen. "THE SQUAW MAN" followed suit—crawled right up over the edge of the screen, and then magically appeared at the bottom and started working its way up again. "STARRING DUSTIN FARNUM" jiggled and crawled up the screen with the supporting cast. So did the opening scenes of the picture.

Cecil stopped the showing and went into a huddle with the operator. After fifteen or twenty minutes they tried once more, but the images still wouldn't stay put. The invitation preview of Hollywood's first feature film had to be called off and the audience went home.

Cecil was at his wit's end and I was in despair. We brooded and discussed the situation until three or four o'clock in the morning. We had used up all our capital, spent all Sam could collect as advances from states'-rights men, and there remained unpaid bills. And all we had to show for it was a film that wouldn't project. It appeared that the local experts had either botched the processing job through ignorance or that someone working in the lab for interests who didn't want us in business had willfully sabotaged it. In either case we might only make matters worse by taking the film back and giving them further opportunity to cripple it. With so much at stake Cecil decided the only thing to do was to take it to the best laboratory in the country and see whether they could salvage it. The Lubin Manufacturing Company in Philadelphia, founded on optical equipment, had an unassailable reputation both as a leader in commercial film printing and for its own short subjects.

I had to go to San Francisco to straighten out some trouble with one of my vaudeville acts, "Lasky's Redheads," which was playing the Orpheum there, and Cecil and I agreed that I would continue on from there while he would start from Los Angeles with the negative and print, joining me in Chicago for the remainder of the journey.

It was a dismal trip. We sent wires back and forth between the Southern Pacific and Santa Fe trains every day to buck each other up. We didn't dare tell Sam what had happened or that we were on our way East, fearful that he would blow a fuse. Meantime, he was only having apoplexy. With the states'-rights men breathing down his neck he was frantically wiring us in Hollywood for release dates on the picture and getting no replies.

We explained our difficulties to "Pop" Lubin and he turned us over to his top technicians. Cecil went into the lab with them and left me pacing back and forth outside, sweating in an agony of suspense, knowing that if the film couldn't be saved we were ruined in a great big way. How I was going to explain our failure to Dustin Farnum, the staff, my wife's relatives who put up money, all our creditors — and Sam, who had now given up his job with the glove company! It was beginning to have the earmarks of another fiasco like the Folies Bergère. I wished Sam had never mentioned pictures.

After the most harrowing half hour I've ever lived through, Cecil rushed out beaming, threw his arms around me, and hugged me. There was nothing wrong with the negative. We went downtown and got tight.

It had taken Lubin's men only a few minutes to spot the trouble. We had purchased Eastman perforated negative stock, but as an economy measure Cecil had used unperforated positive stock and a hand-operated punch which spaced the holes differently from those on the negative, with the result that the projected frames constantly crawled upward.

We had an accurately perforated print made and took it to New York for an invitational trade showing at the Longacre Theatre on February 17, 1914. As soon as the screening was over we could tell from the reactions of the states'-rights men that our first production was a hit. . . .

While we pioneered the long film in Hollywood, Adolph Zukor's new company had produced its first feature in New York — *The Prisoner of Zenda,* starring James K. Hackett. The day after our screening I was flattered to find among the congratulatory wires one from the president of Famous Players.

I had never met Zukor but I remembered going into his Penny Arcade on Fourteenth Street ten years earlier, while playing at Tony Pastor's with my sister. The arcade was filled with automatic fortunetellers, strength testers, and other fascinating gadgets cleverly designed to pick your pocket. But a row of peep-box dispensers of thirty-second dramas was collecting the steadiest stream of coins. It was evident that the proprietor of this copper mine had a bonanza. I learned later that 10,000,000 pennies went through Adolph Zukor's sluiceways that first year. . . .

I called Zukor to thank him personally for his telegram. He proposed that we meet for lunch. Cecil had gone immediately back to California, but Sam went with me to Delmonico's, where executives of the era were reputed to consummate more deals than they did in their offices.

Zukor was small in stature, but I began to think of him as a titan when he expounded astute theories about the future of the motion-picture business. We found that we had a community of interests, aside from the fact that we were selling our pictures to the same states'-rights men. His vision and quiet dignity still infused me as I walked with Sam to the offices we had taken on Fifth Avenue opposite the Public Library.

"That man is an inspirational force!" I said. "I want to keep in close contact with him."

Sam agreed, and we never failed to have lunch with Zukor whenever I came to New York.

LOUIS REEVES HARRISON
The Squaw Man

Louis Reeves Harrison was one of those observers of the new movie medium who had an optimistic view of its possibilities. His tone here is complimentary and far grander in its rhetoric than his subject deserved. But he manages to tell us most of the events in The Squaw Man *and also to chide the Lasky publicists for calling it a DeMille film, when obviously Oscar Apfel was the one who knew how to direct a movie. This is a review in* Moving Picture World, *February 28, 1914, pages 1068-1069.*

One of the best visualizations of a stage play ever shown on the screen, "The Squaw Man," was a source of surprise and delight to me, and to the able critic at my side during the private exhibition, from beginning to end. Credit must, however, be given almost entirely to the direction and interpretation, the direction in this case embracing both form and treatment of an almost flawless production. To the lucid arrangement and delicate appreciation of dramatic values, to unwavering logic and consistency, to the pains taken in those tiny details which make action realistic, to the pervading sense of beauty, and to highly intelligent interpretation, quickening interest in the outcome, must be ascribed the charm this feature is bound to exert.

I have not seen Oscar Apfel's name made prominent in connection with this winner, but I recognize his handiwork without difficulty. Cecil DeMille, I am told, put his heart and soul into making "The Squaw Man" an unqualified success, but his unbounded enthusiasm could only act as a support to the unhampered skill and decided native ability of the active director. First honors must go to the gentleman whose discriminating judgment cleared the path of this notable production of a thousand thorny errors. Dustin Farnum's unobtrusive and masterly characterization ranks next in value—he was largely responsible for the "surprise and delight" already mentioned—for he has certainly grasped the essential principles of screen interpretation. His performance is so manly, so apparently devoid of stale artifice, that I could only regret that he was not representing a typical American.

The general theme, that of frenzied self-sacrifice on the part of a blameless man for the sake of a villain who happens to be a member of the same family, "for the family honor," whereby he blasts his own career, has been very popular with lady novelists since Ouida used it, and variations of it have been seen on both stage and screen until it has become almost as familiar as "Mary had a little———" but it is time that it should be shelved, along with a lot of overdone expedients. Nothing in the photodrama is less conducive to progress in the new art than this old billposter theme. But it is all the more creditable to the producers that they have presented with exquisite charm what is no longer considered to be within the bounds of common sense. The truth is that they have depended upon a rattling good story of adventure, running with unbroken unity, sustained by a character of magnetic personality, through perils at sea and on shore.

To begin at the beginning, Jim Wyngate, with whom we are better acquainted as Dustin Farnum, agrees to be the scapegoat for his relative, the Earl of Kerhill, who has embezzled the funds of Wyngate's regiment, and, as soon as Jim is disentangled from a lot of other officers that our affections may be fastened upon him, he leaves England in a trading schooner, and the real fun begins. He has been followed by a detective. Every small boy in the audience and a large portion of the big ones will begin to sit up and take notice when Jim gets busy with that detective. Jim is every inch an athlete, and he does not mince matters as they do in stage struggles. He succeeds in making a fool of the spy at the end of a game fight and soon after performs greater feats, when the ship catches fire. The fire scenes aboard ship are made plausible by using an actual vessel, sailing in the open, and there is a delightful fidelity to legitimate requirements not ordinarily seen in the escape of crew and passengers in the boats.

Jim is picked up by an American vessel, landed in New York, and gradually drifts from the lurid White Way to ranch life in the far west, accompanied by "Big Bill," whom he has saved from the deft "touch" of a tango artiste. They arrive at a railroad station that is a veritable gem of its kind—we look through the combination bar and station, where cowboys assemble at train time, to the track on which actual trains are passing. Some of the high scenes occur in this room, and the view of cars running without gives them an unusual atmosphere of realism. Jim gets into difficulties there with Cash Hawkins, and the latter is shot dead in the station by an Indian girl, a veritable one, and a remarkably fine actress, when he attempts to murder Jim in cold blood.

It is not altogether a pleasing spectacle to see white women impersonating Indian squaws, and they are seldom, if ever, successful at it; on the other hand, Indian girls who can awaken and hold sympathy for their roles are few and far between, but Princess Redwing performs her part with exquisite fidelity and great depth of feeling. The play's highest merit is the opportunity it affords this accomplished actress. The love of this child of the forest for the splendid specimen of manhood injected into her dull career forms the most touching and beautiful part of the story, and it was probably the essence of interest in Royle's stage version. So artless, so appealing to the protective instincts of true manhood, so self-abnegating is that love, that it is bound to make heartstrings throb in the audience.

It is quite probable that both Royle and DeMille, when they come to study this characterization from the viewpoint of spectators, will realize that the art of producing moving pictures is to be measured by its own canons alone. Both may perceive that this new method of thought transmission has a grander scope than the boxed-in stage presentation once they are enfolded in the charm of its method of telling a story. Its directness, the lack of intervening utterance, its very silence, all contribute to a fascination long proven to exist, not only for the mixed audience, but for those familiar with superior examples of the older arts. When these gentlemen come to us, as they surely will, with the finest products of their creative talent, unhampered by what they have learned in a totally different medium of expression, with a cause that is compelling, it will be with quickened fondness, for what can give such free release to their forces.

Note the characterization in action of the Indian maid when the man she loves goes snow blind, when she follows the trail of his horse until she finds it where he was thrown, and thereafter trails his steps to the sulphurus crevice into which he has fallen. Note the impression made by witnessing her patient courage and native resource in the almost insurmountable task of rescue, the comparison suggested of her sturdy and simple devotion to the dependent and resourceless man hunter of civilized society, the lady who affects to steer the boat while man does the rowing, who relies on sex attraction rather than sex qualification. The physical superiority and mental alertness of the woman enjoying fewer advantages could never be so forcibly presented in the related narrative as in the pictured story.

Note the compelling beauty and nobility of actual scenery as compared to stage affectations. The complex impression produced is powerful enough to make one subscribe to the view expressed by a great creative critic, "Art's first appeal is neither to the intellect nor to the emotions, but purely to the artistic temperament that guides civilized man back to nature for relief." The same critic said, "I hold that no work of art can be tried otherwise than by laws deduced from itself; whether or not it be consistent with itself is the question." Note the Indian maid "fighting it out alone in the foothills, only nature looking on," the distance tragically mellowed by a setting sun – how fascinated we become by this visible world of form and color, not only because its delicate beauty is so appropriate to a communion of a human soul with the spirit of the Great Invisible, but because of its imaginative insight and poetic aim!

This one scene might well have been the last, discovering, as it does, the finest sentiment of the story, the tortured appeal of a human heart – "will we ever come to our own?" Sickened with pursuit of the unattainable, how often have each of us secretly communed with something we only vaguely recognize as a power that makes all our boasted ones pitiful. Such occasional glimpses may be less intelligible than those more commonplace, but they belong to life in its artistic entirety, enter a sphere of deep feeling, stir the nobility too often dormant within us, rouse our better selves. The touches of great beauty contain a secret of success known only to screen presentation – they cause us to surrender ourselves more completely to the story that is being told and to love this new art for its own sake.

WILL IRWIN
The Low Spot

We're with Zukor again, in the summer of 1913, before the Lasky-Goldwyn-DeMille combine had started production on The Squaw Man *in Hollywood in December. The story is told by authorized biographer Will Irwin, a prominent journalist, in* The House That Shadows Built, *op. cit., pages 184-194. His worst financial crisis is linked with another time of near disaster for Zukor in 1915.*

A firm begins continuous production in January, say; the film can scarcely go forth before June, and it is January again before returns from its sale or distribution reach their peak. Meantime, production, with its heavy expense, is going steadily on. Just before the second January comes the low spot. If you survive until the next June you reach a peak of returns, and all thereafter is well. But that low spot is a slough of despond which has smothered many and many a promising enterprise. Zukor approached it in the summer of 1913. Al Lichtmann, selling states' rights on the road, read a sinister sign in the letters and telegrams from the head office. Early in the week he would flash to New York a low cash offer for a certain piece of territory, and Zukor would spurn it. Thursday or Friday would come a telegram "Accept offer and wire money." This, to Lichtmann's shrewd intelligence, meant only one thing: Zukor was having trouble in meeting his payroll. Once he failed on that—down would come Famous Players like a house of cards.

Other creditors he could put off, was putting off; but his formidable payroll had become a nightmare. Zukor threw everything into the bottomless pit. One week it was the reserve of securities which he was keeping to insure his family against his disposition to gamble with business; already, in the first pinch, he had sold one thousand shares in the Loew Company—these he had been holding against the great multiplication of values which he foresaw. Then he called on Morris Kohn, offering for $25,000 an interest he held in the Penny Arcade business. He had been turning a smiling and inscrutable face to the outer world. Before this relative and old associate, however, he dared let down a little and express his burning anxiety. Kohn, to save time, himself

bought the shares for spot cash. Zukor dumped that into the hole.
Then, by that persuasiveness of his, he wheedled the bank into lending him just a little more. But there, Lee informed him, it must stop. While he believed personally in Zukor and his enterprise, he had the directors to reckon with. Probably, from the banking point of view, the time had come to call a halt. In the vaults of two banks lay at that moment more than $200,000 worth of Adolph Zukor's notes, secured by some secondhand machinery and a few films which, if the "craze" collapsed during the next few months, would be only spoiled celluloid. Into the yawning chasm went this last loan. The next week Mrs. Zukor insisted on selling her jewels. That sacrifice of affection, together with some small scrapings from the corners of his empty estate, met the next payroll. Long before, Zukor had considered selling his car and giving up his apartment. But he dismissed that idea. News travels fast on Broadway; and there, of all places, to be prosperous you must look prosperous. If his car disappeared, if he moved to poorer quarters, the pack would be down on him.

Now, he was up against a blank wall. Two weeks ahead lay the turning point; for then payments would begin to roll in. But for all he could see, it might as well lie two centuries ahead. Famous Players was so busy making history that it neglected to record history. Also, fire afterward destroyed what records there were. It is impossible, therefore, to date this crisis exactly. But it came in 1913, and toward the end of the summer.

In the middle of the week Daniel Frohman dropped as usual into the studio. When Zukor said good-morning that pleasant smile of his looked forced. Frohman watched him as he puttered with the papers on his desk. All the lines of his face drooped.

"What's the matter with you, Adolph?" he asked suddenly.

"Nothing," replied Zukor.

"But there is something," persisted Frohman. "Come on, Adolph – tell me!"

Suddenly Zukor's reserve broke down.

"It's the business," he began. And he poured it out in a burst. So much confidence had his associates in Adolph Zukor that even Frohman, the business man, had never thought much about the financial basis of their enterprise. The Chief was taking care of that. After his initial burst of emotion, Zukor sketched the situation coolly and logically. Salvation lay a fortnight ahead; but they must exist meanwhile. He had exhausted every resource, every device. Nothing for it but bankruptcy – his old personal devil – or a receiver. Himself, he would be squeezed out altogether or reduced to a minor position. The control would pass to bankers, who could never understand what Famous Players was trying to accomplish.

"Well, I'll see if I can do anything," said Frohman as he left the office. Adolph Zukor took this sombrely. He was inured to hollow reassurances.

Frohman started to the Lyceum. On the way his intense human sympathies and his ardent belief in the business came together in a benevolent resolution. When he made his first success in theatrical management he had segregated from his earnings enough money to insure him against poverty in his old age; for he knew well the speculative nature of his business. This he invested in first-class bonds, which he tucked away in his safety-deposit box. Through all his vicissitudes he had held this reserve secret and sacred. Suddenly, Frohman changed his course, walked to the bank, to the safety-deposit vaults.

That afternoon, he returned to the studio, and laid on Zukor's desk a check for $50,000.

"It's a loan, not an investment, Adolph," he said. "Pay me when you get out of the woods."

Fourteen years later, Adolph Zukor, dwelling on the virtues of Dan Frohman, came out with this story. He who heard it met Frohman next day and mentioned the incident. Frohman blushed like a girl.

"Did Adolph tell you that?" he faltered. Himself, he had never told. . . .

In those days, insurance companies looked on the inflammable film with great suspicion. The famous Charity Bazaar fire in Paris, which started in a cinema booth, had accentuated that prejudice. Also, the business was so new that actuaries had not calculated the appropriate premiums. Insurance let the moving picture strictly alone.

Frank Meyer, realizing this, had at the very beginning looked into the matter of a fireproof safe for their precious negatives. He chose a huge affair, protected both with an asbestos lining and vacuum cells. When it arrived it seemed too heavy for a somewhat insecure floor already burdened with a tank. So he had it fastened to the wall by a pair of steel straps. Presently, the fire inspector, looking over this dangerous establishment, noted the arrangement and vetoed it on the spot. It imposed, he said, too much strain on that wall. Some day, wall and safe might come down together and crash through both floors onto the braid factory below. In the event of a fire, it would surely bring down the wall. Meyer, who is something of an engineer, did not believe him. And to move the film safe to another locality would entail innumerable inconveniences. He appealed to the fire commissioners. They had the matter under advisement, when the expected happened—also the unexpected.

On the night of September 11, 1915, Packy McFarland and Mike Gibbons fought in New York for the lightweight championship. The studio, from top to bottom, happened to be mad over boxing. Virtually everyone was going—except Frank Meyer. Mechanical superintendent of the firm, he served also as its filmcutter. Absorbed in a peculiarly intricate problem, he determined to work it out that night and gave away his ticket. As they passed out on their way to dinner, the studio force guyed his enslavement to duty. By half-past six the studio was empty except for a few mechanics working overtime on the lower floor, and Frank Meyer, cutting film on the upper. The safe stood open, and hundreds of thousands of dollars' worth of negatives and prints lay scattered over the shelves. Finally, one of the stage hands, an Italian, was visiting a friend in a flat just across the light-well.

The mechanics looked out of their window. They saw the Italian making wild, dramatic gestures. He was a bit of a clown; they took his performance for some of his characteristic monkeyshines and responded with derisive grimaces. He was trying, as a matter of fact, to give an alarm; he had seen that the braid factory below was a cauldron of flames. . . . Despairing of making them understand, he scrambled down the fire escape and up the one which led to their window. Even as he threw it open, the fire had burst the panes of the braid factory. As they jumped to the fire escape one of the mechanics remembered Frank Meyer and ran back. The fire was rushing up the stairway. He called; Meyer's voice answered. Remembering that a ladder ran from the cutting room to the roof, he leaped back to the fire escape and escaped just in time.

Meyer had sat so absorbed in his work that a choking sensation in his throat gave him the first warning; then the house fire alarm clanged from below. He thought first of the precious, fragile films. Gathering an armful, he ran to the stairway. It was afire. He rushed back to the safe, chucked into it haphazardly the films from his arms, from the table, from the racks. By the time he had closed the safe door he was choking with the thick smoke and the area by the staircase was burning like tinder. He scurried up the ladder, and butted his way through the hatchment. The tar roof was already afire from another quarter, and the opening of the hatchment had created a draught on which smoke and fire, fed now by raw film, shot up like a geyser. As he ran to the edge, the flames seemed to chase him across the roof. He dropped to the next building, and a jet of water from a hose drenched him to the skin. It was a chilly night and as he scrambled down the fire escape he decided to get a taxicab and go home for dry clothing.

Meantime, Adolph Zukor, who himself intended to see the fight, was dining at the Knickerbocker Grill with the adolescent Eugene. Mr. and Mrs. Emil Shauer, who were going to the theatre, sat at another table. They finished, and strolled together out to the car. Traffic on Broadway had stopped, fire bells sounded from every direction, and a glow lit the southwestern sky.

"Quite a fire," remarked Zukor to a policeman at the curb.

"Yes," responded the policeman casually, "general alarm. It's a moving-picture studio on West Twenty-sixth Street."

When Frank Meyer returned in his dry clothes he had some difficulty in crashing through the police lines. Up and down between the engines strode Adolph Zukor, weeping frank, and open, and unashamed tears.

"He's taking his loss hard," thought Frank Meyer. "Well, he's got a licence." At that moment Zukor saw him, ran to him, embraced him, stood off feeling him all over and laughing hysterically with relief. For Frank Meyer was reported missing—when he went home to forefend pneumonia, he had not thought of that possibility. The last heard of him was his voice, calling to the mechanics across the blazing stairway.

All night the partners in this emperilled venture stood inside of the police lines, watching the fire burn to its maximum and decline. That safe, steel-lashed to the wall, held the negatives of seventeen films; many of the most important still unprinted. If the wall fell in and dropped it into the superhot furnace below, fireproof safe or no fireproof safe, they were gone. And so, probably, was Famous Players—just as it was getting onto its feet. Those little rolls of celluloid represented all their product for six months; and they had not a cent of insurance. But the wall held; and toward morning they could see through the smoke the safe hanging aloft like a dovecote. Even then, they could not be sure.

Enter Lasky and Zukor 123

The experts on fireproof safes, arriving next morning, seemed even less sure. Ordinary papers, they said, would resist the heat. But films, being mere celluloid, blazed and exploded at a comparatively low temperature. Had Frank Meyer, when he closed and locked the door, also thrown in the combination? That would make a great difference. Meyer cudgelled his brain, but he could not remember. Choking with smoke, in peril of his life, he had acted on instinct. They could not know until the safe cooled. That would take two or three days.

His associates remark yet on Zukor's calm during this crisis. That very morning he set to work as steadily, as systematically, as though this were a minor incident. He called the company together and assured them that their salaries would be paid on Saturday night as usual. He leased for a studio Durland's abandoned riding academy in Fifty-sixth Street. His competitors, expressing a fine tradition of American business, offered him a loan of all their spare facilities. He sped arrangements for resuming production at the earliest possible moment. His anxious associates wondered if he lacked imagination. In truth, he had too much imagination; he was shutting the door on it lest it overwhelm him. "I wouldn't let myself think that those films might be gone," he said afterward. "I was afraid I'd break down if I did." Even on the fateful morning when mechanics and firemen lowered the cooled safe from the wall and set it in place to open he remained in his temporary office, madly at work.

Frank Meyer laid a trembling hand on the lock. No, he had not thrown in the combination! He took a long breath, opened the doors.

Not even the edge of a film was scorched!

Tradition in the moving-picture business calls this the great crisis of the Famous Players. Zukor disagrees. The company was on its feet now, past the peak, a going concern. Even had these films burned, he believes that he would have fought through. The really dangerous crisis was that "low spot" of the summer before—the episode of Daniel Frohman's check.

This was his last flirtation with financial embarrassment. Henceforth, he struggled not against bankruptcy, but toward leadership and control and power.

TERRY RAMSAYE
Hodkinson and Paramount

> One of the aspects of motion picture production least understood by outsiders is the necessity to have a distribution contract in hand before production starts. Only an amateur tries to collect money to make a movie just on the chance that someone is going to want to see it. Adolph Zukor was not yet in a position to finance his own films. He was certainly not an amateur plunger and he was not the owner of a string of theaters. He was dependent on people who could deliver pictures to theaters on a regular basis. W. W. Hodkinson was such a "buyer" and he had a firm price established ahead of time: an advance of $25,000 (or, as Lasky remembers it, $35,000). Zukor was not happy with this arrangement, as Terry Ramsaye indicates in A Million and One Nights, op cit., pages 628–633.

Now from out of the West came a tall solemn stranger, one W. W. Hodkinson, representing the Progressive film exchanges of Los Angeles, San Francisco and elsewhere along the Pacific slope. He was among the most important of the buyers of the new Independent feature pictures. He arrived in New York in January, 1914, to stay a few weeks making new contracts. He stayed for years and became the central figure in the new reorganization of the business of the motion picture. . . .

Hodkinson entered into negotiations with Famous Players for their coming pictures. The stage was set for a new drama of personalities and struggle.

Hodkinson represented the machinery of motion picture merchandising and distribution. He had been schooled in the rigid discipline of the Trust. He had built upon it and applied it.

Adolph Zukor, head of Famous players, was the most significant single figure in the field of picture production. He was inwardly driven by Napoleonic ambition.

In the terms of these two personalities, production and distribution were due to meet – and clash.

There were endless negotiations.

Zukor was beset by his problems, and fear that distribution was going to control production.

When Zukor thinks he walks. There was a night in this period when he walked from midnight to sunrise. Twice that night in the streets of New York he saw Battery Park, and once he crossed One Hundred and Twenty-fifth street. When the Sioux started ghost dancing it meant trouble along the Big Horn. When Zukor starts walking it is time for everybody on the reservation to look out.

Hodkinson and distribution represented only one of Zukor's problems. Mary Pickford was getting expensive. The whole theory of "famous players" was undergoing revision. It seemed that "famous players in famous plays" was not the perfect idea after all. Zukor's Class A pictures, with the great names of the stage in them, were falling down, while his Class B with this little girl with a curl was getting the money—and she and her mother knew it.

Zukor got peace for a moment with an agreement to pay Miss Pickford a thousand dollars a week. In January, while the distribution pot was coming to a boil, Miss Pickford, with Edwin S. Porter in charge, went to California with a company to make *Tess of the Storm Country*, one of her greatest successes.

When that distribution contract with Hodkinson's Progressive exchanges was ready to sign Zukor had walked a lot of mileage. Hodkinson, in the offices of Zukor's attorney, Elek J. Ludvigh, read it. In his understanding of its terms it would have invaded his pending deal for the pictures of the Jesse Lasky company. It was aimed at control of the business by control of production.

"We'll take care of Lasky," they promised Hodkinson. He did not want Lasky "taken care of." Hodkinson had seen competition taken out of production by control in the Trust, and he had observed the consequences.

Hodkinson walked out, the contract unsigned. . . .

The exchangemen, assembled in New York in 1914 found a leadership in Hodkinson. One day at his office at 110 West Fortieth street, a five part agreement and pact was formed. They decided to pool their power and Paramount Pictures Corporation was born. It was named after an apartment house sign that Hodkinson had seen that morning and the trade mark, now known to the world, was the picture of a mountain that he sketched on a blotter. The Rocky Mountains, through Hodkinson, had a good deal to do with picture history.

Now Paramount had the power. It was the market. For Paramount Hodkinson made contracts with Zukor, Lasky and Garbutt of the Bosworth concern. An advance of $25,000 a picture was to be made. The producer was to receive 65 per cent of the earnings from rentals and the distributor, Paramount, was to take 35 per cent. The figures were based on Hodkinson's General Film Company experience. The 65-35 ratio remained a constant of picture distribution practise for many years.

It was all settled – almost.

Adolph Zukor was now one of three picture producers under contract to supply films to Paramount. And W. W. Hodkinson was boss of Paramount.

Zukor began walking again.

JESSE L. LASKY
"So We Combined"

Now we take up the story of the early corporate developoment of Paramount Pictures, which was not always a smooth operation. First, Jesse Lasky reports on the friendly competition of Zukor's Famous Players and the Lasky Feature Play company, followed by the merger of the two into Famous Players-Lasky. Right away we are surprised by the forced departure of Sam Goldwyn, Lasky's brother-in-law, who had helped persuade him to get into the movie business and had been such an effective salesman of the rights to exhibit The Squaw Man *before it was even finished. This is from* I Blow My Own Horn, *op cit., pages 120-124.*

Sam and I continued to lunch with Adolph Zukor at Delmonico's every time I was in New York, and when I was on the West Coast, Sam kept in touch with him over problems that affected both our companies. Zukor was very farsighted about the picture industry and we were always grateful for his advice. At least I was. Sam frequently clashed with him on matters of policy. But the three of us had a feeling of being partners in a common cause, although our companies were admitted rivals. When Marguerite Clark was a magic name at the box-office, her contract with Famous Players ran out and I tried to lure her away from them by offering her more money – about $5000 a week, as I recall. Zukor topped my bid by a thousand or two and kept her, but then, to show there were no hard feelings, loaned her to us for a picture, *The Goose Girl,* which was one of the most successful of our early productions.

We watched each other's pictures avidly, and if one or the other company introduced a new idea or improvement in technique, the other was so quick to take it up that the originator didn't have time to exploit it before he was imitated. The situation was similar to that of automobile makers all coming out with the same changes at the same time. But Famous Players always bested us in one regard. Whenever they depicted high society on the screen, their elegantly gowned beauties made our dress extras look positively frumpy. Dress extras made only $5.00 a day and had to furnish their own wardrobes. A girl can't build up much of a wardrobe on an occasional $5.00 pay check, so our dress extras were usually qualified seamstresses or other young women clever enough with a needle to make $2.50 worth of material and a Butterick pattern look like a $25 frock.

It always puzzled me how Famous Players could give their pictures a semblance of a style show without spending thousands of dollars on wardrobe. I learned many years later when Al Kaufman became my assistant that, when he had been head of production at Famous Players in New York, he did his casting of dress extras from a little black book containing a list of women friends of Wall Street millionaires. The $5.00 a day meant nothing to those gorgeous hussies – they just liked to flaunt their Paris finery before a camera.

We continued distributing our pictures through the states' rights men until 1915. Then one of them, W. W. Hodkinson of San Francisco, called all the others together in a meeting with the producers in New York – there were about twenty men present – and proposed that the states'-rights men band together in a distributing company in which they would each own stock. Hodkinson himself suggested that the new releasing association be called "Paramount Pictures." I didn't like the name at all. I didn't think it suggested film artistry. It sounded more like a brand of cheese or woolen mittens. But the first organization to distribute pictures nationally was formed under that name, Hodkinson was made president, and I lived to see Paramount swallow up my own name.

The combine would only agree to pay us $35,000 in advance on each picture against 65 per cent of the gross revenue. Now that they had what amounted to a trust, they could dictate terms to us. With production costs rising, plays costing more, and stars and directors making increased salary demands it became practically impossible to finance ourselves on the meager Paramount advances. Famous Players and the Lasky Company both felt the squeeze badly but couldn't move Hodkinson to more lenient terms.

Zukor could see a battle ahead, and revealed his concern even when he was trying to relax. He was learning golf, and at about the twelfth hole would remark, "Well, I guess we're 65 per cent around the course." One day he called Sam and me and proposed that we merge our two companies under the joint banner of "Famous Players-Lasky." Pooling our resources would make us the most powerful force in the industry and enable us to get the kind of bank financing we both needed to produce more ambitious pictures. Famous Players was making more pictures than we were at the time, and their assets were considerably greater than ours. Mary Pickford's contract alone was a property of inestimable value, even at her current salary of $10,000 a week plus bonuses which brought her income close to $700,000 a year. However, Zukor was satisfied to split the stock fifty-fifty between both companies in order to make the proposition attractive to us.

So we combined. Adolph Zukor became president, I was named vice-president in charge of production, Sam was elected chairman of the board, Cecil retained his title of director-general, and Arthur Friend, a young attorney I had met during my courtship at Long Lake, and who had organized the corporate structure of the Lasky Company for us, was made secretary.

We rented another floor over the one we already occupied at 485 Fifth Avenue and the Famous Players staff moved in. We expanded to several floors there before putting up our own building.

Famous Players-Lasky was the backbone of the distributing organization, supplying 80 per cent of the Paramount product. But Paramount also released the pictures of several smaller companies. Two of these, caught in the same desperate plight as we had been, now merged with us—the Oliver Morosco Photoplay Company and Hobart Bosworth's Pallas Pictures, the latter managed by Frank Garbutt, who shortly assumed a post as our vice-president in charge of finances.

I took charge of the studios and production of all four companies, relieving Zukor to devote his genius to the financial end and later to building a world-wide network of film exchanges and theatres. Our strengthened position made it possible for him to borrow all the working capital we needed from the Irving Trust Company. With Wall Street backing motion pictures entered the realm of big business.

Our pictures had been customarily introduced on the screen with the words "Jesse L. Lasky presents—" followed by the star's name, the title of the picture, and the rest of the cast. Few directors and no scenario writers were given screen credit in those days. Famous Players followed the same practice, starting the main titles with "Adolph Zukor presents—." After the merger it was decided to continue the same way, Zukor presenting all the pictures made in the East, while my name would appear on the Coast product.

My first significant duty in the new setup was to see that our most important asset wasn't sitting around twiddling her thumbs. I made an error of judgment in hastily assigning Hector Turnbull to do an original for Mary Pickford based on the lyrics of the song "Less than the Dust." America's Sweetheart was miscast as a halfcaste, and *Less than the Dust* was probably the lowest-grossing and least-popular picture she ever made. It might have ruined a lesser star.

Thus I started the association with Zukor on a blunder that would be hard to top—but Sam managed to top it! He came in while I was conferring with Mary Pickford during preparation of the story and blurted out, "Jesse, don't let Zukor butt in on this picture. He's okay as an executive, but we've always made better movies than Famous Players, so see that you keep the production reins in your hands!"

Mary, naturally feeling more loyalty to the man who had made her the favorite actress of the screen than to the new and untried custodians of her career, reported the remarks to Zukor.

The next day at lunch Zukor was unusually quiet. "Mr. Lasky," he finally said, "I'm sorry to tell you this, but Famous Players-Lasky is not large enough to hold Mr. Goldfish and myself. You brought him into the company and therefore I don't want to ask him to leave. But you'll have to choose between Mr. Goldfish and me. I'm going to the country for the weekend, and I'll await your decision there."

I've never had a harder decision to make, and I had to make it alone, since Cecil was in Hollywood. I hardly closed my eyes for the next forty-eight hours. I had tremendous respect for Zukor's courage and qualities of leadership. I felt sure that with him at the helm our company had a glorious future. But Sam was my sister's husband, and while he lacked Zukor's experience, he also was a brilliant strategist. He was the one who had goaded me into the picture business in the first place. He had helped plan and build this organization, which had now grown beyond the point where it concerned only ourselves. We now had many stockholders, and their best interests had to be considered—which pointed to Zukor's guidance of the company, unhampered by internal dissension. I had to admit to myself, whatever obligation I felt toward him, that Sam was not geared to take a back seat for anyone. He was and still is the kind of dynamic personality that functions best alone, with all the power in his own hands.

ADOLPH ZUKOR
Operating in a Turmoil

Here is Zukor's version (The Public Is Never Wrong, op. cit. pages 178–180) of the departure of Goldwyn from the combined corporation, Famous Players-Lasky. Zukor was known as a quiet little man, working most often behind the scenes. Here Sam Goldfish [Goldwyn], who was both taller and heftier than Zukor, is described as throwing his weight around and making a good deal of noise. After this episode, he tried two other connections before finding his successful role as Hollywood's most independent producer. Zukor appears to believe that Goldwyn had "no hard feelings," which was not the case, and also that DeMille (who remembers it differently) took part in the decision to ask Sam to go.

In his own autobiography (1959), DeMille reproduces part of a letter from Jesse Lasky at the time which indicates that there was a clear majority of the board for Zukor (because of Lasky's decision) therefore it was decided to keep Cecil "out of the controversy." He was a member of the board but also a contractee as director-general. DeMille says he was glad he was kept out of it, but evidently at some point he proposed to bring Goldwyn out to join him "in the production end of the business." Eight years later Zukor cut back on DeMille's contract advantages so sharply that he, too, was forced to leave.

Every hour on the hour, and sometimes the half hour, Sam Goldwyn sent a shock through the organization, in the manner of those pneumatic drills which shake all the buildings in the vicinity. It was Sam's nature. A man of boundless nervous energy, he was always in a terrific hurry, had to keep things whirling in what amounted to a frenzy. . . .

Before long I was convinced that Goldwyn disagreed many times only for the sake of argument. It is no disservice to him to say that he liked operating in a turmoil, inasmuch as in the nearly forty years since that time he has become celebrated for it. But I liked to move with greater care. My aim was the building of a large and wide-flung organization, while he operated in the moment.

Sam was not a believer, one might say, in parliamentary procedure. A chairman of the board does not ordinarily concern himself with the day-to-day details of operation. Sam did, and by temperament he had to, though I didn't know it at the time. One day, for example, I had just completed a contract with Jack Pickford, Mary's brother, calling for five hundred dollars a week. Sam canceled it, saying the figure was too high. His post didn't give him authority to do that. But, as I say, rules meant little to Sam when he was excited.

And so within a few months I knew that one of us was out of water in Famous Players-Lasky. The decision did not come easy. It is true that when confronted with a problem I always took to the streets and walked. For that matter, I walked five or six miles every day—nearly always to and from the Switzerland Apartments at Riverside Drive and 156th Street to which we had moved.

Faced with this problem, I would find myself late at night down at the Battery and then, seemingly a few minutes later, entering Central Park, miles uptown. In the end I decided to put the solution in more objective hands, those of Lasky and DeMille. If they believed that the chances for Famous Players-Lasky was better with me gone, I would depart without rancor. I was perfectly confident of my ability to start over again.

The matter came to a head while Lasky was discussing Mary Pickford's next film with her. They held their conferences in our combination library and board room. Goldwyn kept dashing in with suggestions and exiting with door slamming.

One evening after Goldwn and Mary had both departed, I walked into the library.

"Jesse," I said, "I have come to an unhappy conclusion which may distress you more than it does me. It is a hard thing to ask you to choose between your brother-in-law and me. But many a film company has failed because of internal dissension, and I can see it happening with us. The decision will rest with you and DeMille. You do what you think best and I will go my way, whichever you choose, without a bitter thought."

I communicated the same thought to DeMille and he came on from the west coast. They asked me to stay. Goldwyn had no hard feelings, nor did I. We had several conversations and agreed that our temperaments and methods were too different for things to continue the way they had been. A division of stock was arranged and Goldwyn's share, which we purchased, came to a little under a million dollars—a neat enough sum for four years in the picture business.

SAMUEL GOLDWYN
A Bitter Chapter

From Warsaw, where he was born in 1882, Samuel went by himself at the age of 11 to England, seeking out relatives to stay with. Two years later he was in America, where the name of Goldfish was assigned to him at immigration. After his departure from Famous Players-Lasky, he put together with Edgar Selwyn a company combining their names (Goldwyn) and later took that name for his own. In his rather rambling memoirs, published in 1923 (N.Y., George H. Doran Co.) he tells on pages 23–24 of his aspirations, on pages 105–107 his claim that he was responsible for bringing Zukor and Lasky together and his shock at being asked to resign. A postscript from a later period of fame and success is added (pages 260–261) to show his feelings about the way of life he chose.

. . . I had been a poor boy – poor and often homeless. Of formal schooling I had practically none. At the age when most boys take arithmetic and a roof and three square meals as a matter of course I was fending for myself. When I got these things it was through odd jobs in blacksmith shops and in glove factories. Sometimes, of course, I did not get them at all. For example, I remember how once as a boy of twelve I wandered for a whole week through the streets of London with no more ardent guaranty of the future than a loaf of bread.

My early boyhood was spent in Europe and I was just fourteen when, absolutely alone and with no friend or relative to greet me, I arrived in New York City. From the city I went to Gloversville, N.Y., and there, after about four or five years spent in a glove factory, I succeeded in persuading a firm that I could sell gloves. I can say without arrogance of heart that I did sell them. But there was no miracle of ease about this process. I travelled from coast to coast; I often worked eighteen hours a day; I put over my product in districts where it never sold before. As a result of all this I was making about fifteen thousand dollars a year at the time when I chanced in upon that little motion picture theatre. I also owned stock in my company and, thanks to an expanded income, I had been able to supplement my fragmentary schooling by many lectures and concerts and by frequent trips to Europe.

But, although at thirty I was a comparatively successful man, I was not satisfied. I can remember how when a boy in the cutting department I used to walk by the leading hotel in Gloversville and look at the "drummers" who cocked their feet up in the big plate glass window. How I envied them—those splendid adventurers with their hats and their massive cigars both at an angle! For to me they represented the everlasting romance of the far horizon. And when at last I myself was admitted to this peerage I was sensible, of course, of another, greater goal. I have made many mistakes in my life, but I can honestly say that they were all results of an unceasing effort on my part to reach the bigger thing just beyond. . . .

It had long been apparent to me that a merger of the Lasky and the Famous Players organizations promised many benefits. It would put an end to the costly competition for stars and stories and it would effect a corresponding reduction in other expenses. To all such arguments, however, Mr. Zukor turned a deaf ear, and it was not until 1916 that I succeeded in overcoming his reluctance. Then, under the name of the Famous Players-Lasky Company, these two enterprises which only a few years before had launched out with a capital representing conjointly less than one hundred thousand dollars, were incorporated at twenty-five million!

It was a radiant day for me when the vision of this gigantic unification, held so persistently for many months, finally took form. But, as so often happens, the fulfilment of my most cherished dream proved to be a weapon turned against me. Mr. Zukor was the president of the new organization; I was chairman of the board of directors. I shall not enter here into the differences which sundered us, both men accustomed to domination. I shall merely relate that only a few months after the formation of the new company I resigned my interests in the Famous Players-Lasky organization.

But before leaving this phase of my career I want to pay my heartfelt tribute to the man whom I consider responsible for much of the success won by Lasky films, Cecil de Mille!

Although I have had occasion to mention several instances where his judgment was at fault, I have never once lost the sense of how disproportionate these rare flaws were to the sum of his achievement. As a matter of fact, DeMille is seldom wrong in his valuations of either performer or story. Again and again his judgment proved superior to both Lasky's and mine. Then, too, he adds to the qualities which make him a big director, a gift for personal relations which I have seldom seen equalled. Farrar was only one of the many Lasky stars who "got along" wonderfully with our chief director. The courteous, self-controlled, kindly De Mille – who, indeed, could dislike him?

Certainly my own thought of him always reaches far beyond our mere professional association. To me at a time when I most needed it De Mille was a true friend, and the memory of his truth and loyalty illumines one of the bitterest chapters of my life. . . .

[I urged H. G. Wells] to come to California as my guest, look over the situation. But, although I assured him that such a visit would leave him perfectly free to decide whether or not he cared to enter the picture lists, Mr. Wells did not accept my invitation.

As I left his home that day I remembered suddenly that twenty-five years before, I, who had just been entertained by the most celebrated of the younger English novelists, had wandered without home and without money through these very London streets. There was no self-congratulation in that swift contrast of present and future, but there was a deep wonder at the mysterious flux of life.

Another feeling dominated this wonder. It was my gratitude to the work which has so shaped and coloured my destiny. To motion pictures I owe all the wide ranges of contacts which have made up to me for a boyhood handicapped by so many unfavourable circumstances. To it I owe also the greatest blessing which can befall any one of us – an impersonal interest so vivid and compelling that it survives any personal grief or maladjustment.

Almost everyone who has been connected with picture production understands the fascination which it exerts. I always think, indeed, of the answer which Charlie Chaplin once made to somebody who asked him what he most wanted from the future.

"More life," said Chaplin promptly. "Whether it comes through pictures or not – more life." And then he added half sadly "Still I can't think of myself out of pictures. Whatever I do, I find myself wondering, 'Now, will that be good for my work or not?'"

Although, in comparison with this great creative artist, my own sphere is so humble, my understanding of this one dominating interest is sufficiently complete to justify me in applying his words to myself. Like Chaplin, I cannot think of myself out of pictures. For to do that would be to turn my back on the far horizon which has always called me to it.

JESSE L. LASKY
The Power and the Glory

Lasky continues here his account of Famous Players-Lasky and the consolidation of power by Zukor. The distribution company started by W. W. Hodkinson is taken over by the more powerful joint production companies. There is a casual reference to the takeover later on of Triangle, with its directorial stars, Griffith, Ince, and Sennett. Frank Woods is hired, and B. P. Schulberg. Lasky's diplomacy is revealed by his offer to place both Zukor's name and his own at the top of the screen. The chapter title is his own and forecasts the title of a movie he produced independently at M-G-M in the years after he left Paramount. (I Blow My Own Horn, op. cit., pages 124–126, 129–130).

I continued to commute between the coasts and to lunch with Zukor every day I spent in New York. Over the years our lunches shifted from Delmonico's to Sherry's to the Astor, then the Ritz, as each in turn became the fashionable spot for executives to doodle the backs of menus with million-dollar deals. Yet we never called each other by our first names until almost forty years later.

These luncheon dates meant far more to me than the pleasure of being in the company of a kindred spirit. I sought Zukor's judgment and advice on every important move we made in the production end. He kept a finger on the pulse of our business and his keen financial analyses determined the upper limits of the budgets we could safely allot to our pictures. He was always ready to do battle for bigger and better pictures.

One day he said, "Mr. Lasky, we are being throttled, strangled to death! I have fought with Hodkinson to increase the cash advances and the percentages of the gross for our pictures. The man has ice in his veins. He won't see that unless we get more money we can't make pictures of better quality and attract the best talent in the field. It has come to this—we've got to get control of Paramount or we'll be forced out of business. But don't worry—we're not going out of business!"

Zukor quietly bought up the shares of several Paramount stockholders, including Hiram Abrams, who had been one of the New England states'-rights men, and then maneuvered Abrams into the presidency before Hodkinson, conducting what he

Enter Lasky and Zukor   137

thought was a routine election of officers, realized that he was unseated. With control of the company in our hands from that moment we acquired the rest of its stock and Paramount became a subsidiary distributing company owned 100 per cent by Famous Players-Lasky, Inc. Nevertheless we retained the name Paramount for its trademark value, and used the slogan "If It's a Paramount Picture It's the Best Show in Town."

Not long after this coup Zukor sent word that he wanted me to plan a group of features with higher budgets than ever before. Whatever they earned would now be ours to spend for increasingly better pictures. This enabled us to go forward with confidence that we could remain in the vanguard of the fast-growing industry, which by this time included Carl Laemmle's Universal Film Manufacturing Company, the Fox Film Corporation, Metro, and Triangle, which released the productions of D. W. Griffith, Thomas Ince, and Mack Sennett.

I quickly wiped out the memory of *Less than the Dust* and recovered Mary Pickford's prestige by sending her to the Coast with orders for her pictures to be done on a don't-spare-the-brains-or-cash basis, and Zukor shortly set up another subsidiary company, Artcraft Pictures, to handle them and other high-budget films which couldn't be released at our regular block-booking rates. Cecil directed two of Mary's productions, *A Romance of the Redwoods* and *The Little American*. Then on a happy hunch I delivered her into the hands of Marshall Neilan, a young director who had first worked for us as an actor in an Edgar Selwyn play, *The Country Boy*. He was responsible for some of Mary's best-remembered and most typical successes at the height of her popularity—*Rebecca of Sunnybrook Farm*, *The Little Princess*, *Stella Maris*, *Amarilly of Clothes-line Alley*, and *M'liss*. William Desmond Taylor also handled a number of her pictures. Simultaneously we were starring Mary's brother, Jack Pickford, in such stories as *Freckles* and *Tom Sawyer*.

Having the two acknowledged queens of Hollywood, Mary Pickford and Marguerite Clark, on one lot made for some tempestuous times. The same kind of parts suited both to a T, and no matter what prized story property was bought for one star, the other coveted it. Mary was making $10,000 a week and 50 per cent of the profits from her pictures when she decided to abdicate her shared throne and set up a monarchy of her own.

Marguerite had the field to herself on the Lasky lot until she married Harry Williams, a young Social Registerite of New Orleans. Williams told me that his wife might continue her screen career, but that he would not permit her, ever again, to kiss a leading man. This was the kiss of death in reverse for Marguerite Clark's popularity. We starred her in two or three more pictures, respecting Williams' injunction, but it was no use. Every film in those days adhered to the unwritten law of a saccharine clinch at the end. Marguerite's fans expected this as their due and simply couldn't accept their idol as a frigid heroine. Without wasting any time or more dimes at the box-office they got themselves other idols.

Before long we were able to build up our premium rental line, Artcraft, by absorbing the three giants of the Triangle Company, along with their top stars, Douglas Fairbanks, William S. Hart, and Charles Ray, and their ace writing team, John Emerson and Anita Loos. We developed another brand labeled Realart, using it for pictures in a lower budget and lower rental bracket, to build promising personalities like Bebe Daniels, Vivian Martin, and May McAvoy until they were starring material for the Class A Paramount productions. With this expansion I found myself with a schedule of 104 pictures in 1917, including 52 standard Paramount issues, 18 Artcrafts, and 34 Realarts. The bulk of them were made at the Vine Street studio, but we also used the Morosco Studio in Los Angeles and the Famous Players Studio on Fifty-sixth Street in New York, a former riding academy that, like the original Lasky Barn, had been converted from horseflesh to ham. . . .

Making pictures at such a merry pace, I wasn't able to assign writers to the stories and stories to the directors, along with my other duties and necessary traveling. So I had brought in Frank Woods, an expert in silent screen-play construction who had worked with D. W. Griffith, to take charge of this phase of studio operation. But the responsibilities got too heavy for him to handle alone, so we created a new kind of executive to oversee writing and production of individual pictures, I dubbed them "supervisors" and delegated Hector Turnbull to ride herd on them.

The word "supervisor" has long since passed out of existence in the Hollywood hierarchy and "producer" is now substituted to designate the link between management and production. Those categories are combined in an independent producer such as Sam Goldwyn, who is a company unto himself. But Pandro Berman, for instance, is one of several producers at M-G-M, all of whom are responsible to the production head of the studio. Some production heads confine themselves to supervising producers. Others occasionally engage in production themselves.

Among our early supervisors were Tom Geraghty, Lucien Hubbard, E. Lloyd Sheldon, Ralph Block, Walter Woods, Julian Johnson, William Le Baron, Howard Hawks, Waldemar Young, and Louis "Buddy" Lighton. For some time they didn't even get screen credit, but they were the first members of a profession now represented by the Screen Producers Guild of 180 members.

Soon Turnbull was more than swamped, and as Frank Woods was also overworked and nearing retirement age anyway, I had to look around for still another ringmaster to keep things moving at a furious clip.

Joseph Dannenberg, editor of the Eastern trade paper *The Film Daily*, suggested Ben Schulberg, who had been in the publicity department of Famous Players before the merger and was now producing low-budget independent pictures starring his promising young discovery, Clara Bow. I conferred with Schulberg and offered him the post. As an inducement to expedite his acceptance I magnanimously agreed to take the Clara Bow contract off his hands for a consideration of $25,000. This was the equivalent of volunteering to relieve him of a million dollars, but neither of us realized the sensational popularity Clara Bow was shortly to enjoy and he gladly accepted.

With Schulberg overseeing half the pictures and Turnbull the other half there was inevitable rivalry between the two and conflicts over the selection of stories, directors, stars, writers, and supervisors available on the lot. But the assembly line did move faster under this divided authority. Production also continued at the Famous Players Studio in New York under Hugh Ford, assisted by Albert Kaufman. The output of pictures from the West Coast was stepped up so drastically, however, that "Jesse L. Lasky Presents—" appeared at the top of the screen about five times as often as "Adolph Zukor Presents—." I thought I detected a slightly reproachful look in the eyes of my luncheon companion. In the interests of better digestion I suggested a change of policy, and from then on all our pictures, whether made in the East or on the Coast, were "presented" by Adolph Zukor and Jesse L. Lasky in tandem.

JESSE L. LASKY
Production Problems

> *In his turn at the podium at Harvard, Jesse Lasky challenged the students with the basic conflict between (1) the production values a story needs and (2) the limited money which may have been allotted for its filming. Should the studio production chief be more of an artist (like Lasky) or more of a hardheaded businessman? How far should he go in pursuing perfection? Will spending more make it any better? He gives us here one of the best statements ever offered of the role of the creative producer in Hollywood. (The Story of the Films, op.cit., pages 112-116.)*

Our real problem in production is how to improve the quality of the pictures and at the same time maintain cost or business control. If I were asked for a problem to put up to you gentlemen, I think it would be this: Suppose you were going to organize a motion picture studio, who would be your dominant factor? Would you have a man of my type who was a visionary, half a dreamer and only half a business man, who was keen about the quality of the product and might well lose touch with the cost? Or would you put at the head a thoroughly trained business man? In the latter case, the business man would dominate me and when I wanted to dream he would say, "No; here is your budget, $200,000, Mr. Lasky; that is what you have to spend; our income is going to be so much." Then there would be the inevitable clash. I would say, "This is a great story and it cannot be done that way. We don't get many good stories. When we do, let us tell them." "Well, tell this one for $200,000." "You can't." "Why can't you?" "Mr. Businessman, listen. I will prove it to you." And so the argument runs on.

The expense of every picture is segregated. Let me illustrate by reference to actual cost sheets as they are worked out in the studio. Here is a picture we are not ashamed of, because it was kept well within its original budget, "The Grand Duchess and the Waiter." The star was Adolphe Menjou. The scenario charges amounted to so much. Never mind the exact figures. I am merely showing you our methods. Under the head of direction we itemize the director and assistants, camera men, cutting the film, and property men. In the acting group some of the items are wardrobes, props, new sets, total settings, scenery. Under locations we place the expense of sending the company out to take outdoor scenes. Then there is the cost of lighting the sets and the wages of electricians who throw light on the objects to be photographed. There is the development of the negative, the writing of the titles, and the changing of the captions to get them as interesting as possible, the studio overhead, the cost of the story. The total cost in this instance was $110,000, and the studio had estimated it at $135,000. You see how everything is figured in detail and the whole fund apportioned to the various departments.

But here is a bigger picture, "Beau Geste," which was planned to cost $500,000 to $600,000. In spite of a very carefully arranged budget of $600,000 the unforeseeable factors which had to be met, such as transportation delays, heat on the desert, people sunstruck and overcome—it was photographed near Yuma, Arizona, one of the hottest places in America—raised the cost to $992,000. Fortunately, in the end the finance department had good reason to applaud our judgment.

Where the scenario charge of "The Grand Duchess and the Waiter" amounted to $12,894, the scenario charge of "Beau Geste" was $28,000. The story cost, which represents the purchase of the picture rights, was $20,000 or $30,000.

You may ask, "Why do you pay $28,000 for the writing of a scenario? Doesn't that sound extravagant?" Well, this is what frequently happens. We take one of our best scenario writers and say, "Here, Jim, you like this kind of fiction. What do you think of it?" "I think it is great." "Would you like to write it?" "Yes." We assign him the task of writing that scenario. He is supervised by an editor with whom he is in daily contact. When he has his scenario ready, the director reads it and says to the head of the studio, "I don't want to make that picture." "Why not?" "Because it doesn't contain the vital elements of the story." The management reads it and calls in experts, and the experts agree with the director. Perhaps the writer had a good scenario but he has lost the romance, the drama, the heart interest. A few weeks' time of high-salaried people has been consumed and already there is an investment of $5,000 or $6,000. You try another scenario writer or maybe you get a team to collaborate and work together. Your writing department's overhead goes on until finally you get something that is really worth an investment of $600,000, but in the process you have expended $28,000. The average scenario costs $5,000 or

$10,000, but we must allow for lost motion and mishaps and in a preliminary estimate we may figure $15,000. We say that ought to be ample, but the net result of a very earnest effort to do something fine has in this instance cost $28,000.

Once more, the problem I put up to you is this: Suppose you are the business head and have the last word, and I say to you, "This is a great story if only we can present it right; it will be a great success and make a lot of money. But I have already spent my allotment of $15,000 and I have not got the story the way it should be. I may not have it next week or the week after, but I will get it eventually. Can I go on?" You, business manager, have a right to say, "No; you have had enough time; you have spent your $15,000; go ahead and shoot." If you insist, the director will direct the picture, the camera man will turn the camera, the actors will act, and you may get one of those things that have made the public say, "What is wrong with the movies?" In that instance I should say that the thing that was wrong with the movies was the domination of business control.

So you see we have a peculiar industry. I call it an industrial art or rather an art industry, for I put the art first and I am always going to. If that is so, why shouldn't I dominate you and say, "Mr. Businessman; you are right as far as you go. I have spent my $15,000, but I see something that ought to be done and it is going to cost us more. We have overstepped our allowance, but I feel that we were justified." After all, I risk my job every time I do that, because you cannot make many mistakes of an overexpenditure of hundreds of thousands of dollars and be retained in your position.

However, men have come into our business and attempted to analyze it; they have gone through department after department and said, "You are extravagant here; you are wasteful there," and then they have devised economical methods which put the control in the hands of hard-boiled business men until business dominated the artistic side. Under that policy you get the negatives at a reasonable cost, but you get pictures of average or mediocre quality. You get no brilliancy, no outstanding successes, and, if that sort of unimaginative restriction should continue, I believe in time the industry would dry up with monotony.

I put that problem up to you. How would you handle it? Would you have a controlling board of two? If the two do not agree, what are you going to do? Our solution is to try to retain an executive at the head who has sympathy for the artistic side of production but who also has a lot of good, common business sense. We say to him, "You are to determine these problems finally. Give as much rein to production as you can. Keep constantly in mind a fine competition, a fine aggravation of the two departments; keep them at each other's throats; let them go as far as they can before separating them." That is what we do. It means that life is a constant turmoil for the executives.

JESSE L. LASKY
Cruzing over the Santa Fe Trail

"We had never produced a history-making cinematic mile-stone," Lasky told himself ruefully, after making 360 features in nine years. His story of *"our first superspecial road-show attraction,"* The Covered Wagon, *is an outstanding example of the fruitful intervention of an executive in the production schedule. He claims it was "one of those incredible, irrational accidents that make show business so unpredictable," but it was also the conscious choice of a rationally rash human being. It also must have been one of the happier high points between the Hollywood studio and the New York office. For historians it is an example of personal, anecdotal source material which explains more than any balance sheet or organization chart.* (I Blow My Own Horn, *op. cit., pages 159–164, his own chapter title.)*

We had made 360 features in nine years since *The Squaw Man* and there wasn't an epic in the lot of them. Of course if I relied on our exploitation brochures of the period to reinforce my memory I could readily believe that each and every one of these masterpieces put *The Birth of a Nation* to shame. A maudlin little number with Agnes Ayres and Jack Holt was casually referred to as "the greatest of all dramas." *Find the Woman,* worshipfully touted as "the greatest mystery ever screened," is still such a great mystery that I seriously doubt if you can find the woman—or the man— who could tell you who was in it or what it was about. Exhibitors were solemnly warned: "Picture theatres that miss Charles Ray in *The Egg Crate Wallop* will have an aching void that no other picture can ever fill." Several thousand picture theatres have an "aching void" today, but I wouldn't attribute it to not having played *The Egg Crate Wallop*.

Despite these sales blurbs my memory tells me that these three particular pictures and the other 357 didn't live up to the effusive promises of the press books. We were the most successful picture company on the face of the globe, our product improved from year to year, and we kept well ahead of our competitors, but I knew in my heart that we had never produced a history-making, cinematic milestone—and the guilty knowledge was always a source of extreme annoyance and personal embarrassment to me. The seven-year-old challenge of *The Birth of a Nation* still stood, a silent reproach that, with all our facilities and the pool of creative talent we commanded, we couldn't, or at any rate hadn't, done anything that overwhelmed picture patrons the way Griffith's masterpiece had. The fact that Griffith himself never again matched his first triumph was small consolation.

The way our first superspecial road-show attraction grew out of a cheap, run-of-the-mill program filler is one of those incredible, irrational accidents that make show business so unpredictable that no rules, no yardsticks can be applied to it. I suppose it started with the highly colored tales my grandfather told me in my early boyhood about his crossing the plains in a covered wagon in 1848, to settle in Sacramento, where my father was born. The skirmishes with Indians, the crushing hardships endured by the pioneers were branded forever on my imagination even before Edison invented his peep-show Kinetoscope.

I had to do so much commuting between my offices in New York and Hollywood that I felt like a transient in both places. Sometimes when I arrived on the Coast, waiting telegrams would demand my presence in New York for a conference, and when I got back there, some trouble would pop on the Coast that called for immediate personal attention. The only office I had that gave me a feeling of permanence and security for more than a few hours was a drawing room on the California Limited. Whenever I left New York, Jeane Cohen, the bright, shrewd secretary who had finagled me into buying *The Sheik* and later casting Valentino in the lead, would load me up with scripts, synopses, and business papers to read on the train. After changing from the Twentieth Century to the Santa Fe in Chicago, the three-day stretch without interruptions enabled me to do some of my best thinking and planning while crossing the prairies of Kansas into New Mexico and Arizona.

As I departed on one of these trips, Jeane handed me a copy of Emerson Hough's novel about the westward trek of the pioneers, *The Covered Wagon*. "What's the idea of giving me this book, Jeane?" I chided. "I can't waste time reading a story we've already bought."

"Please read it," she insisted, "so you'll appreciate it. You only read a synopsis when you authorized its purchase and no synopsis could do it justice."

"I've got more important things to do," I objected, slightly nettled. But I picked up the book somewhere over the plains of Kansas and became so absorbed in the struggles and adventures of the pioneers determined to reach the West or die in the attempt that for the whole day I became again a child at my grandfather's knee, listening to the most exciting tales a boy ever heard. And every time I glanced out the train window at the rolling prairies, the mountains, the desert, I saw the vast panorama of sky and earth forming a backdrop for those heroic souls whose first wagon train actually took much of the same route three quarters of a century before—a procession that united the West with the East, a migration but for which I myself would not have been born in my beloved California. Superimposing the past on the present by reading about that trek while actually retracing it myself, as I looked out the window of a speeding luxury train at the same scenery my grandfather had viewed from a lumbering Conestoga, was an emotional, almost mystical experience.

It was routine when I arrived at the Coast studio for Schulberg and Turnbull to give me a schedule of the new pictures in preparation, with tentative casts, directorial assignments, and estimated budgets. I would make changes I thought necessary and send it to Zukor, who would submit it to the sales department and other executives and return it with their criticisms and consensus of opinion and his own suggestions. I then gave it back to Schulberg and Turnbull, who jointly carried out the program.

I noted with dismay that *The Covered Wagon* was entrusted to George Melford, a director who could always be relied on to bring in a picture on time and within his budget, but I couldn't help feeling that his artistry was suspect, because he wore a large elk's tooth as a watch charm! I was even more alarmed to learn that Mary Miles Minter, a disciple of the brittle, china-doll school of acting, was to be given the role of Molly Wingate, the hardy, pioneer heroine. *The Covered Wagon* was not the ideal vehicle for

Mary Miles Minter. A Rolls-Royce was more her style. The picture was budgeted at $110,000, a normal expenditure for a Western.

"Boys," I said, "I want this picture taken off the list."

"I'm glad you're going to shelve it," Schulberg admitted with evident relief. "It's been a headache. Minter is sulking because she doesn't want to play in a Western and two directors turned it down flat. Melford only agreed because he takes anything that comes along."

"I'll talk to them," I said. "And I'm not taking it off the list permanently. It's going to be the greatest show we've ever made but not the way it's set up now."

Schulberg was flabbergasted.

I sent for Melford.

"George," I said, "why do you let them shove things like this *Covered Wagon* on you? You're too good-natured. With all the experience you've had, you shouldn't have to direct Westerns. That's for unknowns who haven't proved themselves."

Melford beamed. "This kind of assignment doesn't bother me," he confided. "I can knock them off with my left hand. But to tell the truth, I *would* like a story I could get my teeth into."

"I'll personally see to it that you get a fine drawing-room play, and you can forget *The Covered Wagon*," I promised.

"I wish you were here on the Coast all the time," he sighed.

Next I called in Mary Miles Minter. Although she was the wrong type to play a rugged pioneer woman, she was a very popular star and had to be handled with considerable tact. "Mary," I said, "I see they've cast you for *The Covered Wagon*," and I don't like it. You're at the stage where every picture you appear in is important. You'd be wasted in a horse opera—gingham dresses and no make-up. You should be showcased in Paris gowns, moving in an atmosphere of society and sophistication."

"You mean I don't have to play in *The Covered Wagon?*" she asked incredulously.

"You don't have to play it," I assured her.

She leaned over and kissed me in bubbling gratitude and rushed out of my office to spread the good news.

I had knocked the props out from under the picture. Now I could reconstruct it as I wanted. Who could direct with an authentic primitive feeling and vigorous touch the sweeping scenes of cattle fording the river, the wagon train winding endlessly through unpopulated spaces, the Indian fights, the buffalo hunt? I remembered that James Cruze, a young character actor who had recently been made a director, was supposed to have Indian blood. If so, he was closer by inheritance to the pioneer days than any of our other directors and should have had a natural instinct or affinity for the courageous drama of the barren plains. To this day I don't know whether he really had some Indian forebears — I never checked on it — but hearsay to that effect was what prompted me to call him in for a conference. I gave him the Emerson Hough book, and he read it overnight.

I can still see him as he barged into my office the next morning wearing riding breeches, brown shirt, and his cap on backward in the approved directorial style. He had such explosive enthusiasm and inspired imagination for the spectacle aspects of the story that I put it in his hands with full confidence. He had ridden all over Nevada and was mentally earmarking perfect locations for the dramatic high spots. He even knew where the necessary buffalo were to be had. To play the main character, Will Bannion, he suggested J. Warren Kerrigan, a matinee idol who had slipped almost into oblivion for no apparent reason.

Lois Wilson, a wholesome young actress we all liked but who had never had a real opportunity to show her worth, was decided on for the heroine. Ernest Torrence was cast as Jackson, the tough, hard-bitten old plains trader who joined the caravan and figured prominently in the overland journey, and Tully Marshall as the immortal guide and pathfinder, Jim Bridger.

The new conception demanded that everything be done on a lavish scale. We couldn't cut corners. We began to throw money around like confetti. All the ranches within a hundred miles of our location in the Snake Valley of Nevada were combed to find four hundred wagons, which were rented and transformed into covered wagons by the prop department. We hired horses and all the oxen we could find. We made financial arrangements to use the buffalo herd and the necessary locations. I asked the estimating department for a revised estimate on the basis of our expanded plans. They quoted, with some misgivings, the figure of $500,000. That would be equivalent to $5,000,000 today.

A few days after I sent my quarterly budget East, Zukor phoned. "Mr. Lasky," he said in his quiet way, "we've gone over your proposed pictures for the next quarter and we all agree the list is very good. But there seems to be a typographical error on your budget for a Western called *The Covered Wagon*. It says $500,000. Isn't the decimal point in the wrong place?"

"No," I said, "it will cost half a million dollars to make *The Covered Wagon*."

There was a ponderous silence. "But Mr. Lasky," he protested unemotionally, "don't you realize Westerns are dead? Even Bill Hart's *Three Word Brand*, which we released three months ago, will hardly break even. The top boys in distribution think you've lost your mind or that you're out of touch with the changing times for wanting to make another Western at all."

"Mr. Zukor," I said anxiously, "they don't understand—but you will. This picture is more than a Western. It's an epic."

"An epic?"

"E-P-I-C," I elucidated, trembling in my boots for the money we'd already spent without authorization, preparing for an elaborate production.

There was a long pause. Then the still-calm voice came over the wire. "An epic, eh? Well, that's different. You go ahead and I'll take care of the sales department." That was all the argument needed to convince the champion of bigger and better pictures. If Adolph Zukor hadn't been in the driver's seat, *The Covered Wagon* would no doubt have stopped dead in its tracks right there. When the carnage was over in the sales department, he wired me: "BUDGET APPROVED. REGARDS AND GOOD LUCK."

The company of 127, a large technical staff, a thousand locally hired extras, and 750 Indians worked for eight weeks in a 500-tent camp 85 miles from a railroad. Then they moved to Antelope Island in the Great Salt Lake for the buffalo hunt.

When I saw the completed picture in the projection room, I wasn't satisfied with the way the story ended near Fort Bridger, before the wagon train split. So I had it rewritten to show both the California and Oregon contingents continuing to their goals, and had the company reassembled and the wagon train rebuilt in Sonora, California, for the necessary snow scenes.

Actually I went over the original and revised budgets combined. *The Covered Wagon* cost $782,000, but it was one of the largest money-makers in silent-film history. We recovered our full investment from two theatres alone—the Criterion and Grauman's. It played the Criterion to standing room on a two-a-day schedule at $1.50 for fifty-nine weeks, breaking the world record of forty-four weeks for *The Birth of a Nation* nine years before. It could have run on for three years, but there was such a clamor for its release to other New York theatres that the first run was ended while still doing capacity business.

Robert Sherwood, at that time a leading dramatic critic, called it "the one great American epic that the screen has produced."

It pioneered a new type of extravagant, spectacular Western; it inaugurated a policy in our company of one tremendous roadshow attraction every year which could be booked like a stage play with reserved seats at more than twice the usual admission prices; it gave J. Warren Kerrigan a new lease on his professional life, and made stars of Lois Wilson, Ernest Torrence, and Tully Marshall, and lifted Cruze to the ranks of screen immortals.

I'd like to think the destiny that wove magic around the greatest picture Famous Players-Lasky ever made was compounded of less capricious and gossamer stuff than my grandfather's telling me lies that I believed in my childish innocence, my secretary handing me "something to read on the train," George Melford wearing an elk's tooth, and a rampant rumor that Jimmie Cruze was part Indian. But I've been too long in this unfathomable business to expect to find rhyme or reason to it.

BRUCE BLIVEN
The Covered Wagon

Bruce Bliven, one of the editors of The New Republic, *found* The Covered Wagon *to be pretty much what Lasky hoped for, his review emphasizing spectacle and the attempts at historical realism. Neither script nor acting were up to the other elements, but it was a big show and brought in the crowds. Our extract is from the review published April 25, 1923.*

... *The Covered Wagon's* story fits the motion picture because it is an epic: the epic of Westward, Ho! across the plains in the roaring forties. Before our eyes a great wagon train assembles on the west bank of the Mizzoury river, opposite where Kansas City stands today. We travel with this train all the way to the Pacific slope: out along the slow, heartbreaking trail to Oregon, which was the homesteader's bright fixed star in 1848 before the Gold

Rush. Our wagons bump behind the snail-like crawling oxen across uncounted miles of prairie; we have a heartbreaking struggle, and lose some of our cattle in crossing the terrible flood waters of the Platte. A few of us, faint hearts, give up and turn our oxen's faces toward the East—back to Pennsylvany and safety from Injuns and prairie fire, cyclone and water-starvation; but most of us press on—a great, slow, sure migration of people who have half a continent to loot and know it, and bend willing shoulders to the task.

Over and over, in this picture, you stand at the head of the long line of prairie schooners, temporarily halted, dwindling off toward the horizon. A bugle sounds; a leader on horseback makes a semaphore of himself, and slowly the whole great train lumbers forward in its dust. The twenty-foot whips crack above the oxen; the women and babies peer out from the puckered canvas doorway, the lads on their ponies gallop ahead. You get an irresistible feeling of the movement of a whole population toward the sunset; of scores and scores of similar trains pouring through every gap in the Alleghenies, moving across the Mississippi basin, sometimes down along the Santa Fe trail in the south, sometimes with Pike's Peak for a lodestar, or through Wyoming toward Oregon. . . .

What I am praising, you note, is the theme of the picture, rather than its execution. Yet the latter is excellent, not only for what it does but for movie temptations resisted. For instance:

The handsome hero, suffering repeated attempts at murder by the villain, always catches him at it, always lets him go. Whereupon the hero's back-woods Faithful Friend (magnificently played by Ernest Torrence) denounces him roundly as a careless fool, a dolt, an idiot; and finally, to the audience's unbounded delight kills that villain—when he isn't looking. You wouldn't, to paraphrase the useful Mr. Kipling, find that in a mere movie.

Point two: most of the males, including a twelve-year-old hellion who is all boy, chaw tobacker; and they chaw it in the unlovely, juice-dripping style of real life.

Point three: The highly virtuous back-woodsman and his truly noble chum, the scout, arrive at a trading post. Thereupon, to the undoubted anguish of the troglodytes on the Pennsylvania Board of Censors, they proceed to get good and drunk. (Incidentally, I defy you, I defy you not to hold your breath when these two rip-roaring drunken old scoundrels proceed, à la William Tell, to shoot tin cups off each other's head at fifty yards.)

Point four: An old lady dies en route, and is buried on the lone prairie. It is easy to see how a director with less passion for historical fact than James Cruze would have done this bit: the lonely little white cross in the illimitable gray waste, etc. Iris out on cross silhouetted against sunset; cut to closeup of coyote's head, howling. Not so Mr. Cruze. It is explained that the Indians who lurk behind every big wagon train waiting for strays and stragglers had just as lief loot a grave as not. Therefore ashes are scattered over the leveled top of this one and the entire wagon train runs over it.

Point five: There are some exquisite scenes showing the pioneers, halted for the night, seated about their campfires. Leaping flames, flickering lights on the canvas wagon tops in the background, and the high wide heavens of the West overhead; a lovely piece—and right in the middle of the foreground, the prairie mothers in hideous rocking chairs, temporarily appropriated from the wagons' cargo. A bit of sheer ugliness which (for me, at least) synthesizes into a whole possessing the beauty of the truth.

Not all of the film lives up to these high marks, of course. We have a hero who, having been dismissed from the army for cattle-stealing, submits to a tongue-lashing from his lady love and never even tries to tell her that he took the cattle only to keep his troop from starving to death in the desert. We have, again, the heroine herself, under no sort of compulsion from her doddering parents, about to marry a villain whom she does not love—an act without a shadow of a reason unless we are to infer a congenital preference in the buxom miss for the worst of marriages as against the best of spinsterhoods. Finally, it annoyed me to see this heroine, in the midst of grime and sweat and dust, always unutterably clean, as immaculate in snowy linen collar and cuffs as a Lucille mannequin, standing out against the crowd like a bar of soap in a coal bin.

These are minutiae, however, and perhaps hardly fair to mention. As a whole this motion picture must certainly rank among the four or five best ever produced, and as a wholly admirable attempt at the task to which the powers of the camera best lend themselves—the recording of an epic story, where the struggle is all on the surface, and with man's first and last enemy, Mother Earth herself.

Ben Hur (1925)

Chapter 4

The Big Five

It was a rugged era in many ways — Albert Smith

By the summer of 1915, D. W. Griffith's film, *The Birth of a Nation*, which had premiered in New York in March, was well on its way to what was to be a 48-week run. This astonishing achievement was proof not only that the art of the film had come of age but that feature-length films were going to make a lot of money for a lot of people in the future.

On the other hand, there were not going to be a lot of companies. A great consolidation shake-out would be taking place during the 1920s. The companies of the Edison trust would all give up the ghost, even the doughty pioneers of Vitagraph. Survival called for vertical integration—production companies which could distribute pictures to their own theaters, theater chains which had their own movie making lots in Hollywood.

One of the grandest gestures in this direction was the Triangle Film Corporation, an attempt by Harry Aitken to follow up the phenomenal success of the Griffith film, which he had largely financed. With Ince, Griffith, and Sennett as his production team, he proposed to place weekly shows in metropolitan theaters leased or owned by his own company.

It seems doubtful that Aitken was suited for that kind of steady entrepreneurship, and Griffith certainly chafed under it. The notion of using New York stage people had already been seen by Zukor to be unsuitable for film, although the name Famous Players still survived. But even more important was the fact that Zukor and the other veteran players had so many good contract players, writers, and directors signed up and competing. Triangle was absorbed by Zukor, the master strategist, within three years.

But meanwhile it had become clear that nobody was going to run the whole show. As soon as Famous Players-Lasky, with Zukor at the financial helm in New York and Lasky at the creative controls in Hollywood, was clearly perceived as the dominant company in film making, forces of competition and counterbalance began to come together. Theater men like Thomas Tally in Los Angeles and John Williams of West Virginia saw the proverbial handwriting on the wall: Zukor was beginning to charge them more and he was beginning to give preference to theaters who took all of his films on his terms. That preference meant a lot because Zukor had the stars. In fact, he had Mary Pickford, above all. He began to be the chief exponent of "block-booking," which meant that exhibitors could have a Mary Pickford picture only if they bought a group of lesser pictures at the same time.

"First National Exhibitors' Circuit" was a brand new company in 1917 and it grew fast – from 100 theaters in 30-plus cities to several thousand loyal franchise holders by 1921. The fear of Zukor was the main driving force, but the decision to reach at once for contracts with top stars was a big factor in drawing membership. A million dollars was handed to Charlie Chaplin for any eight movies he wanted to make, and a profit-sharing deal was signed with Mary Pickford. Thus performers began to be producers, and Chaplin even set up his own studio.

Now things were beginning to heat up, with as much drama as any movie. In this open intercorporate war, prices for talent were going sky-high. The people with the talent began to wonder if they couldn't be the managers, too, saving some costs in the process, keeping more of the profits themselves, and perhaps quarreling less over how to make the pictures.

United Artists became, in 1919, another competitor for Adolph Zukor. Mary Pickford, Charlie Chaplin, Douglas Fairbanks, and D. W. Griffith were the founders, and when they rebelled in this way against their old managers (Zukor, First National, and Aitken) it was said by the irate and agonized outsiders that "the lunatics had taken over the asylum." At any rate, this new form of organization didn't put a stop to show business quarrels. There were profits for each of the "united artists," but distribution management was not an agreeable task. Differences of opinion went right on, endlessly and monumentally, especially between Pickford and Chaplin.

Meanwhile, back at Famous Players-Lasky, our former struggling immigrant hero, so careful, quiet, and patient—watcher of audiences, contractor with stars—has turned into a different character. He is looked upon as a monopolist and a menace, not too far from a trust builder in the manner of Edison. He has been stopped from playing that role: First National and United Artists have seen to that. But now he sees himself menaced by others, and the competitive race turns angry.

The obvious way to fight First National was to buy more theaters. From 1919 to 1921 Zukor acquired or built 300 large houses in major towns and cities. Paramount representatives were called "the wrecking crew" and "the dynamite gang" by aggrieved independent theater owners around the country. The pressure was brutal. If an independent didn't want to sell out, he would soon find a sign on a nearby building or vacant lot announcing a new Paramount theater.

Meanwhile William Fox was expanding his theater holdings and Marcus Loew, who already had some of the best first run movie houses in the big cities, was preparing to buy a couple of production companies in California—Metro and Goldwyn (with Goldwyn already out)—and to hire L. B. Mayer as studio head. He thereby picked up such film properties as *Ben Hur*. The chariot race was on. The former partners, Zukor and Loew, were full size corporate competitors now.

By 1926, when Adolph Zukor presided over the dedication of his own Paramount building on Times Square in New York City, there were five major companies in the American motion picture business: Universal, Fox, First National, Loew's Inc., and Famous Players-Lasky, soon to be renamed Paramount-Famous-Lasky.

First National, however, already was on its way out: its big Balaban and Katz theater chain in Chicago had been acquired by Paramount. Its California studios would be taken over soon by the Warner Brothers, who had started with theaters in Pennsylvania. Another newcomer, Radio-Keith-Orpheum, would take over fifth place during the sound period when Universal gave up its theaters. Universal, Columbia, and United Artists would come to be known as the "minors" in the 1930s, and the majors would be Paramount, Loew's (M-G-M), 20th Century-Fox, RKO, and Warners.

KENNETH MACGOWAN
The Triangle of Griffith, Ince, and Sennett

Here is Kenneth Macgowan's attempt to explain, in a few pages, the debacle that was Triangle. If Paramount was the lengthened shadow of a careful planner like Zukor, Triangle seems to have been the short and sad reflection of Harry Aitken's misjudgments. This is from Behind the Screen, *op.cit., pages 171-178.*

By the summer of 1915, when Zukor and Lasky had laid the foundations of what was to become Paramount Pictures, three other men were planning an even more imposing edifice. They were Harry E. Aitken and the partners Adam Kessel and Charles O. Bauman, who released through a company called Mutual. Aitken had lured Griffith away from Biograph to supervise his Majestic unit. In the Reliance company, Kessel and Bauman had a rising young producer-director named Thomas H. Ince, and they controlled Mack Sennett with his Keystone Comedies. Aitken, Bauman, and Kessel left Mutual and took their considerable assets with them. These they united in a new and gargantuan project in both production and distribution, the Triangle Film Corporation. It was the most ambitious, promising, and potentially creative organization in the history of the silent screen — and the most disastrous.

Triangle had a truly impressive program. Its films were to be produced by three of the outstanding film makers of the day. One production unit was to be headed by Griffith, and another by Ince, while on the third point of the triangle Sennett was to balance adroitly. In addition, the company signed up some two dozen stage stars, ranging from Beerbohm Tree and Taylor Holmes to Marie Doro and Billie Burke, and from DeWolf Hopper and William Collier to Raymond Hitchcock and Eddie Foy. In some of the biggest cities, Triangle took over and redecorated "legitimate" theaters, and presented its films at "legitimate" prices — then two dollars for the best seats. A large orchestra played a classical overture and accompanied the films with special musical scores.

Few remember that Triangle spread the sorry business of the "double bill" across the nation, but at least the company made no "B" pictures in our meaning of the term. Although the films were no more than five-reel program features, they were carefully made, and boasted stars of the screen as well as the stage. Each bill—which ran a week at the special Triangle houses instead of only a few days—included one feature from Griffith's unit and one from Ince's, with a two-reel Keystone thrown in. The opening performance at the Knickerbocker Theater on September 23, 1915, drew an audience of Broadway's "first nighters" as well as the leaders of filmdom. The opening bill included *The Lamb*, from Griffith, with Douglas Fairbanks and Seena Owen; *The Iron Strain*, from Ince, with Dustin Farnum, Enid Markey, and Louise Glaum; and Sennett's *My Valet*, with Raymond Hitchcock, the Broadway comedian, as well as Mabel Normand and Sennett himself.

The basic policy of Triangle was that Griffith, Ince, and Sennett should *produce* pictures, rather than direct them personally. They were called director generals, and they combined the status of Lasky with that of his "supervisors" when he had to turn out 104 pictures a year. While Lasky hired lesser men to ride herd on scripts, directors, and cutters, Triangle made into supervisors three of America's four leading directors. . . .

There is a good deal of confusion about just who actually directed some of Ince's productions. One authority says that W. S. Hart was responsible for eighteen of the Ince pictures in which he appeared, and all but one of the seventeen for Triangle. Another says that various directors were in charge. In Hart's autobiography, he credits an ex-cowboy, Clifford Smith, as co-director with him after his first few films. As to other films besides Hart's, Ince sometimes added a certain confusion by announcing first that a film was "produced and directed by Thomas H. Ince," and later, merely "produced" by him.

Griffith was as busy as Ince, though for a shorter time. In the six or eight months before he became completely absorbed in *Intolerance*, he supervised around forty pictures for his unit. Among the best and busiest of his directors were Christy Cabanne, who made eight films, Allan Dwan, who took care of six, and John Emerson, Broadway actor and playwright, who directed six. These men and W. S. Van Dyke, Raoul Walsh, Jack Conway, and Chester and Sidney Franklin—all working under him—suggest that Griffith had better judgment than Ince in choosing directors, or felt that he had to depend more on what he called his "sub-directors."

Three-quarters of Griffith's pictures were made from original stories written expressly for the screen. He himself supplied eleven original stories, seven under the pseudonym of Granville Warwick. One of his early discoveries, Anita Loos—who was to write the best seller *Gentlemen Prefer Blondes*—had the aid and encouragement of Frank Woods, Griffith's story editor, and of her future husband, John Emerson, in developing a talent for oddly amusing plots and witty subtitles. As director and writer, Mr. and Mrs. Emerson were responsible for some of Douglas Fairbanks' successful pictures after he left Triangle.

Although Griffith and Ince saved money—and did the screen good service—by developing original stories, Triangle nevertheless came close to financial disaster within two years, and was out of business by 1919. Since almost all its films were well written and well directed, why did the company fail so quickly?

The stage actors usually take the rap. It is true that they were unknown to the great bulk of movie audiences. Almost all of them seemed unsuited to the screen; without the spoken word, their stage personalities were lost. And their salaries were frightfully high. But, if these actors were a major liability to Triangle, why does nobody blame the man or men who picked them out and paid them too much? Was it Aitken, Kessel, or Bauman—the managerial brains—or should Griffith, Ince, and Sennett share some of the blame?

There can be no question that the salaries paid to the stage stars added greatly to the costs of production—and in two ways. Paying Beerbohm Tree $100,000 for six months' work, and signing Joe Weber and Lew Fields at $2,500 each per week and De-Wolf Hopper at $1,500 were samples of Triangle's inflationary policy. Such salaries were bad enough, but when screen players heard about them, they insisted on getting on the gravy train, too. In 1913, screen players like Clara Kimball Young and Blanche Sweet, Francis X. Bushman and J. Warren Kerrigan, had been happy enough if the paycheck ran from $200 to $600 a week. Two years later, they had discovered that the studos had to depend on the screen stars for effective performances and financial success. So they demanded more money and they got it.

The high cost of both stage and screen actors wasn't the secret of Triangle's failure, for Paramount and other studios also paid through the nose. No, something else accounted for the sad fact that after the first flurry of interest in Triangle's bold and ambitious program, the public grew chilly, and looked elsewhere for its entertainment. The debacle of Triangle was indeed spectacular. Exhibitors in thousands of theaters began to cancel contracts. The income of the company's own theaters was too meager and their expenses too great. Even though they were in the largest cities, moviegoers willing to pay two dollars for a couple of "program" pictures and a two-reel comedy weren't plentiful enough to fill a theater through a week's run. So the masters of Triangle made the most violent reversal of form known to the economic history of the screen. Within two months they dropped the admission price in their own houses to ten, fifteen, and twenty-five cents, and showed only one feature, with a Sennett comedy, each half-week.

In spite of Triangle's starry crown—supervisors Griffith, Ince, and Sennett—its failure would probably have been inevitable, even if the company hadn't loaded itself down with expensive and ineffective stars. With its modest program pictures, Triangle was moving against the current of the American screen and of Europe's before the war. Between Zukor's beginnings in 1912 and the five-reel releases of Triangle in 1915, there had come portents of a new order. The public had developed a taste for longer and more spectacular films. In 1913, *Traffic in Souls* in six reels and *The Sea Wolf* in seven were outstanding successes. The next year, *The Spoilers* did even better with nine reels. Italy had already sent us spectacles that culminated in *Cabiria* (1913), which lasted a full three hours. Then, in March, 1915, came *The Birth of a Nation*.

Oddly enough, it was this twelve-reel spectacle that seems to have lured Aitken, along with Griffith and Ince, into the mistaken belief that millions of Americans would pay the equivalent of more than $5.00 in today's money for a very different kind of entertainment—two five-reel program pictures. Aitken, who had helped finance and distribute *The Birth of a Nation*, must have been fascinated by the crowds, both in New York and on tour, that paid Broadway theater prices for the best seats. Unfortunately, he seems to have ignored two important facts about this film. It was a towering spectacle that lasted two and three-quarter hours. Also, it wasn't embarrassed with stage stars. I suppose I am not the one to scoff at this mistake of the otherwise astute Aitken, for I remember with what enthusiasm I looked forward to

160   THE FIRST TYCOONS

the launching of Triangle, and praised its films.

In spite of the trend toward longer films, one may argue that Triangle could have been a success if more of its stage actors had been as effective on the screen as Douglas Fairbanks, Sr., W. S. Hart, and Frank Keenan. For after the company stopped producing new films in 1919, many features in which these actors had appeared were reissued under new titles—some of them three or four times—as late as 1923. . . .

Even seventeen features with Hart and thirteen with Fairbanks in less than two years couldn't save Triangle from dissolution. The laughter of the gallery gods of Broadway must have greeted the news, in 1917, that Zukor had taken over all its assets—Griffith, Ince, and Sennett, Fairbanks, Hart, and "Fatty" Arbuckle, Emerson, Loos, and Woods.

BENJAMIN B. HAMPTON
The Rise of First National

Benjamin Hampton was vice president of the American Tobacco Company when he was asked to inquire into the movie industry as a possible area for investment. Like Jeremiah Kennedy in 1908, he became fascinated with the contradictions of business and art. He even thought he might be able to rationalize it all by consolidating together Vitagraph, Famous Players-Lasky, and a few others. These large visions conflicted with the views of both Hodkinson and Zukor, but Hampton was emboldened to enter the business as a film producer for a few years. Musing about Zukor's role in all this, he was encouraged by friends to write what became the best analysis we have of early business relationships.

On pages 174-185 and 190-196 of The History of the Movies, *op. cit. he gives us his considered estimate of the acumen and skills of Adolph Zukor in the context of his critical confrontation with First National. "The secret of his rise to the top of the motion picture industry," Hampton says, "may be found in his uncanny flexibility in meeting emergencies as they arose." Hampton does not speculate on what might have happened to Paramount and to the industry if Zukor had not reached for profits and power by beginning "quietly and persistently to increase Paramount and Artcraft rental rates." Would First National not have been created? Would Mary Pickford not have left him for his new competitor?*

By his consolidations and acquisitions, Zukor had made himself the largest producer and distributor of features in the world. More than half of the most popular stars were on the Paramount list, and Artcraft had Mary Pickford, the magnet that drew more money to ticket windows than several other favorites combined. When theaters accepted the Artcraft increase in Pickford picture prices and advanced their admittance rates, Zukor was in a position to dominate studios and exchanges. The Paramount group of companies did not constitute a trust—at least not in the common acceptance of the term; they exercised no monopoly and controlled no more than twenty or twenty-five percent of the total volume of rentals. But Zukor had something more effective than a monopolistic corporation—he had the stars that controlled the audiences, and he believed audiences would permanently control the theaters.

He began quietly and persistently to increase Paramount and Artcraft rental rates, and presently representatives of these companies were giving preference to theaters that would use Paramount-Artcraft films to the exclusion of features made by other producers. Theater owners such as Robert Leiber of Indianapolis, Thomas Tally of Los Angeles, Jones, Linnick and Schaeffer of Chicago, Eugene Roth and Turner and Dankin of San Francisco, had followed a practice of using part of the Paramount output, supplying the remainder of their needs with pictures of Selznick, Goldwyn, Hodkinson, Fox, Metro, V L S E, Universal, and other producers. Such theaters, usually showing fifty-two pictures a year, might buy twelve, twenty-four, or thirty-six features from Paramount, dividing the other weeks between other manufacturers. In this manner, leading producers were assured of first runs, and the practice served exhibitors by maintaining competition and restraining the prices charged by producers.

Selznick and other manufacturers were not slow to follow Zukor, keeping their charges as close to his as possible without losing business. Some theaters could pay the advanced prices, and some thought they could not; however, looking beyond a consideration of prices, intelligent exhibitors foresaw that, as the logical result of Zukor's new method of giving preference to theaters showing nothing but his features, mere "preference" might soon be followed by insistence. If theaters should accede to his demands, other producers would starve to death, and Paramount-Artcraft could enforce whatever prices Zukor should elect to charge.

Only two or three years earlier, important first-run theaters would have met such a situation by throwing out the impudent manufacturer's product and showing none but pictures made by his competitors. Some exhibitors now followed this impulse and discarded Zukor's pictures, only to learn to their sorrow that control of their own houses had passed out of their hands – audiences definitely dominated the screen, the stars controlled the audiences, and many of the popular stars were employed by Zukor. Theater owners who discarded Paramount or Artcraft saw the pictures eagerly accepted by competitors at Zukor's prices and in accordance with his demand for preferential exhibition of his product. Good pictures could be obtained from other producers; about half the favorite stars were independent of Zukor; new stars were arising; but there was, nevertheless, definite box-office value connected with Mary Pickford, and the prestige of Paramount and Artcraft was steadily increasing. . . .

Leading exhibitors, often owning a chain of several theaters, had acquired wealth and influence in their home cities. The pride and business sense of such men urged them to find means of repressing Zukor before he could acquire dictatorial power. Thomas L. Tally, of Los Angeles, now rich and prominent, but still filled with his old fighting spirit, found the way out. His idea was to create an organization of exhibitors, one member in each principal key city, which would buy, or make, and distribute pictures of its own. Such an association would be profitable in itself and would restrain all producers from asking exorbitant prices. John D. Williams, a West Virginian who had been selling and exhibiting American films in various parts of the world for a number of years, was in Los Angeles. Tally outlined his plan and Williams liked it so well that they united to put it into effect.

"First National Exhibitors Circuit" was the title given to the project, and it was to have twenty-five or thirty members, each owning the franchise for his district, and each paying his share of the cost of production. Tally's neighbors, Turner and Dankin at San Francisco, and Jensen and Von Herburg at Seattle, joined promptly, and as quickly as Tally and Williams could travel to the east the plan was approved by owners of theaters in almost every key city. Jones, Linick and Schaeffer of Chicago, Finkelstein and Rubin of Minneapolis, Stanley and Jules Mastbaum of the Stanley Company of Philadelphia, the Hulse chain in Texas, the Sanger-Jordan circuit in New Orleans, Abe Blank in Iowa,

Rowland and Clarke in Pittsburgh, John Kunsky in Detroit, the Nate Gordon interests in Boston, the Fabian circuit in New Jersey, all joined Tally's organization. The first meeting was held in New York in April, 1917. Robert Leiber of Indianapolis was elected president, Harry Schwalbe, of the Stanley group of Philadelphia, secretary, and John D. Williams, manager.

First National exhibitors owned about a hundred theaters, and in each of thirty or thirty-five key cities at least one of their houses was a leading first run that was an important customer of Paramount pictures. The association issued sub-franchises to theaters in neighborhoods and outlying cities, and within a few months several hundred important exhibitors had joined the movement. In time five or six thousand theaters were in its organization. Ownership and control of the corporation, however, remained with the two dozen original stockholders. . . .

Nothing like the storm that arose when First National was organized had previously been known in the industry. Tally, Williams, and Schwalbe wasted no time in buying or building studios or studio organizations, but directed their efforts solely to bidding for the big box-office names of leading producers. As noisily as possible, they announced that First National would obtain the greatest stars, and the plain inference was that First National would pay the greatest salaries. This was indeed a startling shift in the attitude of exhibitors. In 1916 they had threatened to scalp Zukor for having raised Mary Pickford's compensation and thereby increasing the burden of the exhibitor. Now, in 1917, suddenly becoming producers, they manifested their intention to boost actors' earnings far above the figures they themselves had declared to be outrageous. The industry, by now long inured to the extravagant boasts of producers, took these announcements at something less than their face value, but it was genuinely aroused when First National took Charlie Chaplin from Freuler at a salary announced as "more than a million a year."

Soon it became known that the new organization had adopted a plan calculated to be more attractive to stars than that of Artcraft. First National was not, at the beginning, an employer of players or an operator of studios. Under its contract with Chaplin, the comedian became his own producer, agreeing to make for First National eight two-reel comedies a year. First National was to advance $125,000 to make each negative, and in this sum was included the star's salary. Chaplin was free to make pictures longer than two reels, and First National would advance $15,000 for each additional reel of negative. . . .

First National now controlled many first runs. It had bought Charlie Chaplin. It was bidding very high for Mary Pickford. With Pickford and Chaplin in its possession it would own the two greatest first-run attractions in existence, and many high-class exhibitors would protect their theaters by using First National pictures. Inasmuch as Paramount and Artcraft were the principal distributors of first-run products, they would be the chief sufferers.

Zukor was so agile, resourceful, and unexpected in meeting emergencies that a horde of legends regarding him have sprung up. In accordance with our standard American practice of describing our national figures as noble heroes upon whom the Almighty has bestowed miraculous gifts, or as demons intimately leagued with Hades, Zukor has been portrayed as a modern combination of Napoleon and Machiavelli with dashes of oriental subtlety; or as an inspired genius, who, while selling furs in New York and Chicago shops, shrewdly planned to make himself dictator of the entertainment world and ruthlessly forced his way to the top. . . .

The truth about Zukor is far more interesting — and significant, as a lesson in the ways of our civilization — than the far-fetched legends concerning him. The decade in which Zukor was learning what makes the wheels go round was the famous "trust era" and trusts were the most popular subject of contemporary discussion. Trust-busting politicians raged at Rockefeller, Duke, Ryan, Havemeyer, Harriman, and other "malefactors of great wealth," calling on the Federal government to send them to prison. The muckraking magazines and the newspapers regularly attacked and exposed the iniquitous monopolies of illegal combinations. The government responded with a series of antitrust lawsuits that acquired the popularity of sporting events, but a mind much less keen than Zukor's could not fail to observe that the prosecutions invariably came slowly to a common termination in the courts' the trusts were torn apart, "the eggs were unscrambled," "the octopus was cut to pieces," but no "malefactor of great wealth" ever got near a jail door.

The public was satisfied. The game had been played and ended. But Zukor, noting that each fragment of a dismembered trust promptly became a healthy and profitable octopus on its own hook, was convinced that America loves its industrial and financial magnates, its Big Business Men, much as the English love their nobility. Wealth, honor, and glory were waiting for any young man who would play the game of business in accordance with the somewhat nebulous rules of the Supreme Court, which seemed to be that one could dominate to one's heart's content if one didn't make the mistake of too blatantly piling corporation on corporation.

Zukor's industrial philosophy is the result of his youthful observations. He was able to appraise accurately the American attitude towards wealth, but even more important was his willingness to work terrifically at any task he undertook, and his eagerness to learn from other men and to expand his mind to absorb whatever they could teach him. He had no detailed plan that led from a penny arcade to a skyscraper in Times Square. The secret of his rise to the top of the motion picture industry may be found in his uncanny flexibility in meeting emergencies as they arose. While others were debating the wisdom of departure from established customs, Zukor would quietly change his opinions and move swiftly along new and apparently dangerous lines to deal with crises.

Zukor, Loew, Selznick, Nicholas and Joseph Schenck, Rowland, Fox, Laemmle, Patrick Powers, Walter Irwin, Goldwyn, John D. Williams, and other film men prominent in the revolutionary period of 1914-18, played the business game with the ardor of sportsmen and gamblers. Lewis Selznick used to say that each fellow thought he was "smarter" than the others, and he describes his own victories as triumphs in "outsmarting" his competitors. It was a time of clever, cunning, daring operations. The plain, undecorated truth about Zukor is that he persistently "outsmarted" all other players of the game.

Although theaters, studios, and exchanges in 1917-18 represented investments of several hundred million dollars, and gave employment to a hundred thousand people, Mary Pickford remained the industry's most valuable asset. Women's place in business has grown enormously in importance in the last three decades, but Mary Pickford is the only member of her sex who ever became the focal point in an entire industry. . . .

The Artcraft contract with Mary Pickford was to expire in the autumn of 1918. First National began its negotiations with her in 1917, so Zukor knew long in advance that he would have to increase her compensation or lose her. Artcraft was paying her half a million a year and half the profits of her pictures. First National offered her $225,000 apiece for three negatives, with allowances for stories and other items that brought the price to about $250,000; Charlotte Pickford was to receive $50,000; and profits were to be divided equally between Miss Pickford and First National. . . .

A hard problem. Zukor solved it characteristically—by listening carefully to another man, and modifying his own point of view. . . .

Cecil B. DeMille was one of the first directors to insist that a good motion picture is based on a good story. Associated with him was Jeanie MacPherson, author of screen stories and an expert continuity writer. In 1918, DeMille, with Jesse Lasky's approval and cooperation, made an experiment to prove the soundness of his theories, producing a new negative of "The Squaw Man" with an "all star" (which is, of course, non-star) cast at a cost of $40,000. "The Squaw Man" was rented as a single picture, that is, distributed on the Artcraft system instead of the Paramount program or series method. It earned $350,000 gross. DeMille followed this with "Old Wives for New"; the negative cost was $66,000, gross earnings $380,000.

The making of Mary Pickford pictures had been transferred from New York to Los Angeles, so that discussions of a new contract between the actress and Zukor in 1918 were held in Hollywood.

DeMille pointed out to Zukor that, in a period of unlimited competition, with hundreds of men eager to break into the movies and with capitalists at last aroused to the commercial possibilities of the industry and equally eager to supply the money, the steadily mounting star salaries would sooner or later bankrupt anyone who played the game to the finish. He offered to select obscure players, and by good direction to make box-office names for them in two or three pictures. Famous Players would be sure of continual profits instead of facing the constant gamble of whether or not a star would earn his keep. To support his argument he used the figures of "The Squaw Man" and "Old Wives for New" in comparison with the costs and earnings of Mary Pickford's pictures: "Squaw Man," cost $40,000; "Old Wives," cost

$66,000; Mary Pickford's average costs $165,000 to $170,000 with gross earnings about equal, $350,000 to $380,000 each.

DeMille's point of view seemed unassailable, but Lasky and Zukor had to consider as well the problem of whether or not Paramount-Artcraft could maintain its ascendency if the star system was weakened or destroyed. . . .

Zukor pondered for several weeks, and then followed the course so often successful with masters of opportunism—he evolved a compromise plan: Mary Pickford could go, and De-Mille could proceed to put his theories into practice. If the public approved the results, Famous Players-Lasky could extend the all-star method indefinitely. Meanwhile he and Lasky would maintain the star system and let time decide which of the two was the best business practice.

Still reluctant to allow First National to acquire Miss Pickford, Zukor tried one more plan.

"You've worked very hard for years," he told her. "Why don't you take a vacation? If you will stop making pictures for five years, I will give you $250,000."

"Oh, I couldn't do that, Mr. Zukor," she answered. "I love pictures, and I'm just a girl. I couldn't quit now."

They said good-by, and Mary Pickford went to First National.

MAE D. HUETTIG
The Battle for Theaters

> *Mae Huettig was one of the first of the researchers on the film business to realize that suits at law tend to bring out interesting facts and documents. In this selection from her book,* Economic Control of the Motion Picture Industry *(Philadelphia, University of Pennsylvania Press, 1944, pages 34–39), she shares with us a confidential report by a top financial firm which was offered in evidence when the Federal Trade Commission tried to bring monopoly charges later on. It shows quite clearly that Famous Players-Lasky was justified economically in going after theaters: after all, that was where the big percentages of profit were. Then she goes on to give in some detail how the Paramount buyers roamed the country wiping out independent exhibitors.*

Mr. Zukor decided in 1919 to go into the theatre business. His decision was not, however, motivated solely by fear of the various types of exhibitors' combinations. The hearings on the Federal Trade Commission charges against Famous Players-Lasky contains a report on the industry made in 1919 by H. D. H. Connick to Kuhn, Loeb and Company, on the basis of which the financial firm decided to support Zukor's entry into the business of owning theatres. The report states:

> ... the largest returns of the industry result from exhibiting pictures to the public, not from manufacturing them. The Famous Players-Lasky Corporation Sales Department estimates that the gross annual return of the 15,000 American theatres during 1919 will be $800,000,000 and that the total amount the producers will receive in the form of sales and leases of film and accessories will not be over $90,000,000. It is apparent to anyone who has had theatrical experience that this is not an equitable division. Producers claim that even when full consideration is given to the extra cost of the large orchestra and attractions required of the picture houses, they should receive from 22 to 25% of the gross theatre income. . . . From an examination of such records of theatre operation as are available and assuming that the sum required to amortize the building will not exceed 2% of its cost, and that the amount of the ground rental per annum does not exceed $30 per seat, and with prices of admission ranging upward to 60 cents, a preliminary guess has been made that a theatre with 3,100 seats will return at least 25% on the investment in addition to the usual first run rental charge in their district for the use of films. That the 25% is conservative is indicated by the fact that the Grauman Theatre of Los Angeles is

now earning profits of 100% a year; the Rialto in New York at the rate of about 80% a year; the Stillman in Cleveland at the rate of over 100% a year.[38]

On the subject of the size of theatres in relation to their profitability, the report states:

> There is no doubt as to the financial advantage of the theatre with a large seating capacity over a small one. An examination of the cost of operating theatres shows that with the same standard of exhibition, the only increase in operating cost in the case of the large houses occurs in the comparatively low-priced items, such as ushers and cleaners. The big items—management, film rental and orchestra—remain the same. There are differences of opinion as to the size of theatres that should be constructed.[39]

With facts such as these at his disposal, together with ease in obtaining capital through the facilities of Kuhn, Loeb and Company, Zukor decided to become a theatre owner as well as the producer and distributor of films. And on no small scale either. His plan was described as "selling the product direct to the people."

> Mr. Zukor, president of the Famous Players-Lasky Corporation, has developed a plan to increase the earnings and percentage of profit to the corporation. Should his plan be carried out they will become the most important exhibitors of motion pictures in America as well as the leading producers and distributors. . . . He plans to build or acquire about 50 theatres properly located in the important cities of the country and several additional ones in the theatrical districts of New York and sell his products direct to the people and take the resulting profits. . . . This circuit of key theatres will enable his corporation to dominate the motion pictures industry in this country and at the same time increase the percentage of profits.[40]

In connection with this program of theatre acquisition, Kuhn, Loeb and Company floated ten million dollars' worth of the first public offering of movie securities. By August 31, 1921, Zukor's company had acquired 303 theatres.

A gauge of the success of the plan is found in the increasing difficulty experienced by independent producers in securing first-run releases for the pictures. Goldwyn Pictures Corporation, finding that good releases were increasingly difficult to obtain, announced in 1921 that it had acquired a half interest in approximately thirty theatres in order that it might secure proper exploitation for its films. At approximately the same time Loew's, Inc., a $25 million theatre company, bought Metro Picture Corporation, an impoverished producing and distributing company, which had also been experiencing difficulty in obtaining first-run showings. (Metro, it may be observed in passing, had been organized in 1915 by a group of exchanges struggling to break through the Patent Company's near-monopoly of films.)

Apparently sufficient evidence of the success of Zukor's plan existed to warrant the filing of a complaint against the corporation by the Federal Trade Commission in 1921, charging unfair trade practices and restraint of trade through monopoly control of the first-run theatres in the country. The following quotation from the Commission's statement of findings describes the situation:

> On July 22, 1919, the board of directors of Famous Players-Lasky Corporation . . . for the purpose of modifying, perpetuating and making more effectual its said distributional policy, i.e., block-booking, as distinguished from the lease of individual pictures, and for the purpose of intimidating and coercing exhibitors to lease and exhibit films produced and distributed by Famous Players-Lasky Corporation, adopted a progressive and increasing policy of building, owning or otherwise controlling theatres, especially first-class, first-run theatres in key cities to be used to give to the best picture films produced by Famous Players-Lasky Corporation first-run exhibitions under the most favorable conditions, to advertise and exploit said films, create a popular demand for their exhibition by the patrons of the theatres of the better class in territories adjacent to said several key cities, and to make leases for their exhibition indispensable to the successful operation of such class of theatres. . . . Because of the dominant position of Famous Players-Lasky Corporation in the motion picture industry, its methods of competition, policy and practice are necessarily followed, adopted and maintained by all competitors of Famous Players-Lasky that are strong enough to acquire and operate first-class, first-run theatres to exploit their most meritorious pictures. . . . Therefore, it is made difficult for small and independent producers or distributors of films to enter into or remain in the moving picture industry or market, or to lease individual pictures on merit. . . . By said methods, Famous Players-Lasky Corporation has unduly hindered, and is unduly hindering competitors, lessening competition, and restraining trade in the motion picture industry, with a dangerous tendency toward the creation of a monopoly therein in the several parts of the United States.[41]

Within the industry, this phase of the integration process is described as the "Battle for Theatres." Descriptions of the period sound like a journalist's account of a war. Indeed, at times the intensity of the drive against resisting theatre owners was out of all proportion to the value of the objective, as was later admitted by the majors. The admission was reluctantly made in the form of the return of many of the theatres to their original owners when centralized operation proved unprofitable.

From the point of view of the producer-distributors, the acquisition of theatres served two immediate purposes: It gave them an assured outlet for their films, and it gave them, rather than the independent theatre owners, the revenue from the box office. In most of the smaller towns it was not necessary to acquire all the theatres, since movie attendance was likely to be concentrated in one or two houses. In the larger cities, more extensive operations were considered advisable in order to obtain a substantial portion of the box office.

The technique of theatre acquisition involved an encircling movement in which the choice given the independent theatre owner depended upon the earning power of the property. If his was an undoubtedly lucrative house and one which the major company had determined to acquire, he had the alternative of either selling on terms offered or of meeting threatened competition from a new theatre to be located in the immediate vicinity. He could expect as a matter of course that the new theatre would have first choice of product and play dates. Usually, when an agent of one of the majors approached an independent theatre owner to discuss the purchase of his theatre, he would have with him an option on an admirable theatre site across the street. Most theatre owners, faced with the choice of selling or of competing with an affiliated theatre, sold. Other instances were handled differently. If the theatre was not notably profitable, its importance was chiefly as a buyer of films. In such cases, the theatre owners were often persuaded to give preference to the product of the particular major.

At first Zukor's company was the principal menace to the independent theatre operators. It seems quite clear that the pattern of the relationship between the majors and independents was established by him at this time. Roving representatives of Paramount were soon dubbed "the wrecking crew" and the "dynamite gang" by the theatre owners.[42] Much of the bitterness of the exhibitors against the majors goes back to this period of strong-arm dealing and no amount of "public relations" or good-will advertising has

172   THE FIRST TYCOONS

quite succeeded in restoring mutual trust to the relationship. One of the first tangible results of the warfare between the independents and the majors was the formation in 1920 of a national trade association of theatre operators, the Motion Picture Theatre Operators of America. By 1921, a membership of over ten thousand was claimed.

Zukor, however, was not the only menace to the independents. By 1923 Loew and Fox had also expanded their theatre holdings considerably. The independently owned first-run theatre was rapidly becoming extinct through absorption either by one of the major producer-distributors or one of the unaffiliated circuits. The latter were also growing steadily in strength and numbers.

> Scores, eventually hundreds, of exhibitors, some of whom had been in the industry since nickelodeon days, disappeared as the circuits proceeded on their forward march. . . . Soon the Pacific slope, the Rocky Mountain states, most of the Central states, Texas, the southwest and the southeast, were closed to independents; eastern Pennsylvania and Delaware were controlled by the Stanley Company; Paramount shared New England with Loew and Poli; Loew, Fox, Paramount, and First National controlled New York. Loew and Paramount had already penetrated Ohio and were strong in Cleveland and Cincinnati; they were making alliances in Michigan. There remained New Jersey, Maryland, the District of Columbia and a few sections scattered throughout other states that had not come under the domination of Zukor, Loew, First National and their allies.[43]

Thus the most important present-day characteristics of the industry were already indicated by 1923. Further development merely gave substance to the skeleton structure. There were several completely integrated units with national systems of distribution and important theatre holdings; there were powerful unaffiliated theatre chains counterposed to the strength of the majors; there were numerous individual theatre operators competing with the chains for both product and patronage; the first-run theatres, already largely pre-empted by the chains, were clearly established as the site of power in the market. Paramount, First National, Loew's, and Fox were engaged in production, distribution, and exhibition, but not with equal strength in each activity. Paramount dominated production and was becoming increasingly important in exhibition. First National's strength was in its large number of theatres and its volume buying power; Loew's, in the quality of its relatively small theatre chain. Still to appear on the scene were two more major companies, Warner Brothers and R.K.O. Their story is tied up with the development of sound and belongs to another era.

NOTES

38. *Federal Trade Commission v. Famous Players-Lasky, et al.* Complaint No. 835, p. 903.
39. *Ibid.,* p. 903.
40. *Federal Trade Commission v. Famous Players-Lasky, et al.* Complaint No. 835, p. 961.
41. *Ibid.,* p. 961.
42. The story of this period has been told in considerable detail in B. B. Hampton's *A History of the Movies.* An entire chapter is devoted to the Battle for Theatres.
43. B. B. Hampton, *op. cit.,* pp. 274-75.

The FTC had the responsibility by law of prosecuting as well as studying anti-trust violations. But the result of the case brought against Zukor was only a rap on the knuckles. Blockbooking was declared improper and he was to promise not to do it again. (See **Film Daily Annual** *for 1928 for the report, and* **New York Times** *16 July 1927 for interpretation.)*

ALBERT E. SMITH
It Was a Rugged Era

*Here is Albert Smith (pages 265-270) to testify that not only theaters but producers were subject to the lash. Smith reported earlier (*Two Reels and a Crank, *op. cit.) that Vitagraph had its peak year in 1920 with profits of more than $6,000,000. In 1922, "we estimated our actual losses to be nearly a million dollars" because of the competitive methods of "the biggest film company in the world." (Smith identifies his enemy thus, without naming Zukor.) Famous Players-Lasky, like the trust of old, was trying to freeze out another company by threatening exhibitors who chose to rent Vitagraph films. Smith had promised independent theater owners he would not get into the exhibition business. By 1925, that self-restraint would put him out of the movie business altogether.*

Vitagraph, oldest and strongest of the pioneer companies, was the most important target of the new trust.

Vitagraph owned no chain of theaters. It had kept its promise to its old exhibitor friends.

In that pre-television era a producer's lifeblood was theaters, whether owned by himself or another. Theaters are the windows, the avenues to the public, and without them a producer's films lie unseen in dark vaults.

The new order had an idea, an exciting idea, compelling, foolproof, deadly practical: produce movies *and* own theaters. Then a producer could exhibit his own pictures when and how he pleased.

Acquiring theaters became quite an art, though an effective method was to make an offer so big as to break down the resistance of the sturdiest owner. The approach was not always this direct. Sometimes it was psychological, with periods of waiting, like a detective stalking a criminal.

I remember one case in particular. A young man had come to me in 1910 saying he would give anything for a chance to get into the exhibition phase of motion pictures. Since Vitagraph had no theaters I directed him to a friend, who put the youth in charge of a theater. It was a small house which wasn't doing too well.

In a matter of months patronage increased. The young manager had novel ideas. One plainly was a showman's artifice. He would delay admittance, allowing a long line of customers to form down the street to give the impression the picture was a smash hit. But he did not impose on their good will; he kept them in good spirits by distributing little boxes of chocolates which he had purchased in wholesale lots.

In time the young man had enough money to take the big step—a down payment on a theater of his own on the Pacific coast. I met him shortly after; he was proud and happy.

Under his virtual night-and-day supervision the house enjoyed unusual business. One day a representative of a film combine came to see him. The combine had numerous theaters in that area and was anxious to add the young man's house to its chain. But the youth said he had worked hard to buy the theater, that he had given to it much time and thought.

The representative returned a number of times. He said his principals preferred to buy the house, but if he wouldn't sell they would build another in the immediate vicinity.

The youth still declined to part with his property.

A few weeks later a large sign was placed on a building a short distance from the theater stating that the property had been acquired for the building of a mammoth moving-picture palace to seat thirty-five hundred people and to be opened on a certain date. The young man knew his house would not be able to cope with this kind of competition.

In a later visit the representative informed the young man that they did not wish to eliminate him entirely from the picture. If he would sell they would keep him on as manager.

Finally, pressed with worry and attracted to the large salary offered him as manager, the young man agreed to the sale. He was paid a small amount of cash and given the balance of the sale price in stock of the corporation owning the theater chain.

Things went smoothly for a time, then a series of incidents and shifts in responsibility slowly ate away the authority of the young man's position. Lesser employees were instructed to make certain decisions heretofore reserved to the manager, until finally, greatly humiliated, he resigned.

By 1922, Vitagraph's position in the world film market was under serious assault by a producing company which had set out to acquire as many theaters as possible. The competitor, with four hundred first-run houses in key American cities, was the biggest film company in the world.

We felt its power more severely with each passing month. Then, certain maneuvers became apparent. There were whispers at first, and, later, letters marked confidential reached us from exhibitor friends of long standing.

Though we had suspicions, it was puzzling at first why our business was falling off so sharply. The gross from pictures shown in America and Canada dropped twenty thousand dollars a week.

By September, 1922, we estimated our actual losses to be nearly a million dollars—because of the trade practices of this competitor.

Two months later Vitagraph filed suit for six million dollars.

A series of acts over quite a long period of time was behind our decision to take the drastic step. One of the first of these tactics occurred in 1918.

We had hired George Randolph Chester, creator of the fictional character, J. Rufus Wallingford, perhaps better known as "Get-Rich-Quick Wallingford." We let it be known that Chester would produce and direct several motion pictures centering around the Wallingford character.

In 1921 we made *The Son of Wallingford*. Two months later this competitor released a picture called *Get-Rich-Quick Wallingford;* our loss on *Son of Wallingford* as a result of this competition was approximately one hundred thousand dollars.

We had bought the motion-picture rights to John Arthur Fraser's version of the famous James M. Barrie story, *The Little Minister*, and in 1912 filmed it as a three-reeler under the same title. Now, this competitor announced plans to produce a picture called *The Little Minister* based upon the Barrie play. We notified them that we had certain rights in *The Little Minister*, and for weeks a controversy raged over the matter. We then decided to film a second version of *The Little Minister* in five reels with new players, but using substantially John Arthur Fraser's story line. By the time it was completed and ready for release, the competitor had released its own version of *The Little Minister*.

Now there were two *Little Ministers* showing. The competitor distributed circulars calling attention to this fact. One of the circulars stated:

"Show this one and you will make money and build prestige—show the other and you will lose both."

The circular further read:

"One is notable—the other negligible."

Also:

"One is the best in American stagecraft—the other is poor beyond the ordinary."

In selling their *Little Minister* this competitor offered an unusual price advantage, stating in a letter to exhibitors:

"Don't delay this, as *The Little Minister* is now going big and you can get the benefit if you hustle in your date. Leave the price to us, IT WILL BE ALL RIGHT, and to your advantage."

Also, this competitor sent letters to all its branch managers with the apparent design to force exhibitors to refrain from dealing with Vitagraph.

One of these letters was sent to us by a friendly exhibitor in Denver. It contained this sentence:

"This is to advise you that I want you to kick out every Vitagraph account that you can find, irrespective of the terms you may have to make, just so you cancel the contract and get them out of the way."

The letter was circulated among the competitor's district salesmen. It was accompanied by a note which read in part:

"Please do not permit anyone to read this communication, and work quietly on this subject but get the results. You will note that he (an official of the competitor company) lets down the barriers regardless of the terms which you might have to make, but you must have convincing proof that you will be able to kick Vitagraph out."

This campaign against Vitagraph had immediate, disastrous effects. It induced many exhibitors to breach or cancel their contracts with us. Trade practices of this competitor did not appear to be based upon any difference in the grade or quality of the product, but indicated an intent to establish a monopoly and freeze out Vitagraph, in a manner that seemed in the opinion of counsel to violate the Clayton and Sherman acts.

One day, after our suit was filed in the New York federal district court, I had an important visitor. He was Will Hays, the big gun of the Motion Picture Producers and Distributors' Association, of which this competitor was a member.

He said:

"Look here, Mr. Smith, I've devoted a lot of effort to cleaning up the mess in the motion-picture business and just as I get everything to looking all right you start one of these multi-million-dollar suits."

"What am I supposed to do — sit around and let them destroy Vitagraph with their underhanded tricks?"

"I don't blame you but I can get this situation cleared up. I'll remove the troubles you complain about. If you call off the suit, I'll see to it that they don't continue."

I told him I would discuss it with Will Seabury, my lawyer. Will favored maintaining the action. We discussed and argued it for days, and Hays kept coming back with fresh reasons for my calling off the suit. I didn't know what to do. I was tired, problems had begun to pile up at the studio, and on the outside the nagging contentions and little rivalries were twisting routine matters into major puzzles. Too, the suit would be a long time trailing through the courts. So, when Hays said he had been assured that the competitor would discontinue its practices in connection with Vitagraph, and when agreements were signed to that effect, I agreed to call it off. In less than a month the competitor had broken these agreements, and even more openly was renewing its attack on Vitagraph.

> Diary entry—July 20, 1924: Sea Battle for *Captain Blood* between *Arabella* and enemy ship—full-size square riggers bought for $5,000 each. Battle filmed with government permission in channel between Catalina and mainland. Property man instructed to put 200 lbs. dynamite in *Arabella,* but used 5,000 lbs. at suggestion of dynamite salesman on theory it would improve scene. Instead, ship exploded in seconds, and went up in matchsticks. Too fast. Camera recorded only blur.

It was a rugged era in many ways. We paid Sabatini thirty thousand dollars for *Captain Blood* and turned it into one of our most expensive productions. On the night of its *première* in New York I was standing outside the theater shortly before the start of the performance.

A motion-picture critic on a New York daily, an old acquaintance of ours, strolled up. He had just been to a dinner presided over by one of Vitagraph's toughest competitors—a man who for years held a high place in the industry. His guests were reporters and the town's leading film critics.

The critic friend of mine drew forth a wrist watch—quite a luxury in those days.

A sly smile crossed his face.

"Our host gave everyone there a wrist watch," he said. "Must cost between a hundred and a hundred fifty dollars each. He said something else. He said his feelings wouldn't be hurt if we decided that *Captain Blood* was a lousy picture."

MICHAEL CONANT
Bankers and Theaters

Michael Conant has written what is probably the definitive study of Antitrust in the Motion Picture Industry (Berkeley, University of California Press, 1960). On pages 24–27, in a chapter called "History of Innovations and Combinations," he gives us a summary of the intricate relations between financial houses and movie companies as the "battle for theaters" between First National and Famous Players expanded into a wild scramble by other companies to acquire real estate.

In April, 1919, First National affiliates controlled 190 first-run theaters, 40 subsequent-run theaters, and indirectly controlled 366 others by subfranchise agreements. By January, 1920, they controlled 639 theaters, including 224 first run.[15] In the autumn of 1921, First National had 3,400 subfranchised holders, but the requirement to take all First National releases caused the number to drop to 2,700 in the spring of 1923. In 1918 First National signed a million dollar contract to finance and distribute the production of Charlie Chaplin. Mary Pickford's productions were also brought into the firm, and in 1923 First National constructed studios and began producing pictures. As shown in table 7, First National's share of domestic releases rose from 2.6 per cent in 1919 to 8.7 per cent in 1923.

Zukor's Famous Players-Lasky reacted to First National's control of exhibition by a decision in 1919 to enter the theater business. Zukor would thereby avoid paying monopoly premiums to local theater circuits and also eliminate many of the uncertainties of bargaining for sufficient first-run exhibition to cover costs. Such a large venture could not be financed internally. Kuhn, Loeb, and Company was brought in to sell a $10,000,000 issue of Paramount Famous-Lasky Corporation preferred shares. Paramount preferred and common were listed on the stock exchange. By mid-1921, Paramount owned 303 theaters, insuring first-run exhibition in many areas. Paramount had acquired interests in three large circuits affiliated with First National. In 1925 it signed an operating agreement with one of the largest, most active First National affiliates — Balaban and Katz Corporation, a 50-theater chain in Chicago and northern Illinois — in which it acquired controlling interest in 1926.[16] Following this, First National began to disintegrate, many of the component companies selling out to Paramount.

Other firms turned to Eastern bankers to finance the race for theater acquisitions. The John F. Dryden-Prudential Insurance group backed Fox Film Corporation, which had acquired 27 theaters by 1925. In that year it acquired one third of the common stock of West Coast Theatres, Inc. Goldwyn Pictures Corporation acquired one-half interest in approximately 30 theaters in 1921. Goldwyn was financed by the Duponts and Chase National Bank. Loew's Incorporated, which in 1920 operated 70 theaters in the New York City area, acquired Metro Pictures Corporation and entered production and distribution of films. Loew's external financing is indicated by two of its board members, W. C. Durant, head of General Motors Corporation, and Harvey Gibson, president of Liberty National Bank. In 1924 Metro Pictures Corporation merged with Goldwyn Pictures Corporation and later acquired the assets of Louis B. Mayer. The new Loew's subsidiary was named Metro-Goldwyn-Mayer Corporation. Universal, under Laemmle, was backed by Shields and Company, investment bankers, in organizing Universal Theatres Corporation to expand in the exhibition field. First National had been financed in its expansion backward into production by floating an issue of preferred shares through Hayden, Stone and Company, and Richard Hoyt of that firm became an active participant in First National. Warner Brothers was incorporated in 1923, and its great studio expansion was financed by securities underwritten by Goldman, Sachs, and Company. In 1928 it acquired the First National Studios[17] and the majority stock of Stanley Company of America with its 182 theaters and control of 51 others.

Although the major circuits controlled the majority of first-run theaters by 1925, they continued and accelerated the battle for theaters. Each major producer-distributor knew that his ability to bargain for good first-run exhibition depended on his controlling a theater chain as a reciprocal bargaining weapon in dealing with the other major integrated firms.

TABLE 8
AFFILIATED CHAIN THEATERS, 1931

Company	Number of theaters
Paramount Publix Corporation	971
Fox Film Corporation	521
Warner Bros. Pictures, Inc.	529
Loew's Incorporated	189
Radio-Keith-Orpheum Corporation	161
Universal Theaters Corporation	66
Total	2,437

SOURCE: Howard T. Lewis, *Motion Picture Industry*, p. 345, as compiled from *Film Daily Yearbook*, 1932.

As shown in table 8, Paramount ended the era of the greatest theater expansion with nearly 1,000 theaters, and Fox and Warner each had more than 500. Loew's and RKO circuits had more than 150 theaters each, and Universal had 66. The six firms had a total of 2,437 theaters. Since these included the great majority of first-run theaters in major cities, the market control represented was much greater than ownership of one-eighth of the total theaters would indicate.

Universal sold its theaters after its receivership in 1933. The other five firms continued to build and acquire some theaters until 1940, when further acquisitions were enjoined by the consent decree in the *Paramount* case. As stated in chapter iii, the five major integrated firms had controlling interests in 3,137 theaters in 1945. The box-office declines after 1930 convinced them that large chains of subsequent-run theaters were not necessary to control exhibition, for monopoly profits could be channeled into first and second run. In fact Paramount learned by bitter experience the diseconomies of centralized control of more than 1,000 theaters. It filed voluntary bankruptcy in 1933. In its subsequent reorganization, the theater branch was completely decentralized, and some theaters were sold.

NOTES

15. Howard T. Lewis, *Motion Picture Industry* (New York: Van Nostrand, 1933), p. 17.

16. In mid-1926 Famous Players-Lasky had interests in 368 theaters. *In Matter of Famous Players-Lasky Corp.*, F.T.C. 187, 210 (1927).

17. A suit to enjoin this stock acquisition under section 7 of the Clayton Act ended unsuccessfully with a dismissal in 1934. *U.S.* v. *Warner Bros. Pictures, Inc.*, Eq. 51-121 (S.D.N.Y., filed 1929).

NORMAN ZIEROLD
The Films' Forgotten Man: William Fox

Destroyed as a power in the motion picture industry after the stock market crash of 1929, William Fox (unlike Jesse Lasky) did leave his name on one of the major companies that survive today, and he lived till 1952. But he was more or less forgotten by the trade and by the newspapers, Zierold suggests, because he had been such a loner and was so "poor at public relations." Laemmle had not only friends but relatives in his own company. Zukor and Loew were old friends from the days of the fur trade. Lasky and Goldwyn were related by marriage before they were forced apart by Zukor, and Lasky and Zukor evidently had a pleasant working relationship even after that.

Fox was both physically handicapped and exceptionally bitter in his unhappy memories of tenement life. Unlike the others, he arrived in America when he was less than one year old. He chose movies at an earlier age (25) than any of the others, but of all the tycoons, he was the most intractable individualist. He found one man he could trust, and Winfield Sheehan stayed with him until Fox tried to be king of the hill in 1929. Norman Zierold has evidently drawn largely from Upton Sinclair's 1933 biography of Fox in this chapter in his lively and knowledgeable book The Hollywood Tycoons *(London, Hamish Hamilton, 1969), pages 215–220, 222–25.*

At the time of his greatest power, in the 1920's, Fox ran a motion picture empire with a value estimated at around $250 million. He was then a sallow-complexioned man, bald-headed, unsmiling. His prominent Jewish nose, dark, intense eyes, and black moustache relieved a face that was close to being round. Fox liked to wear white shirts and sweaters because they were to him a symbol of prosperity, and he could never forget his poverty-haunted childhood. His left arm was withered and hung limply at his side. As a child he had fallen off a delivery truck on which he was hitching a ride to save carfare. The family could not afford a good doctor, and so a makeshift operation removed the elbow joint and left the arm permanently useless. Despite the handicap, Fox became an excellent golfer, using only his right arm. Golf was a gentleman's game. Fox would never carry a watch because he didn't want to know what time it was. He worked until there was no more work to do, driving himself and those around him with a savage intensity. The blinds in his huge office were kept drawn, again to make time stand still, to allow all his energies to flow into the erasure of that poverty which he had once known.

The Fox family—the name was Americanized from Fried— came from Hungary, although both parents were of German-Jewish descent. William was less than a year old when the move to the United States was made in 1880, with the first residence a rear tenement on the teeming lower East Side of New York. Here twelve other children were born, six of whom died in childhood.

William worked as a boy to help support the family. He sold newspapers; he sold stove polish which his father made up in the house; he sold candy lozenges with riddles inside; he sold sandwiches and pretzels in Central Park and spent a night in jail because the wrappers made an illegal mess on the ground. More permanent employment came in the garment trade. Young William was eleven when a sweatshop operator gave him a job cutting linings for men's suits. The hours were from seven to seven, the wages $8 a week. From one firm to another he went, his salary going up to double his beginning scale. All the pennies and dollars were saved. With a partner named Sol Brill he opened his own business to examine and shrink cloth from mills. The cloth-sponging firm succeeded. . . .

Sol Brill told him of a penny arcade and picture show for sale at 700 Broadway in Brooklyn. Fox was intrigued by the peep boxes, weighing machines, punching bags, chewing gum machines, and phonographs which needed only a single attendant to collect the coins. Upstairs in a darkened room a recent invention called a "moving picture" was shown. . . . His savings of $1600 went into purchasing the place from J. Stuart Blackton, the clever, snappily dressed Englishman who was one of the founders of the Vitagraph film studio. His reason for selling, he told Fox, was the studio's increasing demands on his time. As it turned out there were other factors. As soon as he began operating the house, Fox found the crowds of customers thinning to a trickle. Blackton had hired plants to people the premises on the day of Fox's visit.

Brill was so agitated that he moved out of the fledgling business. Fox determined to make it go. He refurbished the rooms, installed more comfortable chairs, and used vaudeville acts to lure people in off the street and then up to his moving picture show. In between the film showings he let a piano player sing illustrated songs, with the audience often joining in.

His first little theater, bought in 1904, became a success, and Fox bought another, checking the location more carefully this time. He soon owned 15 theaters in Brooklyn and New York, and money was flowing into his pockets at a spectacular rate. Even so, he saw that the people who leased him the films were making far greater sums. As a consequence he went into the distribution field, forming the Greater New York Rental Company.

To demonstrate how greatly the initial $1600 had already grown in a few short years, it is only necessary to look at Fox's battle with the Trust. . . . They offered Fox $75,000 for his group of theaters. To their outraged astonishment, he asked for $750,000 and was adamant. The Trust thereupon canceled his license on the ground he had shown some of their films in a house of prostitution. Like the Blackton "customers" at the first theater, the situation was rigged. In retaliation, Fox brought a lawsuit against the Trust for $6 million, saying the companies involved constituted a trust in restraint of trade, thereby violating the Sherman Anti-Trust Act.

The "big ten," headed by blunt, bellicose Jeremiah J. Kennedy of Biograph, were upset by the charge. They contacted Fox, who offered to settle out of court for one million dollars. This further infuriated Kennedy. Fox came down to $800,000. The Trust negotiator offered $200,000. It was Fox's turn to be enraged and walk out. The Trust came back with an offer of $300,000. Fox accepted. . . .

William Fox's fight against this tough combine showed him to be fearless and capable of battling with giants on their own cutthroat terms. His theater chain grew, as did his leasing firm. In 1914 he also entered the field of production. He bought a story called "Life's Shop Window" for $100 and made it into a feature costing a total of $4500. Filmed on Staten Island, it starred Claire Whitney and Stuart Holmes. Fox's sharp metallic eyes narrowed as he watched the initial offering unreel in the projection room. At the end he was silent for several minutes. "Let's burn the damn thing," he finally said. Dissuaded from destroying the print, he released it for showing in his theaters, where audiences were delighted with it. . . .

The most sensational success of the new company involved a wholly fabricated star personality, the first such case in the history of Hollywood. Fox bought a stage play called *A Fool There Was*, which derived from Kipling's poem "The Vampire," inspired in turn by a well-known painting by Burne-Jones. To play the lead, a wildly sensual *femme fatale* who uses men to satisfy her needs and then tosses them callously aside, director Frank Powell chose an unknown – not unknown for long, however. . . .

The first showing of the film, in January, 1915, was preceded by a dramatic reading of Kipling's poem. The audience was therefore prepared for the havoc in the lives of men which the heroine was going to wreak. A frenzy of applause greeted the last image on the screen. Overnight, Theda Bara was a star. Her line, "Kiss me, my fool," became a household favorite, and the word "vampire" and its derivative, "vamp," entered the common vocabulary.

For the next four years Theda Bara vamped at a rate that makes the mind boggle. She made 40 pictures in which she seduced unwitting men, her ample bosom heaving, her curvaceous figure draped with semitransparent silks, her undulating walk an invitation to unbridled passion. Once the men were won away from wives or lovers and completely under Theda's spell, she began to reverse her course, scorning the advances of her conquests, driving them mad with frustration. . . .

Thinly clad Betty Blythe gave a torrid performance in a superproduction called *The Queen of Sheba*. Annette Kellerman, reputed for her physical culture exercises, left Universal for Fox, where she made another early spectacle, *A Daughter of the Gods*, with leading man Stuart Holmes. The film was directed by imaginative, extravagant Herbert Brenon, who talked Fox into letting him shoot on location in Jamaica. Fox groaned as the bills came in – more than $100,000 for a complete Moorish city constructed near Kingston, $7000 for a caravan of camels imported to appear in a fleeting sequence, additional thousands for a tower from which athletic Annette would dive into the sea. The final version ran so long that Fox hired an outside editor to trim it down and took Brenon's name off the credits. When Brenon insisted he wanted no credit for what he considered a butchered version, Fox put his name back on. Their arguments became virulent. Fox issued orders to bar Brenon from attending the premiere. To his annoyance he later learned that Brenon, wearing a disguise capped by false whiskers, saw the film from one of the best seats in the house – and furthermore seemed to enjoy it. The two men continued their spirited scuffling over the years.

The star who led the Fox ranks after the sinister seductions of Theda Bara and the cycle of lush spectacles was Western star Tom Mix. Born in Mix Run, Pennsylvania, he left for foreign adventures at an early age and then went to the American West, serving as a sheriff, a deputy U.S. marshal, and a Texas ranger. In 1910 the Selig Company hired him as a technical consultant and began using him in films. He hit his real stride, however, after William Fox signed him to a contract which wound up ten years later paying him $17,000 a week.

Although Mix had actually started earlier, William S. Hart beat him to stardom. Fox decided that his new player should develop an original new personality of his own rather than imitate Hart. The Mix screen character was accordingly worked out with care. He never drank or smoked or used profanity. He would never kill his enemy but conquer him by clever horsemanship or lasso work. Breezy comedy entered into the characterization. The story line was direct and clear and the motivations realistic.

Tom Mix became a great favorite in such films as *Durand of the Badlands*, *Rough Riding Romance*, and *Tumbling River*, along with his horse of the moment, Tony, Old Blue, or Tony Jr. More than 60 features rolled off the assembly line, filling the pockets of the star and his mentor. . . .

William Fox took some of the profits from the cowboy sagas and plowed them into artistic ventures, such as the 1927 production of *Sunrise*. This was directed by noted European film maker F. W. Murnau and starred Janet Gaynor and George O'Brien. . . . *Over the Hill* dealt with children and their neglect of parents. It was based on an original idea by Fox, who spent $100,000 to make it and netted $3,000,000. . . .

In addition to his commercial films, Fox was a pioneer in other areas. His Movietone process was installed in a Chicago hospital to record the first surgical operation on film. Fox wanted to use talking films to aid medical studies. He also hoped to introduce audio-visual teaching in the areas of science and mathematics, and to make film libraries available for home use. Similar applications were under study for churches throughout the country. The overall plan was grandiose—to make film, under the direction of William Fox, a contributing, formative factor in the life of the nation.

In his majestic business manipulations Fox was a loner, but a key figure in the commercial film empire was Winfield Sheehan, a blond, blue-eyed Irishman who went from newspaper work to a job as secretary to New York's police commissioner. When bribery scandals rocked the department, Fox rescued Sheehan and made him his secretary at $100 a week, then his general manager. Eventually he rose to become chief of production for Fox films, earning $130,000 a year. Fox enjoyed his flamboyant protege, and Sheehan was always ready with a show. He married opera diva Maria Jeritza and built her a splendid showplace in Beverly HIlls, with lovely sunken gardens, frescoed ceilings imported from Europe, and landscaping that included trees from each state of the union. Sheehan acquired a stable of rare Lippizaner horses, which he liked to show off to guests. He and those he invited ate off solid gold plates and drank from solid gold goblets.

Fox himself lived well in apartments that were increasingly luxurious and at Foxhall, a well-kept estate in Woodmere, Long Island. Here he could well afford works of art by the great masters, but conspicuously on display was a reproduction of a painting by LeBrun which had been acquired years ago by submitting Babbitt's soap coupons. It had graced the first modest Fox apartment and served as a reminder of those times of struggle. For the company Fox built a four-story structure on New York's West 56th Street. His own wood-paneled office was immense, with tall, colored-glass windows, thickly carpeted floors, and desk behind which he sat in solitary grandeur, receiving visitors like the powerful potentate he was. . . .

BENJAMIN B. HAMPTON
William Fox Improves His Position

In the late 1920s, Hampton says, Fox found himself surrounded by successful competitive entrepreneurs and seemed to wake up to the need to take some steps. He sought capital to acquire more theaters and also sent Winfield Sheehan to stay in Hollywood and revitalize the production program. But before that he had secured his flagship theater in New York City. These steps are described in A History of the Movies, *op. cit., pages 332–339.*

Hampton relates the story of the Roxy Theater with special relish. It was built by a little-known picture producer, Herbert Lubin (no relation to the Trust member, Sigmund Lubin). He was heavily in debt but was possessed by a vision of the largest and finest theater in the world. He somehow persuaded various financiers to back this "off-Broadway" house which, with 6200 seats and costing about $12,000,000, became the biggest in New York. He also persuaded the best manager in the business, Sam ("Roxy") Rothapfel, who had moved from the Strand to the Rialto and then to the Capitol, to preside over the stage shows and movies at a theater to be named after him.

Paramount owned the Rialto and the Rivoli, and was building a magnificent 4500-seat theater and skyscraper office building in Times Square at a cost of six or eight million dollars. Loew was completing a large, modern house just across the way on Seventh Avenue, and through Metro-Goldwyn-Mayer controlled the Capitol. First National had the Strand. Motion picture experts, bankers, and capitalists were exceedingly dubious about a venture that proposed to compete with these powerful corporations. Even if Lubin should succeed in building his giant house, there might be no producer from whom it could obtain a steady supply of high class pictures. Each of the big companies would use its best productions on its own screens, and as Fox, the only important producer not already represented in the Broadway district, had announced his intention of building a new theater, his films would not be available to the Roxy. . . .

Erection of the Roxy started in 1925; the theater was completed and ready for opening in the spring of 1927. Building and equipping theaters is work of such infinite and peculiar detail that contractors will not undertake such construction for a specified sum. The Roxy was built on a cost-plus basis, and when the opening day drew near, Lubin knew that he faced a deficit—or an "overrun" in costs—of about $2,500,000, and an overrun is not a pretty thing to finance. . . .

During the later months of construction, A. C. Blumenthal, theater scout for William Fox, frequently visited Lubin, and joked with him about the hard job of gauging an overrun in advance, the difficulty of this last piece of financing, and the uncertainty of obtaining pictures when all principal producers had their own theaters. He tried to induce him to sell his stock to Fox and to retire on his profits. Lubin invariably replied that he was perfectly willing to sell to Fox, but he insisted that the Roxy would prove to be a very profitable theater and he demanded an apparently impossible price for his holdings. Lubin's own belief was that the Roxy's boxoffice receipts would average $100,000 a week, a figure that would show a handsome profit on the total capitalization, including the common stock.

Blumenthal could not agree with this prediction of earnings. Theater receipts had increased enormously in the last few years, but, reviewing the intakes of the largest, most popular New York houses, very great optimism was needed to see the soundness of Lubin's contention. The Capitol had been remodeled and its seating capacity increased to 5300. Its normal gross receipts were $50,000, running as high as $65,000 perhaps once a year, because of some extraordinary attraction. The Strand, with 2900 seats and normal receipts of $25,000 to $35,000, broke all records the week that Charlie Chaplin's "Gold Rush" brought $72,000 to the boxoffice. The Rivoli had 2200 seats, and its normal receipts ran $20,000 to $25,000, exceptional weeks bringing in as high as $35,000. The bankers who had underwritten the Roxy bonds and stocks had accepted the calculation of experts that the Roxy could expect normal gross receipts of $65,000 to $70,000, and in exceptional weeks, $80,000 to $85,000.

As the theater neared completion, the owners of several chains throughout the country looked with longing eyes at this titan and negotiated with Lubin for his stock, but they backed away when they learned the price. Blumenthal persisted, scarcely a day passing in which he did not plead with Lubin to "get down to earth and name a figure that a sane man will pay."

One night, a week before the theater was to open, Blumenthal took William Fox into the Roxy. A regiment of workmen was rushing day and night to complete the interior decorations, lay the last carpet, screw down the last chair. An orchestra of 110 pieces was rehearsing. In a practice room a ballet master was training two hundred dancers. The superintendent of ushers was polishing his crew of 120 young men to the highest lustre of courtesy. Everywhere were the sights and sounds of tense activity so that at the appointed hour 6200 selected patrons would witness the inauguration of "the cathedral of motion pictures." In the list of invited guests were high officials of federal, state, and city governments, great bankers, famous business men, notables from the world of science, literature, art, drama, music.

William Fox strolled quietly through the vast edifice, observing everything, and saying little. Perhaps memories crowded his mind. Thirty years is not a long time. His own first little show shops—a shooting gallery with kinetoscopes—a nickelodeon. The audiences of all his early theaters could have been seated in one section of this auditorium. The cost of the Roxy represented a sum larger than the total investment in all his theaters, his studios, his exchanges, only a few years ago. Once, nickels were pushed into a flimsy ticket window by workingmen and children; and now first nighters were paying speculators $10 to $25 each for seats with the distinguished audience that would fill the Roxy next week. The movies had traveled a long journey in the three decades since William Fox first knew them.

Somewhere in the turmoil and confusion of the army of artisans and workmen, Blumenthal led his chief to a small man in shirt sleeves, perspiring and dust-stained, his normally husky voice hoarsened to a croak with nervous tension and lack of sleep—somewhere they found Herbert Lubin, and in a few minutes William Fox had bought the controlling interest in the Roxy corporations for about $5,000,000. After debts were wiped out and settlements were completed, the Fox payments would deliver to Lubin more than $2,000,000 for his promotional labors.

The success of the Roxy theater exceeded the most optimistic expectations. Its gross business one week in its first year was $135,000; its average intake was in excess of $100,000 a week. The large attendance at the Roxy did not reduce attendance at neighboring theaters. Loew's new house and the new Paramount, opening prior to the Roxy, were filled nightly, and the Capitol, the Strand, the Rivoli, and the Rialto continued to roll up big records.

Acquisition of the Roxy was an important event, but only one of many important events taking place in the affairs of William Fox. Able showman and vigorous fighter, Fox had always played a lone hand from the time he left the garment trades to become the antagonist of the patents trust and General Film. Year after year his own studios manufactured successful box-office pictures with star material discovered or developed by Fox—William Farnum, Theda Bara, Tom Mix, Gladys Brockwell, and others—and Fox made large profits by exhibiting the films in his own houses and renting them to other theaters. No stars except Mary Pickford and Charlie Chaplin ever earned more money per dollar of investment than Farnum and Theda Bara, and it is probable that Tom Mix brought more profits to his employer than any other star ever in the movies.

William Fox, Saul E. Rogers, his attorney from earliest days, and Winfield Sheehan, right-hand man and general factotum, comprised the inner cabinet, and these three were always sufficient unto themselves to cope with every emergency that arose in the turbulent trade. When large capital was needed, Fox had obtained it from financiers, but always retained control of his corporations, none of the voting power ever leaving his hands.

After the memorable milestone, Armistice Day, when a new generation suddenly asserted its power and remade the movies to suit current desires, the closely knit Fox film family began to feel the pressure of the changed order. Young people considered Fox stars out-of-date, and Fox pictures began to slip behind in public favor; his corporations continued to make money, but for a while they were dangerously near standing still, and in the film industry a lack of progress, or hesitation for a short time, had usually meant retrogression and defeat. While the changing tastes of the box office were diminishing his earnings, and the increasing costs of pictures were sending studio expense-sheets to the sky, Zukor, Loew, Mastbaum, and First National were hammering away at Fox's theater position. Fox had been expanding steadily, but not at a pace sufficient to keep abreast of Zukor and Loew, and in many cities they had gone ahead of him by acquiring or building new houses that threw his own into the second class.

Suddenly and dramatically Fox seemed to awaken to the hazard of his position, and moved forcefully to reorganize his affairs.

Winfield Sheehan was dispatched to Los Angeles, to take charge of the studio, and to live there and create a new order of picture-making; Fox, bestirring himself to observation and analysis of the theater field, brought A. C. Blumenthal from the west coast to Fox headquarters to hunt out desirable existing houses to be purchased and locations upon which others could be built.

One by one, Fox celebrities faded from the firmament. Fickle youth had distributed its diluted affections among so many exotic ladies, from Barbara LaMarr to Pola Negri and Greta Garbo, that Theda Bara, most famous siren, had disappeared while her professional ability was yet at its height. Married to Charles Brabin, a director, the great Theda retired to their home in Hollywood. William Farnum, with health none too sturdy, returned to the stage; Gladys Brockwell became a free-lance character actress in Los Angeles and built a new reputation for herself; Tom Mix remained with Fox until 1928, when he transferred to F B O (Radio-Keith-Orpheum) for a year, and then "joined out" with Miller Brothers 101 Ranch and Wild West Show—which he had left years before to go with Selig. Later, when his friend John Ringling bought the Sells-Floto circus, Mix became its star.

Lee De Forest, scientist and inventor, had been experimenting for years with sound waves, trying to devise a method to record them on photographic film so that sound and pictures could be projected simultaneously. Theodore W. Case, an engineer in the Fox organization, had been tinkering away at the same problem. William Fox decided that talking pictures must arrive before long; Case was provided with funds and equipment to speed up his experiments, and Fox acquired an option to buy De Forest's patents.

Within a year Fox had made a new program and new policy for himself, and the revolution wrought in his operations was as drastic as that of Henry Ford in sending the old model flivver to the boneyard and designing a modern, stylish car to meet the new demands of the American people. Winfield Sheehan's administration of the Hollywood studio was quiet and non-sensational, but his results were startling. Somewhere in his career as reporter, Manhattan police-department official, and general handy man for William Fox, Sheehan had acquired an uncanny understanding of the popular mind and a sure hand in devising entertainment that would please it. Fox pictures again leaped into the first rank of popularity, and his profits increased half a million to a million dollars a year.

Sheehan, arriving in Los Angeles at the time when the star system was beginning to crumble under the assaults of the all-star idea, abandoned the individual star method, concentrating on a search for good stories that could be made into effective continuities, and then selecting players who he believed could portray the rôles. The actresses and actors might be famous stars or leads, or they might be new and unknown aspirants; Sheehan cared nothing about their reputations if they were able to play the parts. Minor rôles were cast as carefully as the leads, as for example, in "What Price Glory?," in which two experienced actors, Victor McLaglen and Edmund Lowe, and an unknown girl from Mexico, Dolores Del Rio, divided the honors so evenly that none could be called the star. Another stage play, "Seventh Heaven," by Austin Strong, was adapted to the screen by Benjamin Glazer, a Philadelphia lawyer turned playwright, and made into a picture by Frank Borzage. Two unknown youngsters, Charles Farrell and Janet Gaynor, were found on the Fox lot working in small parts. Sheehan gave them the leads in "Seventh Heaven," and the public made stars of them overnight.

In the theater department of his personal revolution, Fox expanded with a rapidity that took him into Wall Street to obtain twenty-five to fifty million dollars through public financing. Halsey, Stuart and Company became his investment bankers and shares of Fox corporations were listed on the New York Stock Exchange and the New York Curb Market. Wherever he needed theater representation, or where Zukor or Loew or First National had better houses than he, Fox speedily moved to place himself in position to cope with any competition. He built modern houses in important cities from the Atlantic to the Pacific, from Canada to Mexico. With a succession of splendid pictures coming from Winfield Sheehan to the screens of fine theaters, Fox soon recovered his lost ground and in a few years was in a position to rival Paramount.

Fox's attempt in 1929 to take over Loew's Inc. was so dramatic and overweening that it might well deserve our attention as a side-trip in financial legerdemain. But it was a failure and therefore had no long-term effect on film history. Some observers speculate that an irate L. B. Mayer might have got President Hoover to apply the antitrust laws. Two other things went wrong. Fox's pile-up of loans to pay for it (including a massive $10,000,000 payment to Nicholas Schenck, Marcus Loew's successor as president) was so tied to stock values that there was no way to recover after the October disaster on Wall Street. Meanwhile Fox was in an automobile accident which kept him out of action for nearly three months. He sold out in 1930 and his legal tangles after that led not only to Federal tax claims but personal bankruptcy in 1936 and finally an indictment on a charge of bribing a judge, followed by a six-month term in the penitentiary. He eventually paid off the claims and was able to support himself and his family.

ARTHUR L. MAYER
The Origins of United Artists

Arthur Mayer was an insider, a publicity man for Paramount at an early stage of his career and later one of the owners of the Rialto Theater on Times Square. He would have known personally many of the people he refers to in this breezy account of the founding of United Artists. This article in Films in Review *(Aug-Sep 1959, pages 390-399, based on an article in* Vanity*) may have been a sketch for a full length history he once planned.*

Mayer, like Macgowan, was a Harvard graduate who wrote knowledgeably about the motion picture business in professional and general magazines. In his later years he was a lecturer in alternate semesters at Stanford, Dartmouth, and USC.

When Richard Rowland, then president of Metro, heard that Mary Pickford, Douglas Fairbanks, Charlie Chaplin and D. W. Griffith were starting their own company, he wise-cracked: *"So the lunatics have taken charge of the asylum."* Actually, the founders of United Artists displayed the same brand of lunacy as Rockefeller, Morgan and DuPont.

Adolph Zukor once said of Mary: "She could have risen to the top in United States Steel if she had decided to be a Carnegie instead of a movie star." Joe Schenck, almost as competent a judge of business sagacity as Zukor, said of Fairbanks: "Don't go up against Doug in a business deal. He's poison even to California real estate men and they are tough birds." As for Chaplin, *he* was reputed to keep half a million at all times in cash in a safe deposit vault. According to his fellow comic, Chester Conklin: "Charlie always declined anything that threatened to cost money."

Mary Pickford had started her movie career in 1909 at the mature age of 16 and was a film veteran of ten years when United Artists was incorporated on April 17, 1919. She had begun at Biograph for $5 a day, but soon attracted the attention of D. W. Griffith, who reluctantly raised her to $40 a week. Mary's golden curls, dimples, winsome smile, thespian talents and masculine determination quickly made her the richest and most famous woman in the world. She was lovingly nicknamed "America's Sweetheart," but her real heart was that of a financier. . . .

"The Big Four," as Pickford, Fairbanks, Chaplin and Griffith were usually called—there were some who added the word "flushers"—tried to get Hollywood's fifth leading figure, William S. Hart, the good-bad man of the early Westerns, to join them in establishing United Artists. Hart participated in most of the preliminary meetings, but when it dawned on him that the artists proposed to put up their own money instead of being bankrolled by investors, his enthusiasm waned. An offer of $200,000 per picture from Zukor also served to strengthen his loyalty to Famous Players.

In whose fertile brain did the idea originate that it was folly for stars to toil for others when they could retain all the profits by working for themselves? Fairbanks, faithful in his fashion to Mary long after he had ceased to be conventionally so, assured me once that the original idea came from "America's sweetheart."

There is considerable evidence that Oscar Price, who was in charge of press relations for William G. McAdoo, the Secretary of the Treasury and President Wilson's son-in-law, on several occasions urged Pickford, Fairbanks and Griffith, while they were on a World War I Liberty Bond tour, to make and distribute their own pictures.

However, the man who first envisioned something akin to United Artists was Ben Schulberg, father of Budd and Stuart. As sales chief of Famous Players-Lasky he was well-acquainted with the terrific boxoffice potentialities of Pickford pictures. They were grossing for Artcraft, one of Zukor's less-than-secret subsidiaries, between $300,000 and $500,000 each, and he was confident that, if sold individually instead of being used to soften up exhibitor resistance to less desirable product, they could bring in between $600,000 and $1,200,000 each. Pickford, however, was only making three to four pictures a year, which were not enough to maintain a profitable distribution organization. Schulberg realized she must ally herself with other outstanding attractions.

The most outstanding in Hollywood, next to Mary, were Chaplin, Fairbanks, Griffith and Hart.

Matters came to a head in '18 when Hiram Abrams, then one of Zukor's top executives, did not see eye to eye with his boss. Men whose business vision seemed defective to Zukor did not linger on his payroll. Abrams resigned before he could be fired, and Schulberg, out of loyalty to his immediate superior, *as unusual in picture annals as it proved unrequited,* resigned also. They promptly submitted Ben's United Artists brainstorm to Fairbanks, who proceeded to sell it to Pickford, Chaplin, Griffith and, above all, Mrs. Pickford.

Fairbanks also contacted McAdoo, who was then recuperating in his Santa Barbara bungalow, and urged him to head the new organization. The canny McAdoo declined, adding, however: "If you will get Price, I will help you organize and be your counsel." It was not until a later date that he specified that his services in that capacity would, in his opinion, be worth $100,000 a year and one-fifth of the company's profits.

Price signed up as president at $18,000 a year and a small percentage of the profits and offices were rented in New York at 729 Seventh Avenue for $12,000 (UA is still located at 729). Hollywood was soon buzzing with rumors about the new company, which its promoters did little to soft pedal. On one occasion Mary, Mrs. Pickford, Douglas, Charlie, Griffith and Hart dined with a minimum of secrecy and a maximum of publicity at the Alexandria Hotel. Sleuths of the major companies kept strolling through the dining room and Chaplin, seated facing the door, would mimic — and there never was a more perfect mimic — the head of the company the sleuth was working for.

Most of the early gatherings of the partners were marked by levity. Doug's idea of subtle humor was to disappear under the table and terrify an honored guest by grabbing his, or preferably her, calf, or he would wire a chair so as to give some visiting VIP an unexpected shock. There were plenty of such visitors, particularly attorneys. So meticulous were the artists in the protection of their interests that it required 10 eminent legal lights to draw up the initial contracts. Mary used to listen to all of them carefully, shake her lovely curls and say: "I disagree with you gentlemen and I will tell you why." The "why" was invariably connected with unnecessary expenditure. She was usually right.

When Douglas was not playing pranks he was indulging in eloquent speeches, maintaining that the stars could only keep their popularity "by building an organization of their own that would insure liberty and freedom of marketing." He would add that they were "being strangled by artist's restrictions, machine-made pictures and mediocre stories." At that time he was making $500,000 a year and Chaplin and Pickford were doing even better.

Although they were in perfect accord concerning the injustices to which they were subjected, the personal relationships between the stars had not always been entirely cordial, and the seeds of future dissension were already planted. Griffith regarded Fairbanks as a buffoon, lacking both dramatic talent and artistic appreciation, and he had lost no time after Pickford left his employ in announcing that Mae Marsh would soon be a far superior performer. Chaplin was so suspicious of even his closest approach to real friends (Mary and Doug) that he was invariably reluctant to sign his name to any document. Fairbanks referred to him as a chronic "kicker." Chaplin retaliated by saying Douglas was only a "jumper."

With Pickford and Fairbanks, however, it had been love at first sight. They were united in the holy bonds of matrimony soon after they were joined in the less sacred bonds of business enterprise. A considerable number of the company meetings were held at their home, "Pickfair." Mary sat at the head of the table in those happy early days and Doug was always seated at her left. They never danced with other partners. That is, never until 10 years later when Doug's eye became as restless as his feet.

Mary and Doug jointly bought a studio on Santa Monica boulevard, in which Sam Goldwyn, after he joined United Artists, became the principal tenant. He and his landlady, Mary, got on even less amicably than most landlords and tenants and couldn't agree even on what color the studio should be painted. As a consequence, it remained a local eyesore for many years. Chaplin, in this as in all other matters of personal conduct, was a staunch individualist. He bought his own studio at Sunset and LeBrea.

McAdoo and Price soon discovered that Abrams, who had been employed as sales manager, was taking over all of their prerogatives except their private offices and salaries. Their wails of anguish, however, evoked little sympathy in the breasts of the artists. The Washington window dressing had served its purpose of starting the new company and was now of definitely less value than Abrams' uncanny talent for selling pictures for more than they were worth. Before long, the ex-statesmen became ex-movie executives and Abrams was elected president, a position he held until his death in '26.

The man who benefited least from the formation of United Artists was its original proponent, Ben Schulberg. He and Abrams had an oral agreement by which they were to be equal partners in any new enterprises in which they engaged. Abrams neglected to cut Ben in on his UA profits and Schulberg eventually had to sue him and thus obtain a substantial out-of-court settlement.

The production of pictures bearing the recognizable stamp of the talents and ideals of their makers rather than those of big studio executives obsessed with mass production techniques, is an inspiring conception. It must, however, to be practical, be combined with the capacity to secure quantity as well as quality. In its first 20 years of existence UA released around 300 pictures, less than one-third of what any of its major competitors were handling. The worst offenders were the original owner-producers themselves. If United Artists had had to rely exclusively on *their* contributions it would not have survived.

The first United Artists picture was Fairbanks' *His Majesty The American*. Its world premiere in New York City on Oct. 24, 1919, served also to open what was then the world's largest theatre, the Capitol. It was tumultuously received, but Doug by this time was fed up with the clean-cut, all-American boy character, hand-tailored for him by John Emerson and Anita Loos. He was determined to go on to more colorful roles and more sumptuous productions. *The Mark of Zorro* was his first blockbuster and its success in the face of the conviction of all the experts that costume pictures were boxoffice poison encouraged him to proceed further with epics in which he could demonstrate his manhood and athletic prowess. He had always regarded himself as in some ways the reincarnation of D'Artagnan and *The Three Musketeers* was the natural selection for his next production. It was followed by *Robin Hood* and then *The Thief of Bagdad,* most opulent of all. *Thief* cost three times as much as *Zorro* and grossed considerably less.

Pickford's first United Artists picture was *Pollyanna* and it is famous, or infamous (depending upon whether you are a distributor or an exhibitor), as the first film sold on a percentage basis. Abrams hired 20 checkers to keep close scrutiny on the boxoffices of theatre owners whose mathematics he suspected.

Mary continued for several years to specialize in the type of films with which she was identified—*Suds, Little Lord Fauntleroy, Tess of the Storm Country*. Like Doug, however, she had an itch for more ambitious projects. *Dorothy Vernon of Haddon Hall* in '24 was her first effort in this direction and its catastrophic reception proved that in her case maturity was premature. American audiences, intent on remaining young themselves, were even more determined not to permit their "sweetheart" to grow up.

Griffith's first United Artists picture, *Broken Blossoms,* was actually made for Famous Players-Lasky, but Zukor found it a little too much on the artistic side. The critics liked it but the public, as usual, agreed with Zukor and displayed its customary indifference to the "fragrantly poetic" and "fragile." A sentimental, unimaginative picture like Griffith's *Way Down East* in '21 grossed $9,000,000, compared to the $2,000,000 earned by *Broken Blossoms*. Then followed *Orphans of the Storm* and a series of undistinguished films, all indicating a steady waning of the genius of the Old Master. He was, said one sympathetic observer, "a great man living within a circle of isolation, a genius out of touch with the world." In '25, beset by financial reversals and suspicious of the manner in which Abrams was distributing his pictures, D. W. left United Artists, but continued to retain his stock in the company.

. . .

Chaplin did not complete his contract with First National until '23. He then wrote, produced and directed *A Woman of Paris* for United Artists, but appeared in it only for a brief instant in the role of a porter. *A Woman of Paris* is usually regarded as the grandmother of the current school of adult (preferably adulteress) sophistication. Its most sophisticated aspect, however, was the rumor, sedulously promoted, that the story was based on an incident in the early life of Peggy Hopkins Joyce, with whom Chaplin had reputedly enjoyed two weeks of well-publicized intimacy. In '25 Charlie released *The Gold Rush,* and although he may since have changed his mind, I recall hearing him say that it was the *"picture I want to be remembered by."* It was shot on location in Nevada, but many scenes were not to Charlie's liking and were re-enacted in his Hollywood studio with plaster mountains, snow fields of salt, and whirling soap flakes. It took over 14 months to produce, cost close to a million, and proved a joy to moviegoers in every land, grossing approximately $5,000,000 in the worldwide market. Incidentally, it's doing another b.o. comeback at this writing.

200   THE FIRST TYCOONS

Even such occasional smash hits did not solve the problem of insufficient product. UA had acquired the reputation of being the Tiffany of the motion picture industry, but it was a Tiffany with only an occasional sparkling diamond to sell. Obviously a doctor was needed, and Joe Schenck was equally obviously the most astute and popular doctor in Hollywood for the severe constipation that afflicted United Artists. He brought in not only members of his own family, like his wife, Norma Talmadge, and her sister Constance, but other movie immortals, such as Sam Goldwyn, Rudolph Valentino, John Barrymore, Gloria Swanson and Buster Keaton. Even the disillusioned Bill Hart left Famous Players-Lasky to appear in some UA films.

TINO BALIO
United Artists Takes Shape

Tino Balio provides an interesting contrast in historical writing with this brief extract from his book, United Artists *(Madison, University of Wisconsin Press, 1976, pages 24–29). His interpretation of the estrangement between Abrams and Schulberg is based primarily on those documents and court records which have survived in archives given to the university. Mayer's is based on personal knowledge of the people involved.*

William Gibbs McAdoo . . . had been head of the Federal Railroad Board during the war, Secretary of the Treasury before that, and was a son-in-law of President Wilson. Pickford, Fairbanks, and Chaplin had come to know McAdoo well during the Third Liberty Loan drive when the three toured the country selling millions of dollars worth of bonds to support the war effort. Late in 1918, McAdoo had announced his resignation from government service, effective January 17, 1919, and now was in Santa Barbara for a rest before returning to his Washington law practice. When his private railroad car pulled into Los Angeles, a band serenade and a grand reception at the station greeted him, courtesy of Doug Fairbanks.

McAdoo declined the invitation to become UA's president, but suggested that if Oscar Price, his former assistant on the railroad board, were named instead, he would gladly serve as counsel for the company. This satisfied everyone; McAdoo, in the words of an editorial in *Moving Picture World,* would bring "prestige second to that of no other businessman in the country . . . his association marks another step in the progress of the business side of the screen, and it goes without saying his voice will have large influence in many quarters where large influence sometimes is very necessary."[20] For a while, anyway, the skeptics would be silenced.

Who first suggested the organization of artists that became UA is a matter of dispute. Film historians from the twenties to the present day have credited Benjamin P. Schulberg with the original idea.[21] Their conclusions were evidently based on a 1920 court case in which Schulberg brought suit against UA's general manager, Hiram Abrams, for a share of his commissions.

When this suit was filed in the Supreme Court of New York on September 8, 1920, the press gave it wide coverage.[22] Schulberg's story as taken from the complaint was that while employed as vice-managing director of Famous Players-Lasky, he "devised and developed certain ideas" concerning a distribution plan for pictures produced by ranking artists. In November, 1918, he described this plan to Abrams, the managing director, after which they agreed to resign from Famous Players-Lasky and go to Los Angeles for the purpose of convincing Pickford, Fairbanks, Chaplin, and Griffith to adopt Schulberg's scheme. During "numerous and extended conferences," Schulberg alleged, he prepared and presented to the artists an extended prospectus setting forth the details of the plan and describing its profit potential. In February, 1919, Schulberg and Abrams "succeeded in interesting the said artists in the said plan, and obtained their consent to the adoption and carrying out of the same. . . . Thereupon the said artists caused to be organized . . . the United Artists' Corporation."

The claim for a division of Abrams' commissions was based, said Schulberg, on an oral agreement with Abrams making them equal partners in all ventures they engaged in. Since it was by no means certain that United Artists would succeed, Schulberg did not ask to become a party to Abrams' contract, so that he could devote "part or all of his time to ventures and activities for their joint benefit."

This in summary was the case of Schulberg the plaintiff, and historians have accepted it as fact. But they did so by ignoring the case for the defense. On balance, it should be noted that Abrams denied all of the allegations in the complaint. In a deposition dated May 15, 1922, he testified that "plaintiff had nothing in the world to do with the organization of the United Artists Corporation, and did not at any time confer with any of the witnesses named or influence them in any way in respect to the formation of the United Artists Corporation, and that as a matter of fact, the witnesses named were unwilling and indisposed at anytime to consider the plaintiff in any way in connection with the United Artists Corporation." A brief submitted in Abrams's defense described Schulberg's complaint as "an ingenious fiction." And Dennis O'Brien, who represented Abrams, politely summed up his position of the case when he said, "Schulberg has the tendency of writing, talking, and claiming too much."[23]

On which side does the truth rest? The issues, unfortunately, were not tried in court. Both parties consented to discontinue the action on December 15, 1922, after reaching an out-of-court settlement for an undisclosed amount of money.

When the declaration of independence was released, Miss Pickford made the following explanation: "We are on the defensive, and many people have asked us why we didn't do this thing long ago. The answer to that is that we were never forced to do it until now. But now, with the possibility of the merger of distributors looming before us, a combination that threatens to dominate the theatres of the United States, it becomes necessary for us to organize as a protection to our own interest."[24]

That their fears were justified was borne out when the Federal Trade Commission in 1927 completed its investigation of Famous Players-Lasky for alleged infringement of antitrust laws. In one of its findings, the FTC stated that Adolph Zukor, in 1919, "endeavored to form a combination with First National by which the latter would produce no films, exhibit no films other than those produced by Famous Players-Lasky Corporation, and finally become subsidiary to or merge with, Famous Players-Lasky Corporation."[25] The merger did not go through, as it turned out, but that did not stop Zukor. After failing to lure First National's officers to his company, he continued to struggle for control of the industry by attempting to acquire First National theater franchises. And this battle he won.

Even without this threat, the founding of United Artists was inevitable. A distribution company to fully market and exploit their pictures was but the next step for these artists in achieving autonomy. Pickford, Chaplin, Fairbanks, and Griffith each started out as employees under contract. With star status came the right to form independent production units, which meant more artistic control and a share of the producer's profits. By becoming their own employers, they now would receive all the profits from their pictures. To be sure, they would have to provide their own financing, but a distribution company managed by a topflight salesman would certainly minimize the risks. And it is precisely for this reason that Hiram Abrams was brought into the company as general manager. Acknowledged by all to be the greatest salesman in the business, he was described by *Moving Picture World* as a pioneer who "made the history of this industry's development so colorful."[26] From the time he started out as a successful distributor in the Boston area until he became one of the original organizers of Paramount and its second president in 1916, he worked in turn as salesman, booker, exchange manager, exhibitor, and head of a great distributing company. Now that he was no longer associated with Zukor, United Artists could put Abrams' wide range of experience to good use.

The actual formation of the company was the result of the handiwork of the lawyers, most notably Dennis O'Brien, the counsel for Pickford and Fairbanks. The other lawyers involved were Nathan Burkan for Chaplin and Albert Banzhaf for Griffith. Two sets of contracts were drawn up and signed on February 5, 1919. The first set established the corporation. The four principals agreed to become associated with each other in the marketing of motion pictures and to set up a company with headquarters in New York having the name United Artists Corporation.

The stock issue consisted of two classes: preferred, in the amount of 6,000 shares, subscription price $100 per share and redeemable at 105 per cent of par; and common, in the amount of 9,000 shares, no par value, 1,000 shares of which were issued to each of the four principals in consideration of their signing exclusive distribution contracts with the corporation. McAdoo was to be issued 1,000 shares in consideration of his becoming general counsel.

The common stock had cumulative voting power, enabling each of the stockholders to elect his own representative to the board of directors. Thus control of the management and policies of the company actually rested with the stockholders and not the directors. Nine thousand shares were authorized in the event that other well-known artists could later be induced to join the venture.

Financing the company's operations – opening exchanges, hiring salesmen, and the like – was to be borne by the four producer-owners. Each subscribed to $100,000 of the preferred stock and agreed to pay on demand up to 20 per cent of the subscription every thirty days if needed.

To prevent the company from slipping out of the hands of the owners, the agreement contained a clause giving the company prior right to repurchase the common stock in the event that a stockholder wanted to sell his interest in UA to an outside party. Another clause prevented the stockholders from forming partnerships with each other, so as to ensure complete equality among the parties. And to further stimulate the cooperative spirit of the venture and as a gesture of mutual trust, the owners decided to adopt an unwritten law stating that no proposal, policy, or decision could be effected without unanimous consent.

In the second set of agreements, the artists turned over to the company, upon the completion of their present distribution contracts, the exclusive rights to handle their pictures for five years. Each agreed to deliver nine pictures to the company; Griffith was required to direct his, and the others were to play the leading roles in theirs. Originally, the distribution contract was for the United States and Canada, but later it was amended to cover world rights.

The distribution fee was set at 20 per cent of the gross in the United States and 30 per cent elsewhere. If in the future the company gave one owner better terms, a "most favored nation" clause guaranteed similar adjustments in the other contracts. These fees were well below what Famous Players-Lasky and First National had been charging, because United Artists was conceived of as a service organization rather than an investment that would return dividends. Profits would accrue to the owners as a result of the company's securing the best possible rentals for their pictures. With this in mind, the owners reserved the right to approve through their representatives in the home office all contracts with exhibitors.

A key feature of the distribution contracts stipulated that each picture was to be sold and promoted individually. Block booking was out. In no way could one United Artists release be used to influence the sale of another UA product. Merit alone would determine a picture's success or failure.

On April 17, 1919, UA's certification of incorporation was filed with the secretary of the state of Delaware. The board of directors consisted of Albert Banzhaf, Nathan Burkan, Dennis O'Brien, Mrs. Charlotte Pickford, and Oscar Price, who represented the interests of Griffith, Chaplin, Fairbanks, Mary Pickford, and McAdoo, respectively. Price was named president; O'Brien, vice president; and George B. Clifton, secretary and treasurer.

The law firm of McAdoo, Cotton and Franklin became the general counsel for the annual retainer of $50,000. Price's salary was $18,000 plus a small percentage of the gross. As the man in charge of sales, Abrams received 2 per cent of the domestic gross and 1 per cent of foreign sales in excess of $500,000. Headquarters were established in New York, at 729 Seventh Avenue, where the company is housed to this day. In a matter of weeks, Abrams had opened exchanges across the country. United Artists was in business.

NOTES

20. *Moving Picture World,* February 15, 1919, p. 899.
21. See, for example, Will Irwin, *The House that Shadows Built* (Garden City, N.Y.: Doubleday, 1928); Hampton, *A History of the Movies;* Mayer, "The Origins of United Artists"; Gertrude Jobes, *Motion Picture Empire* (Hamden, Conn.; Archon, 1966).
22. *Benjamin P. Schulberg v. Hiram Abrams,* Supreme Court of New York, 1920.
23. Letter from Dennis O'Brien to Morris Greenhill, August 20, 1920. 1A/211/3.
24. *Moving Picture World,* February 1, 1919, p. 619.
25. *In re* Famous Players-Lasky Corp., 11 F.T.C. 187 (1927).
26. *Moving Picture World,* November 27, 1926, p. 205.

BOSLEY CROWTHER
Loew Buys a Studio

Bosley Crowther, the New York Times *movie reviewer who wrote the history of Metro-Goldwyn-Mayer in* The Lion's Share, *(N.Y., E. P. Dutton, 1957) introduced us to Marcus Loew when he was first tentatively investing in an entertainment arcade in 1904. Loew's Incorporated has now become the owner of a carefully selected group of first-run theaters in big eastern cities. Our selection (pages 41–42, 51, 71–72, 80–81) attempts to pull together the details of the complicated and fruitful deal by which Loew created the M-G-M studio in Hollywood.*

. . . This duel for power between Zukor and the First National Exhibitors group was leading to new consolidations that were disturbing to Marcus Loew. All through the years of evolution of motion pictures and the film industry, he had remained on the outside, so far as production and distributing were concerned. His People's Film Exchange had been abandoned in 1913, when he let it go to the dying Trust, thus ending his juvenile foray in the distribution of films. And his only ventures in the making of pictures had been investments in small affairs – in a little outfit of Roscoe ("Fatty") Arbuckle called Comique Films and a picture produced by Roland West called *Lost Souls.* Joe Schenck had left Loew's company in 1917 to become a producer on his own – making films for Lewis J. Selznick's company, with Schenck's new wife, Norma Talmadge, as star – and most of the Loew personnel had put in money. But Marcus was not intrigued.

His area of interest was theatres – building, buying, leasing, operating them. By 1919, he had assembled one of the nation's most estimable chains, with houses in Atlanta, Boston, Memphis, Baltimore, New Orleans, Birmingham, Montreal and Hamilton, Canada, plus several new ones around New York. All of them with a few exceptions, continued to operate successfully on his policy of small-time vaudeville and pictures at price scales now up to a fifty cent top.

So long as the business of motion pictures had remained generally categorized, with production, distribution and exhibition maintained in separate hands, Loew had been in a top position.

His theatres gave him first-rate buying power. He was able to make deals for essential picture products more favorable than most of his competitors. Even the new consolidations of production and distribution that emerged, following the Famous Players-Paramount example, were not too menacing to the strong theatre man.

But now, as Loew saw evolution leading to such elaborate forms as bunches of theatres putting out tentacles to gather production facilities unto themselves and, more significantly, the strongest producer-distributor in motion pictures acquiring its own stout theatre arms, he sensed a development of total combines that could well leave him out in the cold. Even William Fox, whose chain of theatres had been expanded during these formative years, had gone into picture making as insurance of product for his theatres. Now Zukor's extension of the segments of his commercial control caused Loew to brood.

His first and instinctive inclination was to increase his theatre strength. Regardless of Zukor, this is what he would probably have done, anyhow. With characteristic candor, he went into partnership with Zukor, himself, in getting the Stillman Theatre in Cleveland. Next he made a deal to acquire the eighteen theatres of the Ackerman & Harris chain on the West Coast. But to do this he found it necessary to have further financing. This was in 1919 – a significant year for Loew.

Now the matter of getting capital was different from what it had been when Loew last went after money, eight years previously. The bankers and brokerage houses were now quite happy to negotiate funds for the better producing companies and theatre properties.

Through two financial houses, Montgomery & Company and Van Emburgh & Atterbury, Loew arranged for a loan of $9,500,00. Loew's Theatrical Enterprises was absorbed into the new Loew's Incorporated, which issued 700,000 shares of common stock at twenty-five dollars par value. Of these, 380,000 shares were transferred to the brokerage houses to secure the loan. The remaining 320,000 shares were used to redeem the common stock of Loew's Theatrical Enterprises at the rate of eight shares for one.

Loew's, Inc., was now Big Business. On its board of directors sat Charles E. Danforth of Van Emburgh & Atterbury, who had arranged the financial deal; Harvey Gibson, the eminent president of Liberty National Bank; W. C. Durant, the president of

General Motors; Daniel Pomeroy, vice-president of Bankers Trust; James Perkins, another New York banker, and Lee Shubert, the theatrical man. Loew was not going to flip matches at meetings of this board.

With his financial house in order and his new theatre acquisitions made, Loew went to his board of directors in December, 1919, with a suggestion that he had been mulling for several months. It was that Loew's, Inc., acquire Metro, a modest producing company from which his chain of theatres occasionally picked up films. He offered two solid reasons for it: first, the industrial trend was obviously in the direction of integrated theatres and studios. If Loew's was to continue to have pictures to put on its vaudeville bills, it should definitely have its own certain and negotiable source of supply.

His second reason was a little more startling. There had recently occurred a change in the policy of selling the more important Famous Players-Lasky films. Now, instead of fixed rental prices for the use of these films, the distributor was going to charge a *percentage* of the first-run theatres' receipts. In other words, the rental would be in proportion to the amount the theatre took in. To Loew, this sounded murderous. He felt the time had come to make his own films.

. . . Loew pondered the proposition of Rowland and Rubin that he buy a half interest in their company.

Then he told them he wasn't interested in half of Metro but would like to buy the whole thing. Rowland and Rubin were interested. They got approval from their stockholders.

And that's how, in January, 1920, Loew bought a studio. . . .

Now, the chance to acquire the Goldwyn company offered these attractive aspects to the people of Loew's: First, the production facilities of the big Culver City studio, with its line-up of stars and directors, were auspicious for the contemplated move toward more and classier pictures that Loew and his associates had in mind.

Further, there was the prospect of acquiring with the Goldwyn company the scattering of affiliated theatres that it had picked up in a period of five years. These included the handsome Miller and California in Los Angeles, the Ascher circuit in and around Chicago and, most particularly, the potent Capitol in New York. Marcus Loew looked upon this house with a peculiarly covetous eye.

But there were two big things to be considered in putting together a deal to acquire the Goldwyn company. One was the matter of cost. Loew's was a frugal organization. Its success was due, in part, to a genius for picking up potentially valuable properties at bargain prices and making them pay. Nick Schenck was expert at this business, and the job of negotiating for the Goldwyn company fell largely to him. Loew was now suffering a heart ailment and was not up to the kind of bargaining he so enjoyed.

The second and more important consideration was that of discovering a man who could head the big producing operation that would be the consequence of the deal. Schenck had already made a thorough check on the management of Metro and had found that Joe Engel, then head of the studio, was not adequate to the job. Studio management, Schenck figured, required a man with a creative bent, but, above all, it sternly demanded competence in handling people and a hard-headedness in business affairs.

Schenck discussed the problem with Robert Rubin, who had come over to Loew's as one of its legal counsel when Metro was acquired. They agreed that the studio head of the Goldwyn company was also weak. Abe Lehr, while a kindly, courteous person, was considered a poor executive. If a deal was made to get the Goldwyn company, a new man to run the studio would have to be found.

Rubin had a suggestion. As legal counsel for Loew's, he was dutifully mindful of its welfare. But he was also mindful of the welfare of another of his clients, his old friend, Louis B. Mayer, with whom he had continued as counselor and financial partner ever since Mayer had gone into producing on his own. When the deal for the Goldwyn Company began to take promising form, Rubin telephoned Mayer in California and urged him to make a quick trip to New York. He figured there might be something doing in the way of a double-barreled deal—a merger of Metro and Goldwyn under the management of Mayer.

This was a calculation that made good sense on several counts, not least of which was the nature and qualifications of Mayer himself. This tough and resourceful go-getter had been doing remarkably well in the five years that he had been making pictures, following his move to the West Coast. The films he produced with Anita Stewart, his first and most fortunate star, had brought him profits and assurance.

... no one, outside the participants (and a few silent advisers, such as Joe Schenck), foresaw the magnitude of the merger that was publicly announced on April 17, 1924.

The major step in the transaction was the absorption of the Goldwyn Pictures Corporation by Loew's, Inc., with the Goldwyn company being purchased through a straight exchange of stock. A new producing company, the Metro-Goldwyn Pictures Corporation, was formed. The common stock of this corporation was given to Loew's, Inc., in exchange for the Metro company. The preferred stock was given to the Goldwyn shareholders in exchange for their shares, one for one. The value of the latter shares was figured at $5,000,000. It was thus, without the passing of any actual monies, that the Goldwyn company was acquired.

By this transaction, Loew's, Inc., obtained, through possession of the voting stock, control of the Metro-Goldwyn Corporation, which was to be a merger of the two studios in the big Culver City plant that was owned by the Goldwyn company. It also obtained the theatres and exchanges of the latter company. In the light of subsequent developments, it was a bargain beyond compare.

At the same time, the Goldwyn stockholders were handsomely recompensed. The preferred stock of the new corporation was to pay a 7 per cent cumulative dividend.

Only one major Goldwyn stockholder refused to accept the exchange. That one was Samuel Goldwyn. He did not approve the deal, and arrangements had to be made by the Goldwyn company trustees to buy in his shares for cash. Thus, through one of those perversities that the unpredictable Goldwyn often displayed, he was not even a stockholder in the new company that continued his patented name.

The second big step in the transaction was the arrangement that was made with Mayer and his associates, Thalberg and Robert Rubin, to direct the production operations of the Metro-Goldwyn company. These three men, constituting the so-called "Mayer group," were put under a personal-service contract for three years, with options. It called for Mayer to serve as vice-president and general manager of the new producing company at a salary of $1,500 a week, Thalberg to act as second vice-president and "supervisor of production" at $650 a week, and Rubin to serve as secretary (with his office in New York) at $600 a week. The physical properties and some of the personnel contracts of the Mayer company were purchased outright by Metro-Goldwyn for $75,000. This employment of Mayer and his associates was the big surprise in the deal.

In order to maintain Mayer's identity, it was agreed that he might choose whether to inscribe the pictures of the studio with the credit line, "Produced by Louis B. Mayer for the Metro-Goldwyn Corporation" or "Produced by Metro-Goldwyn-Mayer." He eventually chose the latter, and thus the familiar name came into common usage and later was adopted as the official name of the studio.

BOSLEY CROWTHER
The Saga of Ben Hur

> Like The Covered Wagon, Ben Hur *was not so much directed as it was produced. It issued forth from a studio system which, even in those early days, was dependent upon the coordination of many departments by a strong central executive and a group around him. The changing company situation added a chaotic background to the decisions of executive producers like Joseph Godsol at Goldwyn and Irving Thalberg at the successor studio, M-G-M, with L. B. Mayer and Marcus Loew, at higher business echelons, also part of the act.*
>
> *Ben Hur as a production case study is a numbing example of a colossal financial gamble carried off in spite of all odds by the will and nerve of stubborn men and women. One caution: The version by Bosley Crowther (The Lion's Share, op. cit., pages 91-95, 98-100) here somewhat shortened, is succinct and dramatic. But Kevin Brownlow, in* The Parade's Gone By *(N.Y., Knopf, 1968) has had access to sources who give a grimmer view of the accident during the performance of the chariot race. There were horses mangled in that scene, and our historian could have been more skeptical of the studio version given to him and to the public.*

Of all the challenging problems that the Goldwyn company brought, by far the most mammoth and momentous was that of the production of *Ben Hur*. This vast and ambitious project, which was already being filmed in Italy, had been started by Godsol at the time he was making a valiant try to save the Goldwyn company. It was a heroic gamble. No production of comparable dimensions had ever been launched. No one had dared start a picture as costly as would plainly be *Ben Hur*.

The history of this production is a saga of motion picture enterprise that stands as a consequential chapter in the overall history of American films. *Ben Hur* marked a notable milestone in the advancement of Hollywood. And in the heat of its achievement and presentation was hammered out a telling triumph for Metro-Goldwyn-Mayer.

Ever since storytelling in movies had been discovered and rendered practical, makers and promoters of pictures had been casting covetous eyes upon General Lew Wallace's famed novel, *Ben Hur—A Tale of the Christ*. This bulging fable of the early Christian era was first published in 1880 and had sold several million copies throughout the world. It was one of the all-time "best sellers," the *Gone With the Wind* of its day.

The story was made for dramatics. A young and wealthy Jew, Ben Hur, who lived with his widowed mother and sister in Jerusalem, was accused by his Roman friend, Messala, of trying to assassinate the new Roman governor. His property was confiscated, his mother and sister were cast in jail, and he himself was condemned as a slave to the Roman galley ships for the rest of his life. In the course of a naval battle with pirates, however, he managed to escape and save the Roman admiral, Arrius, who thereupon adopted him as his son.

Returning to the East a few years later, Ben Hur discovered true love in the person of Esther, the daughter of an old and faithful family friend. Through this friend he was able to recover his fortune and challenge Messala, his cruel nemesis, in a great chariot race for the championship of the East in the coliseum at Antioch. In a thundering, exciting contest, Ben Hur upset Messala's chariot and won. He was then the most famous and wealthy of Roman subjects in that part of the world.

But grief for his lost mother and sister plagued him, and with Esther he tirelessly sought to find them, meanwhile occupying himself secretly in raising a Galilean army to place the man Jesus on a temporal Jewish throne. Then Esther found his mother and sister for him. They were horribly diseased with leprosy. When Jesus cured them by a miracle, Ben Hur abandoned his mission and became a Christian.

The theatrical rights to the story were obtained from General Wallace in 1899 by the powerful producing firm of Klaw & Kerlanger, which staged the dramatization sumptuously with numerous scenes, great mobs of extras, singing choruses and a chariot race with real horses on a treadmill in the center of the stage. The play ran for years on Broadway and was toured widely with road companies all over the world. This was the strong theatrical property that the movie makers were eager to obtain.

One of the novel features of the theatrical contract was that Klaw & Erlanger were bound to produce the play *somewhere* every season or otherwise forfeit the dramatic rights. This was a minor stipulation when the play was having great success and road companies were playing it all over. But, as the years went by and the popularity of the play began to wane, it became more and more of a gamble to send out a company every year. However, the prospect of sharing in the sale of screen rights, which assumed greater proportions as films increased in size, emboldened the producers to continue to mount shows, even when they sometimes lost money. This is the reason *Ben Hur* was played year after year by some company long after it was rendered obsolete by increasingly spectacular films.

The pay-off was worth it, however. In 1919, the eagerness of Douglas Fairbanks to obtain the screen rights caused General Wallace's son, the executor of his estate, to realize that the time had come to sell. After some legal wrangling with Erlanger, Wallace indicated he would part with his entire rights to the novel for $400,000. More interest began to show. There was talk of Adolph Zukor buying the rights for a film to be made by Max Reinhardt, the great German stage director. D. W. Griffith was said to be interested. Whereupon, Erlanger quietly moved to obtain the screen rights for his own disposal. All he needed was the money to swing the deal.

He obtained it in a most surprising quarter. Vincent Astor and Robert Walton Goelet, two of New York's most eminent citizens and wealthy owners of real estate, were interested in a gamble on the prospect. They agreed sub rosa to put up $600,000 – $200,000 from Astor and $400,000 from Goelet. Whereupon Erlanger, in association with Charles Dillingham and Florenz Ziegfeld, formed the Classical Cinematograph Corporation, in which Erlanger, Dillingham, Ziegfeld and Astor each owned a one-sixth share and Goelet owned one-third. With the $600,000 from the two "angels," the corporation purchased the rights to *Ben Hur* from the estate of General Wallace and from the publishers, Harper & Brothers. Now the object was to get someone to make it into a film.

The same came along the next year, 1922. It was Godsol, who

was eager for a story to capture great attention and prestige. Erlanger and his partners wanted at least $1,000,000 for a flat sale of screen rights to *Ben Hur*. The price was out of the question, so far as the Goldwyn company was concerned—or anyone else, for that matter. Fairbanks and Zukor had said "no." So Godsol's only chance of obtaining the screen rights was to make a novel deal, which would be in the nature of an extraordinary gamble. This he decided to do.

He agreed to finance a production of *Ben Hur* as a film, the same to "be of a caliber equal to *The Birth of a Nation* or *Orphans of the Storm* or *Way Down East*," all famous Griffith films—and to share the gross receipts of said production equally with the Classical Cinematograph Corporation. In other words, for the use of the story and title, Godsol agreed to pay *one-half* of all the money earned by the picture. It was, beyond any question, the most fantastic story deal ever made. No wonder Marcus Loew stated flatly, a few years later, to an audience at the Harvard Business School, "It is a contract I do not want to claim credit for."

Since it was in the original contract with General Wallace that the stage production was not to show the figure of Christ nor reenact the Crucifixion, Erlanger insisted that these terms be included in the picture deal. He also reserved for himself full approval of the director, cast, scenario and finished film.

In the course of negotiations, June Mathis, who was head of the scenario department of the Goldwyn company, got friendly with old Abe Erlanger and soon convinced him that she alone was the only screen writer who had the feeling and talent to translate the greatness and grandeur of his pet *Ben Hur*. Erlanger stipulated to Godsol that the ubiquitous Miss Mathis should be in charge of the writing and production of the picture. Godsol willingly agreed.

The assignment inspired Miss Mathis with an enthusiasm beyond any she had known. She was determined that *Ben Hur* should be the greatest and most magnificent motion picture ever made. Nothing would do, she insisted, but that it be produced in Italy, the only place where the spirit and atmosphere of the Roman Empire could be obtained. J. J. Cohn of the studio cost department was sent abroad to reconnoiter the field. He returned with a negative opinion of the practicality of shooting in Rome. However, Miss Mathis was insistent, and she transmitted her enthusiasm to the company heads. "Major" Edward Bowes, vice-president of the Goldwyn company, to whom Cohn reported, was serene.

"We can do it in Rome for $600,000," the always expansive "Major" said.

"How?" inquired Cohn, a stubborn realist.

"That's the director's worry," Bowes replied.

The gentleman upon whom this "worry" quite unexpectedly fell was the handsome and dignified Charles Brabin, one of whose claims to renown was the fact that he was the husband of Theda Bara, the first and perhaps the most famous of all the sultry vampires of the screen.

Brabin and Bowes left for Rome in the fall of 1923. On the ship going over they became chummy and had some stimulating talks about what they wanted to do. Brabin munificently suggested that a reproduction of Jerusalem's Joppa Gate should be built three times as high as the original, so that the mob of people surrounding the far-off figure of Christ in the scene of his march on the road to Calvary would be dwarfed by this symbol of Rome. Bowes thought the idea terrific. This they would have to do. However, he firmly reminded Brabin that the budget for the picture was $750,000 — no more! The director was apprehensive. And he had no scenario, as yet. Miss Mathis had given him nothing but an outline. He began to smell trouble ahead.

The company was finally assembled in Italy early in 1924. June Mathis went over in February. George Walsh, a veteran outdoor star (and brother of Raoul Walsh), whom she had selected to play the key role of Ben Hur, followed in a few days. Francis X. Bushman, who would play the anti-Semite, Messala; May McAvoy, who would be Esther; Carmel Myers, enrolled as the pagan vampire and mistress of Messala who tried to lure Ben Hur — all arrived in the next few weeks, along with technicians and cameramen. Mussolini, in the first flush of his triumphs, gave orders that every assistance be extended to the company.

While waiting for the sets and studio to be ready, Brabin went to Egypt to shoot some desert scenes. And, as spring came, he took his company down the coast to the village of Anzio, the village which years later was to be the locale of one of the bloodiest beachhead struggles of World War II. Here he hoped to shoot the scenes of the battle of the Roman and pirate galleys offshore. Then it was discovered that no barges or anything that might be used to resemble galleys were available.

Just at this time, the merger of the companies occurred, and the completion of the production of *Ben Hur* became the responsibility of Metro Goldwyn—and Mayer.

Actually, Mayer and Thalberg were dubious of the enterprise from the start, considering it to be another of the grandiose and inefficient vagaries of Godsol's extravagant company. Thalberg said he could not see why the film should have been made in Italy. He said that he could do it better in Culver City and at considerably less expense. However, the New York executives were disposed to continue the production abroad. Marcus Loew seemed to feel the foreign venture was a challenge to his new company's prestige. There was also the little matter of the agreements with Abe Erlanger.

Even so, it was obvious that some changes in personnel would have to be made. No "rushes" of what had been shot had come back from Italy, and no one knew what was going on. Thalberg, sensing the stalemate, had secretly assigned the writer, Bess Meredyth, to prepare a new scenario as soon as the merger was certain and had gone into huddles with Mayer about a new director and star.

Then, in June, under a veil of some mystery, a small group left Hollywood for New York. It included Fred Niblo, the director who had made pictures for Mayer on Mission Road; Ramon Novarro, the popular Metro actor; Bess Meredyth, Carey Wilson and Mayer. Wilson, another writer, had been assigned by Thalberg at the last minute to assist with the scenario. It was sensed that something important in the matter of *Ben Hur* was afoot.

In New York, the fact was admitted that they were going to Italy "to look over the situation." Marcus Loew, in his now sententious vein, gave out information that Brabin was "ill" and that possibly Niblo would be selected to "take over this stupendous production." The Hollywood group, minus Mayer, was joined by Mr. and Mrs. Loew, Mr. and Mrs. Robert Rubin and Joe Dannenberg, a favorite pinochle playing friend of Loew, when it sailed for Europe aboard the *Leviathan.* That the die had been cast was fairly clear when Mayer was heard to shout to Niblo, as the ship pulled away from the pier: "And be sure to get plenty of camels in it! Lots of camels!" That was the clue.

When the party arrived, Loew and Rubin broke the news to the nervous company. Niblo was to replace Brabin as director (Brabin had already been sent home), and Ramon Novarro was to replace George Walsh in the title role. . . .

Finally in January 1925, the company was ordered home. All

along, Thalberg had been against the Italian venture. "I could make the whole thing right here for $800,000," he said. A couple of million dollars had been blown in Italy. To cut these unprecedented expenses and confess to a fiasco took decisive nerve. But Mayer and Thalberg were realistic. Marcus Loew now agreed.

Actually, the fourteen months of fiddling in Rome and Italy was not a total waste. In the final assembly of *Ben Hur*, there turned up considerable footage that had been shot abroad. All the scenes of and in the galleys, including the big battle at sea, were those that were shot off Livorno at such tremendous cost. The Joppa Gate sequences, jammed with extras and bulging with spectacle, were made in Rome, as were many other pieces. The only things wasted were money, energy – and time.

And a good bit more of them still had to be put out when the company returned to Hollywood. Immediately Thalberg decided there was no use returning to Rome to shoot the chariot race, as they had expected to do. A bigger and better Antioch Coliseum could be built in Culver City, he said, and he forthwith gave instructions that one should be raised. On a big open lot off Venice Boulevard, at La Cienega, the structure was built at a further cost of $300,000. It was, when completed, the biggest movie set erected up to that time.

While it was building, the company completed the rest of the tie-in stuff – the prefatory story of Mary and Joseph, the raising of the Galilean legions, and such. Thalberg excited some amazement when he selected Betty Bronson to play the role of the Virgin Mary. Miss Bronson's chief distinctions up to then were her cute performances in *Peter Pan* and *A Kiss For Cinderella*. She was later praised for the "soulfulness" of her interpretation of the Mother of Christ.

Incidentally, the Biblical inserts were filmed in the crude Technicolor of the day. These color sequences drew high approval when the picture was released.

When the coliseum was finished, the big day for the chariot race was set, and, after weeks of detailed preparations, all thoughts and energies were now devoted to this conclusive event. Some 3,000 extras were recruited to fill the mammoth set. The going pay for these extras was $3.50 a day, plus lunch.

To play the Roman horse guard that paraded before the chariot race, a crack cavalry troop was borrowed from the Praesidio in Monterey. The soldiers, mounted on beautiful matched bays, wore shining Roman costumes. Stunt men were got to ride in twelve chariots, each drawn by four powerful horses, that were to race around the coliseum track.

Forty-two cameras were located in various strategic spots all over the huge set. These were more cameras than they owned in Culver City—more than had ever been used on one job. When they got all the cameramen together, many on loan from other studios, it looked like a full convention of the American Society of Cinematographers.

When the big day came—it was a Saturday—the extras crowded the old Venice Short Line trolley cars, flocking to Culver City to take part in the big event. Virtually every director and star in Hollywood knocked off that day and went out to watch. There was a festival air about the happening. It was a historic occurrence in the community. The entire motion picture colony had a vital interest in the achievement of this film, not to mention a burning curiosity about this mammoth episode.

Zero hour for starting the shooting was 11 A.M. At 10:30, Thalberg looked at the 3,000 extras banked in the seats of the coliseum and said there were not enough. Studio runners went scurrying madly through the onlookers gaping outside the lot and pulled in another 300.

To be filmed on this day of shooting was the panoramic spectacle of the actual race, the massiveness of the crowded coliseum and the colorful aspects of the Roman holiday. The dramatic close-ups of Ramon Novarro and Francis X. Bushman driving their chariots, which would be cut into the race sequence afterwards, were shot separately from the race itself, of course. To assure that the cowboy stunt men who drove the chariots would make it a real show, a bonus of $150 was offered to the one who came in first.

With everything set, Director Niblo, stationed on a high tower from which he could command the whole business, gave the signal for the race to begin. Buglers blew their summons. Huge tapestries were flung back and out dashed the twelve lumbering chariots. They lined up for the start and were off. As they thundered around the coliseum, dust flew, the crowds roared and the cameras whirred. The excitement was surely as high as it had ever been at a race in Roman days.

Then a phenomenon happened. As the heavy chariots were swinging into a turn, the wheel on one driven by Mickey Millerick, a famous stunt cowboy, worked loose and the vehicle began to careen. On a wild swerve, it banged into another. The two rolled over in a heap, and, as the spectators gasped in sudden horror, two more chariots and teams crashed into the wreck. Four chariots, sixteen horses and four drivers ended up in a spectacular shambles. And not a man nor an animal was hurt!

It was a flash of fortuitous action that no one would have dared try to stage as it occurred — not with the Society for the Prevention of Cruelty to Animals watching the whole thing rigidly. Yet it was a feature that added incalculably to the realism of the spectacle. The cameramen were checked to make sure they had got it. Fortunately, they had.

The rest of the saga of *Ben Hur* is a recount of triumphs and rewards. The vast amount of footage, taken over a period of some eighteen months, was edited into twelve reels. It was provided with a special musical score, written by David Mendoza and William Axt, to be played by the pit orchestra. An elaborate advance publicity campaign on the lines of *The Birth of a Nation* ballyhoo was given it, and its grand première was held at the George M. Cohan Theatre in New York City on the evening of December 30, 1925.

The reception was thunderously approving. A glittering audience of theatrical and society nobs actually burst into shouting and applauding during the chariot race. The film was shown on a two-a-day basis, with two intermissions during its two-hour-and-eight-minute running time — the first intermission after the sequence of the sea battle and the second after the chariot race. *Ben Hur* stayed for a year on Broadway, while it was being road-shown (two-a-day) in other cities. It did not go into general release until the fall of 1927.

Among the perennially popular legends of the motion picture industry have been those concerning the cost and the earnings of *Ben Hur*. The general impression has been that it "cleaned up" for Metro-Goldwyn-Mayer. Actually, the total negative cost of the picture — not including the royalties paid to the Classical Cinematograph Company — was just short of $4,000,000.

On the other hand, the gross earnings (including those from an unsuccessful reissue, released in 1931, with dubbed sound) were $9,386,000. With 35 per cent subtracted from that figure to cover distribution costs, the total net earnings came to approximately $6,100,000. Since this was divided equally with the Classical Cinematograph Company, the ultimate money return to Metro-Goldwyn was almost $1,000,000 less than the negative costs.

However, the total venture was far from unprofitable to the studio and to Loew's. The vast commercial prestige redounding to the company through having this picture was a tremendous, incalculable boon.

But, of course, in the final reckonings, the individuals who really profited from *Ben Hur* were the fortunate gentlemen of the Classical Cinematograph Company, who shared among themselves more than $3,000,000 in royalties—the Messrs. Erlanger, Ziegfeld and Dillingham and especially the "silent" and generally unsuspected partners, Vincent Astor and Robert Walton Goelet.

ALBERT E. SMITH
A Handshake with Harry Warner

*This brief emotional moment brings Albert Smith to center stage again (*Two Reels and a Crank, *op. cit., pages 272-273, 276). Like Jesse Lasky, Smith had a warm and personal family feeling about his studio and the years he spent there. Yet it was not a bad time to bow out. As Vitagraph ends and M-G-M begins, the first echo of sound is only a year away, and everything will be changed.*

It is 1925; a quarter of a century has passed into eternity. The film wars had left their mark. So much now was different, the competition among producers less open and decidedly less frank; one had to surmise what was going on in the background. Vitagraph, the sole survivor of the old crowd, was running smoothly, and the more than hundred exchanges in this country and abroad were a closely knit, effective force. But there were storm warnings. On that day in 1914 we had promised the committee of exhibitors we would not compete with them. Events had turned that promise into a death sentence; unless Vitagraph owned and operated its own theaters, it could not survive for long. The big business was in large theaters, their weekly earnings ranging from fifty thousand to a hundred thousand dollars.

The future actually left us only one course: a move out into the theater field. The warning was clear: Buy theaters quickly. It meant more conflict, more crisis, more "deals," a complete reorganization of the company.

An old doctor friend said one day: "Smith, I'll give you ten years at the most if you keep up this pace. Take it easy, maybe pull out altogether and who knows, you may live as long as your dad."

A ripe old age (Father was ninety-eight at his death) was never one of my secret desires. Still, the prospect of a long rest had a very rosy hue about it. A wishful thought. I put it gently to rest—until the day of that phone call from Harry Warner.

The Warners were in need of a sales organization, and Vitagraph's world network of exchanges fitted their plans.

"You are interested only in the sales organization?"

"Yes," said Warner.

"Would you consider buying Vitagraph lock, stock, and barrel?"

"I don't think so, just the exchanges."

"Sorry, Vitagraph might be for sale, but only in one piece."

He consulted with his brothers. Two days later, less than forty-eight hours after his first call, Vitagraph passed from my hands.

It was almost as simple as this, putting on your hat and walking out, right out of something that has been a part of your life, and repeating to yourself that you were free at last—free to rest, to travel, to follow every whim, and all the time there was that voice inside, a sulky, moody, perverse little voice saying, "It is no longer yours, it is no longer yours."

No matter its age, a child is always a child to its parent, and always needing someone to tuck in that loose shirt end or give its nose a swipe. With Pop gone and Jim out of the management of the company, the chores were mine, and yet they weren't chores, for this was our child.

Three decades had passed, and the child was grown. Though it had not talked, no art had ever said more, or lived more violently or splendidly. One man scratches the earth and a fire immediately burns in the hearts of many thousands. . . .

I remember that day in February, 1925. I shook hands with Harry Warner. He walked out and there was a terrible silence in the room, as if every living hope had gone with him and I was left in a vast empty amphitheater swept clean of memories near and dear. The studio in Flatbush, the bright and friendly stucco stages with their rows of cottages dozing under the California sun, the hundreds of familiar faces in exchanges around the country, the exhibitors who knew the costs of loyalty and had willingly paid the price of it, the day to day crises: a nervous actor, a weeping actress, a temperamental star—Harry Warner took them under his arm and walked out.

The Roxy Theater

Appendices

Appendix A
Author's Note About Motion Picture History

Looking at moving images is now a favorite pastime for almost everyone in the world. It is natural for us to talk to each other about the images we see—what we like and dislike about them, what perceptions and feelings and ideas they seem to us to convey. This means we are all film critics.

Sooner or later we become aware that what we look at in this way, fiction and nonfiction, day after day, tends to shape our consciousness of what life is like. Moving images are given to us by those with the power to pay for them: the cumulative results can change us profoundly. If we care about this, and worry, it means we are willing also to be social critics.

The processes by which works of value are placed before us must be of great interest to every member of society. We are bound to wonder: How do our visual experiences arrive before our eyes? How do the movies we most care for come to be? How are they conceived, created, distributed, and judged?

If we ask these questions, we are beginning to be historians. We are becoming aware that each movie has a history of its own, and that drama in motion pictures has had a long-term historical development as well.

We then find it both necessary and fascinating to study the personalities and the forces which shape the images we watch. We start classifying films into types, noticing changes over time in stories and in techniques. We watch the credits, the stars, and the marketplace. We perceive the roles of producers and directors, and especially, if we are knowledgeable observers, value the primary contributions of writers, whether they are the writers of the "original material" or screenwriters.

Occasionally we think we can see stylistic differences among film makers. If we have dependable information on whether certain contributors to the work (producers, writers, directors, stars, directors of photography, editors) actually had the power to express their personalities, we may find it valuable to speculate about who deserves the most credit for "authorship."

A sense of the past can make us more alert to the times and places in which different films were made. We find ourselves wanting to know more about the whole economic and cultural environment in which these works became possible. Sometimes we even ask, as we compare films from different countries: When is a movie "typically American"?

A sense of the past can help us enjoy movies more. History moves us away from the immediate surface of things. It gives us a sense of depth, of process, of duration, of something like participation in the ongoing experiments of life and of art. As we try to share in imagination the lives of those who gave us the motion pictures of the past, we build a whole structure of understanding which provides a richer background for every image we see. We move beyond the stage of "like" and "dislike" into a more complex appreciation of the forces and efforts involved in a work of art.

By working with history, we are making more effective the circle of communication: our efforts to understand how films come to be are a way of reaching out to meet the efforts of the film makers to reach out to us.

. . . *A note about the method of this book* . . .

The primary purpose of this anthology (and the others like it in the series) is to try to reconstruct in various ways some of the actual experiences of producers, writers, directors, and performers in making American movies. A secondary purpose is to examine, in some degree, the kinds of responses—social and critical—the movies have encountered.

This means depending heavily on reminiscences by the participants, with additional balancing and connecting material by later writers, always preferring those accounts which seem to be most accurate, lively, and brief. The hope is to give the reader a sense of what it was like to be there.

The traditional method of writing a textbook is for the author to gather slowly over several years of reading and teaching all the relevant facts and conflicting interpretations, and then, after many selective judgments, churn them carefully together into hundreds of smooth and impressive paragraphs. These hard-won pages are triumphs of ordered reasoning for the author. Much of our best and most thoughtful film history has come to us in this way.

Yet there are three reasons to be dissatisfied with such after-the-fact narrative writing.

In the first place, history is not experienced in any such reasoned and articulated order. Lists of causes, effects, and meanings, elaborated afterward, give little feeling for the variety and intensity of the actual events human beings lived through.

In the second place, such reasoned interpretations may be painstakingly arranged to fit some theoretical grid or political theme the historian has chosen ahead of time as a guide. This professional pride in diagnosing causes can often take priority over telling what happened, and may even misrepresent it.

In the third place, such gray pages tend to dull the senses of the most attentive reader. Professors and publishers need to have more compassion for all those students in library reading rooms —their hunched bodies and tired eyes—dolefully counting the pages to the end of the assignment.

The academic textbook tradition is not nearly as useful a model for film study as the careful collection of relevant eyewitness accounts, personal recollections, and critical film reviews—the tradition, in other words, of the anthology or "reader." After all, the history of movie-making is a story of crises, anxieties, actions, and passions. Trying to make it out to be a detached process of percentages, trends, and smooth calculations is typical ivory towerism.

We have to face the fact that a large part of what really matters in film history is indeed "anecdotal," because it is about human beings in the very process of deciding and creating. Evidence of that sort is bound to be lost unless someone takes the trouble to recall it subjectively. It is not likely to be found in proper scholarly artifacts like publicity budgets and bills of lading, and only rarely in formal memoranda—although David Selznick and Darryl Zanuck did their best to record some of their attitudes and decisions as executive producers.

Sometimes a turning-point comes to light in the margin of a first-draft script. Sometimes there is a record of a phone call. But important decisions are more likely to be accomplished by people shouting at one another in a moment of chaos. Even in autobiographies this may show up only between the lines. Later researchers, like archeologists—if they arrive in time—can dig up such crisis moments by asking leading questions on oral histories, then try to place them in the chain of events.

Of course that chain of events, however carefully interpreted, will always be controversial. Anyone who gives it a moment's thought must realize that autobiographies are like statistics: they often tell lies. At the very least they avoid some of the facts. Memoirs may be self-protective and certainly forgetful. But they do tell us something specific, some version of events that actually happened at a particular time. They are more absorbing and memorable than textbook analyses, more orderly and more of an "inside story" than ephemeral trade paper reports. Taken together, these recollections probably give us the best human perspective we shall ever have.

Any honorable history must have gaps, even contradictions. Emphasis will differ in two versions of the same event. For every oral history or autobiography with a single source, there needs to be also the testimony of others who may tell more and tell it differently. It is this kind of exposure to conflicting views of remembered events that can give the reader a suitably rough-textured sense of the past. Some sources differ on rather simple facts: it seems useful not to avoid this but to emphasize it, in passing, as a common problem of historical evidence.

Can we hope to piece together the natural flux of events, the lucky high moments, the differences of opinion, the conflicts of personalities, as they actually happened? No. But we can try to find the best existing published materials, written by primary actors and secondary observers on the scene or by later historians who have tried to make things clear. Perhaps, if we are lucky, and if we select and shape the pieces without violating them, we can sometimes recover the feeling of suspense in a single case study. Perhaps, overall, we can sometimes achieve the cumulative effect of a connected narrative.

Since American movies have always been a varied mixture of entertainment and information, this series of readings attempts in its own way to leaven education with pleasure. In film history we should especially strive to include those qualities of drama and character, humor and excitement and unexpectedness, conflict and context, which we praise when we are critics of the storytelling medium itself. Then the reader, stumbling and questioning through these crises and life stories, can face the challenge of trying to put it all together.

. . . A note about what is and isn't here . . .

Obviously nobody can tell all, or make the student (as the newspaperboys used to demand) "read all about it." What is attempted in this volume (and the others in the series) is not an exhaustive account of film making in the United States, but rather a selective file of knowledge about the most important and most representative events and personalities and films. And of course the file has to depend on what has been published.

The narrative method for the series is not chronological but topical, from five different points of view: first, movies as corporate business and as problems of production, then the arrival of directorial personalities, the rise of the star system, the great comedians, and finally the great burst of creative achievement in the 1920s.

There is time overlap in all these topics, but there is also the advantage of getting to know each aspect of the history in a continuous and coherent way. There is a certain rough justice about the topical order, since the business side of movies did come first, the date of D. W. Griffith's first directing job was 1908, and the first "big stars" (Lillian Gish, Mary Pickford, Douglas Fairbanks) became famous in the second decade we call the "teens." Chaplin started work at Keystone in 1914, but the great feature-length comedies all belong to the 1920s.

Of course, as the years recede, we become more selective about what we think we need to know about the past. There will be differences of opinion about what is most deserving of attention. Fans of the silent era may be sorry so much has been skipped: the bibliography suggests some further reading. General readers may feel there is more here than needs to be known. But the selections included have been tested over five years, and student responses suggest that the material holds their interest and does not seem excessive.

One of the hardest problems of selection is where to begin.
Does the history of movies always have to start out with a long list of gadgets like the Praxinoscope and the Zoëtrope? Are we honor-bound to memorize all the things Edison and Dickson did to the machinery (and to each other) before we can go on and find out what the movies looked like? Must we lay on all readers and students learned arguments about the definition of "persistence of

vision" (attributed to Peter Mark Roget in 1824) and whether it really exists as a physical phenomenon or is more precisely psychological?

J. Stuart Blackton, one of the owners of Vitagraph, came back from retirement in 1940 to narrate for the U. S. Navy an instructional film called *Origins of the Motion Picture*. At one point it showed a series of images on the pillars of an ancient Egyptian temple—images which seemed to be in motion if the viewer galloped past on a chariot. It may not have been 24 frames per second. But wasn't this ingenious Egyptian side-show a practical example of persistence of vision and also the very first moving picture, thousands of years ago?

How do we define our subject in practical terms? When did the moving picture become what we know today?

Some people would say that the movies really didn't begin until the American audience made a bestseller out of *The Great Train Robbery* in 1903. Others would say that it all began with the nickelodeon, which proved (about 1903) that movies by themselves could draw paying audiences.

Or did the motion picture arrive in "its essential form" with the Edison patents of 1891, embodied in the Kinetograph and the Kinetoscope? Or was it just a little later (1894) when people actually began peering into the Kinetoscope?

Or did the motion picture "as we know it" appear when Edison bought up Armat's projection scheme and showed it off in 1896 at a New York City music hall?

Or all of the above?

One radical way to cut through this knotty problem is simply to declare technology out of bounds. The pages in old cinema history books that try to cover science and inventions are noble efforts to be complete, but these might better be assigned to the history of science or to cinema's "pre-history." They seem increasingly dated now that the greater part of today's image production is electronic.

For most of us movies become interesting only when they become popular and businessmen start competing for the chance to make them. This begins to occur sometime around 1903, but it doesn't get under way on a large scale until about 1912, with the decline of the Edison patent monopoly and the rise of the feature film. Directorial talent then becomes important and the history of American movies takes off in high gear.

Technology obviously plays an important role in film history. It is the very basis of film making: the director must know what is possible to command, what effects can be achieved. Even the scholar needs to understand a good deal about the production process in order to avoid making mistakes about what happens on the set. In recent years there has been a special theoretical interest in the ways that technical improvements in certain periods have changed the storytelling process.

For the vast majority of readers and students, however, it is a large enough enterprise, and in fact it must be the heart of film history, to be acquainted with the films and the film makers. Just as it is possible, and preferable, for the nonprofessional to study the history of music without examining the methods of constructing pianos or oboes, and to study the history of architecture without knowing all about earthmoving equipment or the stress standards for steel, so it should not be expected that those who come to the study of the motion picture must be inducted into the mysteries of parallax, emulsions, hot splicers, and rear projection. These are subjects of great interest to fans and to specialists. For the student of art and civilization it is far more essential to know (1) the movies themselves (2) how they look (3) how they come to be (4) what they say to us about life. Judgments about the content, style, history, and values of films are a hundred times more important to such a student than knowing the capacities of machines.

If advances in technology were any sort of primary value in deciding what to deal with in film history, then the silent era would deserve only brief attention. What we look for, on the contrary, is the quality of the achievement as a whole, the arrangement of faces and actions and words in the story, and the value of the story itself—whether the film be silent, sound, color, or 3D.

In motion picture production there are two budgetary terms which may be helpful here. On the actual budget document for each new film, a line is drawn across the cover sheet. "Below the line" are the technical functions—from art director and cinematographer down to the last sound editor and production clerk. "Above the line" are the so-called creative people: producers, writers, directors, actors. These are the ones who decide what to do with the machinery.

This is not for a moment to deny that dedicated and inspired technical people have contributed key elements to specific films, to directorial styles, and to the history of genres. Creative talent is widely diffused in motion picture production and often is free to make a contribution.

But those who have played the role of controlling and creative decision-makers have to be the central concern of any serious history of Hollywood. There is of course a history of film technology, as there is a history of unionization and a history of movie houses in Cleveland. Such subjects may safely be left to the specialists. If they were included here at any length, they would take up room needed for our primary subject: the films and the film makers.

Teachers and students and general readers who are especially interested in technological history, visual analysis, or theory of narrative development will find other books which admirably cover these aspects of film study. It is hoped that this book will provide such readers, whatever their primary focus may be, with valuable historical and human insights.

. . . A more personal note . . .

Do I have a theory of history? Some historiographers insist that every writer-observer must be applying some sort of theory, whether consciously or not. Surely it is both irresponsible and vain to pretend to possess at the outset a perfectly prophetic guiding theory and then set about arranging everything accordingly. A theoretical formulation is like a straitjacket combined with blinders: it keeps the writer from moving in interesting directions and it keeps the researcher from taking in those impressions which may reveal unexpected truths.

My intention (if I may be allowed to use such a word) has been to avoid over-all theories, as consciously as possible, until I have done some work. My method, like many other writers (as opposed to philosophers) of history, has been to search through all the materials available, trying always to find and evaluate the kind of testimony which appears to be most richly revealing, without losing sight of the tangled variety of evidence in the changing pluralistic world of human decisions. The word "pluralistic" may seem to signify a particular approach to human events, but it is essentially anti-theoretical.

Barbara Tuchman, in her book *Practicing History* (1981) has given historians an especially valuable guideline:

To find out what happened in history is enough at the outset without trying too soon to make sure of the "why." . . . If the historian will submit himself *to* his material instead of trying to impose himself *on* his material, then the material will ultimately speak to him and supply the answers.

In the 1950s I was a correspondent for *The Christian Science Monitor* in Hollywood. My writing lacked an adequate historical base, but unlike some academic work I have known, it was all original research. At that time, it became clear to me that there are a lot of individual, human decisions and efforts involved in making movies. Of course there are massive limitations—battles with other people, inadequacies of talent and character, vetoes from the New York office, budgets and distribution plans and audience expectations. Marxist theorists refer to something called the "mode of production," which no doubt is a severe limitation. But "mode of production" as automatic causation is conveniently remote. I've never heard of a mode of production that got up in a meeting and said, "Let's do it! Let's make the movie."

Naturally someone will say: "What you are really working with is a 'great man theory' of history." But of course there could never be any valid theory based on such a notion, because it implies that there is nothing else going on in life. There are great men and women (and lesser men and women) who do contribute significantly to history, for good or ill. That is a fact, not a theory. It certainly doesn't explain everything.

When I first set about doing some sort of historical reader, my focus was on the sound period, as it was in my course work. Having just completed editing *The New Film Index: A Bibliography of Magazine Articles in English, 1930–1970*, I foresaw perhaps one modest source book using some of the articles I had indexed. But on sabbatical in the University of Iowa library and at the Library of Congress, I found myself constantly being forced to go back in time. The silent period was where everything began. There was no way to leave out D. W. Griffith and Charlie Chaplin (a general introductory chapter, perhaps?) and when it came to stars, producers, and the production code, the roots were in the 1920s and earlier. How could Irving Thalberg be credited as model for studio executive producers, as he has been for so long, when the models of Thomas Ince and Jesse Lasky were ahead of him? How could one talk about the great stars of the 1930s and 1940s without any reference at all to Mary Pickford or Rudolph Valentino?

232   THE FIRST TYCOONS

By following the line of necessity and responsibility, by listening to the voices of Hollywood pioneers making their own tentative statements about how things work, I did find myself coming up with one tentative, partial proposition about the first thirty years of movies in America. It is a simple observation, so obvious that most observers have forgotten all about it.

Hollywood, starting about 1912, was the beginning of a new frontier of the twentieth century. A lot of people with talent and personal energy and a desperate need to make a living turned up out there, and some of them became rich and famous. The movies were the first phase of those new forms of mass communication, including radio and television, which have become for this century as basic to our way of life as the great westward movement was for the nineteenth century. The old frontier and the conflicts between wilderness and civilization got into the movies, of course, especially into the westerns. And the dominant individualism which came from the frontier tradition entered naturally into the dramatic stories needed by the movies. Most of the stories were about someone winning or losing something. Not till the dark days of the depression in the 1930s and the world war crisis in the 1940s did the values of community action begin to offer a counter-balance to the familiar dramas of ego-centered individualism.

Meanwhile there were certain central figures whose personal experiences in the "real life" of the Hollywood community seemed the very epitome of frontier-style individual leadership. Most of them started at the very bottom of economic life in this country, with little education, almost all of them lacking at least one parent from an early age. Yet they found that they could "get ahead" by expressing their special talents in the movies. They worked at it very hard, and sometimes had good luck, but they certainly managed to fulfill the American dream of individual mobility and success, of fame and fortune.

Determinist theories of history will claim that all this could have happened the same way with other names attached. But it is difficult to take seriously a view of history which ignores personality. Without these very particular people, the first thirty years of American movies would have been strikingly different. Carl Laemmle, Adolph Zukor, Jesse Lasky, Thomas Ince, D. W. Griffith, Erich von Stroheim, Cecil B. DeMille, King Vidor, Lillian Gish, Mary Pickford, Douglas Fairbanks, Gloria Swanson, Rudolph Valentino, Charlie Chaplin, Buster Keaton, and Harold Lloyd were the "great men and women" of the silent screen.

Appendix B
ARTHUR KNIGHT
The Machine for Seeing Better

In "The Machine for Seeing Better," the first chapter of his landmark history, The Liveliest Art, (N.Y., Macmillan, 1957), Arthur Knight accomplished a careful and readable condensation of some of the most important scientific steps in making moving pictures possible. It is provided here for readers who want to know something about these early problems. It also gives us some insight into the international aspects of these early inventions.

. . . If the motion picture has by this time come to be accepted into the sisterhood of the established arts, there is no denying that it was always the child of science. Some of its biographers have insisted on tracing its paternity all the way back to the Greeks' discovery of electricity in amber, back to Leonardo's *camera obscura* and Athanasius Kircher's *magia cystera,* and investigating all the remoter branches of its family tree prior to the 19th century. Once Peter Mark Roget (of *Thesaurus* fame) enunciated his theory of "The Persistence of Vision with Regard to Moving Objects" in 1824, however, the advance toward motion pictures and motion picture projection was rapid and direct. Almost immediately, scientists throughout Europe began putting his theory to the test. Their devices may have resembled children's toys—whirling discs, twirling coins, booklets of pictures flipped with the thumb—but they quickly established the basic truth of Roget's contention that through some peculiarity of the eye an image is retained for a fraction of a second longer than it actually appears.

On this peculiarity rests the fortune of the entire motion picture industry. Essentially, the motion picture is simply a series of still pictures printed on a long ribbon of celluloid—generally either 35 or 16 millimeters (written "mm") wide. Each picture, halted momentarily, is projected on a white screen, then removed in a flash and another picture substituted. Whether run at sixteen frames per second, as in silent days, or at twenty-four frames per second as required for sound films, enough phases of an action appear on the screen for the eye to make the connection between one picture and the next, and to create the illusion of continuous motion.

Roget announced his theory in London in 1924; and at the very same time in France, Joseph Nicéphore Niepce was groping toward the fundamentals of photography. In 1822 he had succeeded in producing a crude but permanent photograph. Soon after the famous Louis Daguerre joined him, and the two men continued to experiment until, in 1839, they were able to outline and demonstrate a complete, practical photographic process. Their method was slow and painstaking, necessitating either still life or, if their subject was alive, the metal headclamp and a rigid, motionless pose held for minutes on end. The subsequent introduction, however, first of the wet collodion process and then the gelatin emulsions both speeded up and enormously simplified the taking of pictures—so much so that by 1888 George Eastman was prepared to market his Kodak camera ("You press the button, we do the rest"), bringing photography within the reach of everyone.

Long before there was celluloid for film, however, before photography had developed to the point where it could be used for animation, the parlors of well-to-do Americans and Europeans were adorned with practical demonstrations of Roget's fascinating principle. Perhaps most popular was the Zoëtrope, a slotted revolving drum. As one watched through the slits, hand-drawn clowns or acrobats, horses or dogs seemed to leap through their paces on the strips of paper fitted inside the drum. A simpler device using a similar technique was the Stroboscope, with the figures drawn upon a slotted disc. The image was seen by revolving the disc in front of a mirror and again peeping through the slits. More elaborate was the Praxinoscope of Emile Reynaud. In its center was a ring of little mirrors; a band of images was placed opposite them against the shell of the drum. As the drum revolved, the movement almost flowed from one mirror to the next to create a particularly charming effect. Reynaud was constantly improving his invention. Soon he added a frame and tiny settings, converting the device into a parlor theater. By combining it with the magic lantern, he achieved a form of home projection. By 1889 he was able to enlarge his pictures sufficiently to present them theatrically, and he increased the number of pictures in his bands, mounting them on reels of seven hundred or more separate hand-drawn images. He was to continue with his little Praxinoscope Theater until driven out of business by the rival movies early in the next century.

In all of these devices, of course, the pictures with their tiny phases of movement were drawn by hand. They are, in fact, the precursors of today's animated films, of Mickey Mouse and Mr. Magoo. No sooner had photography become practicable, however, than it was applied to animation. How much simpler to capture motion with the camera! Although at first each photograph had to be made separately in a sequence of specially posed shots, when such pictures were mounted in their proper order the effect of movement was quite satisfactory. As early as 1861 Coleman Sellers, of Philadelphia, patented a Kinematoscope in which a series of six such photographs were mounted on a paddlewheel and rotated before the individual viewer to create the illusion of movement. Less than ten years later, Henry R. Heyl was projecting similar photographs onto a screen in Philadelphia's Academy of Music for an audience of 1600 people. He called his machine the Phantasmatrope. And in 1877 Eadweard Muybridge and John D. Isaacs used a battery of twenty-four cameras in sequence to photograph Leland Stanford's race horse in motion. In Paris, Meissonier, the great painter of horses, arranged for a projection of these pictures on yet another device, the Zoöpraxinoscope.

With photography and projection already linked together, the next great problem was to create a camera that would take pictures faster than the ordinary still cameras. Perhaps the first successful step in this direction came in France in 1882 when Dr. E. J. Marey, a physician and physiologist studying the nature of movement, developed a sort of "photographic gun"—a rifle that shot a series of pictures upon a revolving drum set into its chamber. Out of this experiment he evolved during the next decade a series of clumsy but original and practical cameras. Other men, scientists and inventors alike, were challenged by the problem of the camera. In England there was the strange, controversial William Friese-Greene, hero of the recent film *The Magic Box* (1952), who according to some single-handedly solved the problems both of photographing and of projecting motion-picture film. There was the mysterious Frenchman, Louis Leprince, who disappeared from the Dijon-Paris Express in 1890, taking with him the designs for a camera that used strips of perforated celluloid as film.

But the most telling contributions to the development of a motion picture camera unquestionably came from Thomas Edison and his talented assistant William Kennedy Laurie Dickson. In 1888, after more than a decade of experiment, Edison produced the phonograph, an instrument for recording and playing back sound on wax cylinders. He had already seen the motion photographs of Muybridge, and the idea of combining moving pictures with sound seems to have been in his mind even before the perfected phonograph was offered to the public. In fact, his first efforts in this direction consisted of a strip of small photographs wrapped spirally about just such a cylinder. "Everything should come out of one hole," Edison maintained. When this failed, Edison turned the project over to Dickson – and with it a new film base developed by George Eastman, thin strips of clear, supple, strong celluloid coated with a photographic emulsion. The film began arriving in August of 1889. It was Dickson who solved the mechanical problem of moving it through the camera, devising the sprocket system that is still standard on 35mm film today. Indeed, this ingenious man even managed to link up the pictures with the phonograph, demonstrating the Kinetoscope to his employer on October 6, 1889, with a brief film in which Dickson both appeared and spoke. What was in all probability the first actual presentation of a motion picture film also marked the debut of the talkies!

Edison's earliest efforts, however, were not directed toward movie projection. He had considerable success with his penny-in-the-slot phonographs, and it was his opinion that a similar device, offering a brief picture at a penny a look, would ensure a steady profit for his invention. The Kinetoscope was a peep show in which ran a continuous loop of film about 50 feet long. For the moment the sound aspects were ignored and Edison and his crew concentrated on supplying little one-minute subjects for these machines – photographed in the "Black Maria," the world's first film studio, which he built near his West Orange laboratories in 1893. By the fall of 1894, peep-show parlors had sprouted all over the United States and soon appeared in Europe as well. Curiously enough, the inventor seems to have had little confidence in the long range possibilities of his machine. When in 1891 he took out patents on his battery-driven camera and Kinetoscope, he neglected to pay the additional $150 that would have secured him an international copyright. Within the next few years he was to regret this oversight. In England, Robert W. Paul copied the Edison Kinetoscope and also produced a hand-cranked portable camera. (Edison's first camera had the general shape and weight of a small upright piano.) In France the Lumière brothers, Louis and Auguste, saw the Kinetoscope and promptly invented their own Cinématographe, a machine that not only took pictures but could also print and project them as well. In Berlin, Max and Emil Skladanowski, also inspired by the Edison novelty, produced their Bioskop. These machines were soon to become a serious threat to Edison's market within the United States.

Thus, within fifty years of Roget's presentation of his theory, the theory had not only been recognized but its principle had been incorporated into various forms of entertainment. Animation, photography, projection—each was an indispensable step toward the final emergence of the movies. Significantly, none of these steps was taken in any single country. Roget read his paper before the Royal Society in London, Faraday in England, von Stampfer in Austria, Plateau in Belgium all experimented with the idea, producing the various toys and devices that incorporated its principle. Uchatius, who first projected painted pictures, was a Viennese, Désvignes, inventor of the popular toy Zoëtrope, lived in Paris. Both Sellers and Heyl were Americans. Photography, developed in France, was carried forward by Talbot in England and, immeasurably, by George Eastman in this country. There were no secrets, and everything was pointing in one direction—the projection of moving pictures upon a large screen. It should come as no surprise, then, to discover that the movies were actually invented almost simultaneously in France, England, Germany, and the United States. The only wonder is that film historians so often seek to establish priority for the inventors of their own countries, resorting to such dubious phrases as "first accredited showing," "first scientific demonstration," or "first public presentation" to bolster their claims. How much better to recognize the indisputable fact that from the very outset the movies were international, that within a single year films were being projected in New York, London, Berlin, Brussels and Paris.

Once the Europeans had grasped the principles behind Edison's Kinetoscope, they moved directly toward projecting their pictures on a large screen. In the United States too, other inventors—Eugene Lauste, the Lathams, Jean LeRoy, Thomas Armat and F. Charles Jenkins—were also building machines that would project the Edison Kinetoscope reels. Throughout 1895 there were demonstrations of their equipment in New York, Boston, Chicago, Norfolk and Atlanta. Only Edison held back. When, somewhat belatedly, he finally turned to the problems of projection, he borrowed freely (as bitter law suits subsequently revealed) from the discoveries of LeRoy and Latham, and joined forces with Armat whose Vitascope incorporated the essential Maltese Cross movement to hold the film strip momentarily at rest in the aperture of the projector. Even so, not until April 23, 1896, was Edison prepared to present his projecting Kinetoscope to the public. The presentation took place during the vaudeville program at Koster & Bial's Music Hall, 34th Street and Broadway, the present site of the Macy store. A few months later the American Biograph, Edison's keenest rival, made its debut at Hammerstein's Olympia Music Hall. Within the year, movies were being seen in virtually every large city throughout the United States and Europe.

Appendix C
HOWARD T. LEWIS
Paramount Famous Lasky Corporation

In a series of volumes entitled Harvard Business Reports *Howard T. Lewis was editor of Volume 8,* Cases on the Motion Picture Industry, *(N.Y., McGraw-Hill, 1930). In this analysis of the production side of a major company, he provides us with policy and procedural background which still interests us today: meetings, story department actions, star contracts, seasonal releases. Especially noteworthy is the quantity control of production by the distribution branch of the company. Although this is just after the arrival of sound, it reflects working processes developed over the 1920s. (A number of blank forms were reproduced which could not be included here; our extract is from pages 182-183, 186, 189, 190-195.)*

In 1919 the Paramount Famous Lasky Corporation owned and operated studios in Long Island, New York, and Hollywood, California. Approximately 70% of the corporation's total production took place at the Hollywood studio. The Long Island studio specialized in short subjects, and in addition, produced from 10 to 12 feature pictures each year.

The production organization of the company was designed to effect the maximum amount of flexibility. Directors, as a rule, were free to proceed unmolested with their respective assignments. Supervision by associate producers was of an advisory nature. It was of little importance in productions assigned to outstanding directors. Studio cabinets, consisting of the studio production manager, assistant production manager, directors, supervisors, and studio executive manager, held weekly meetings to discuss the current problems of the various productions. In this manner each picture benefited from the ideas of all production officials. As a rule, the vice president in charge of production was present each week at either the studio cabinet meeting in Long Island or the one in Hollywood. It was his duty to coordinate the production function with the other major functions such as finance, distribution, and exhibition. . . .

Story departments were maintained in both the home office in New York City, and the Hollywood studio. They were operated as separate units, although the former, because of its proximity to the theatrical, book, publishing, and style center, was considered first in line of authority.

The story departments obtained information and maintained records of current, past, and future stories, magazine articles, plays, poems, and all other materials that might be used as plots for motion pictures. The department managers made contacts with publishers, writers, playwrights, and composers, and endeavored at all times to have current knowledge on matters pertaining to the literary world. To facilitate the proper selection of material, it was necessary for them to understand the story requirements of motion pictures, the censorship laws of the several states, and in particular the type of plot best suited to each Paramount actor, actress, and director.

The story department maintained separate readers to glean material for motion picture plots from magazine articles. Generally magazine articles [stories] were made available to motion picture producers in advance of publication; to be of value as a motion picture plot it was necessary that a serial story be made available long before the last episode appeared in a magazine. Additional material was secured from "fan" mail, actors, actresses, directors, company employees, especially those holding important positions in the production departments, and numerous other voluntary sources.

The two units of the story department submitted briefs of all reviewed material to the studios once each week. It was also customary for the New York division to supply the California studio with the reviewed books and articles. This was necessary because of the lack of literary facilities in Hollywood. If the production heads at either studio were interested in the briefs, the story was studied in detail and a rough script, or motion picture version, was prepared by an adaptor. If the script was approved, it was edited and usually submitted to the Motion Picture Producers and Distributors of America, or some similar organization, for censorship. In some cases censorship was not considered until after the story rights had been purchased. After approval of a story, a price limitation based on the executives' opinion of the motion picture value of the story was set, and the legal department was instructed to complete the purchase. In acquiring story rights careful consideration was given to copyrights and to pictorial, publishing, dialogue, and musical rights. Finally, the script was either assigned for production or catalogued for future use.

Like its competitors, the Paramount Famous Lasky Corporation used various contracts for actors, actresses, and directors. Some contracts stipulated a certain salary for one picture, others a salary for a series of pictures, and still others a stated weekly salary to be paid on the basis of the ratio of the number of hours in which the particular actor was actually employed in a week to the total number of working hours in the week. All stock actors were paid on a flat salary basis.

Aside from contracts for single pictures, those of the Paramount Famous Lasky Corporation were, in general, for six months' duration with subsequent options at the expiration of each six months' period for five years. Usually five-year contracts stipulated definite salary increases operative at each renewal. That clause, however, was not an essential requisite. If for any reason the company should not elect to take up its option, the contract automatically became inoperative, and the actor became a free agent. The actor did not have a similar privilege of rejection. The longest straight contract was for twelve months.

In general all salaries, regardless of position, were paid weekly. Extras, temporary electricians, and others not under contract were paid daily. . . .

As a general rule the Paramount Famous Lasky Corporation planned its production about the first of April. The general manager in charge of distribution stated the number of pictures desired for the coming year. He based his estimates on his own and his associates' opinions in regard to the number of pictures the company could distribute profitably.

Upon determination of the distribution department's requirements, the studio cabinet operative committee, which comprised the chief production executives, mapped out the production program, its classification and total cost, and the material content and cost of each picture. These data were submitted to the president for recommendations and approval. While neither the manager in charge of distribution nor the president of the Publix Theaters Corporation, the Paramount subsidiary theater operating company, was entitled to vote on final decisions, their opinions regarding the submitted program and their recommended changes were influential in the drawing up of the final program.

Motion pictures in general were classified as either starring or special, and were subdivided as sound or silent pictures. In special productions cast with a star of great box office value, the picture became both a starring and a special production. A third classification was at one time made for silent pictures which had a few talking sequences. In 1929, however, because such pictures had practically disappeared from the market, this subclassification was not used.

To facilitate production and release control, the company's 1929-1930 program was segregated into four divisions, classified as Personality Pictures, Commander Specials, Leader Specials, and New Show World Specials. Personality Pictures were the least costly. Their individual budgets were based on a statistical knowledge of the starring artist's value as a box office attraction. Where more than one Personality production was assigned to a star, a total budget was computed from the individual picture estimates. In such cases, the control department was interested only in the total amount, and as a result some pictures profited at the expense of others. There was a wide range in star salaries; it was estimated that the average star received $2500 a week while working. Three or possibly four Personality Pictures represented the maximum number assigned to any one star. Stories for these pictures were selected currently, and in many cases were written by the scenario department especially for the assigned artist. . . .

Commander Specials ranked third in quality and cost of production. As a rule the stories for these pictures were secured prior to the beginning of the production season. The casts of Commander Specials did not contain high-salaried stars; generally they were made up of well-known featured players, none of whom was advertised as the particular attraction. The average featured player earned $750 per week while working.

Leader specials were the company's highest quality regular feature pictures, and often were given extended-run exhibition. All stories for Leader Specials were selected and assigned, and in some cases were in process, in advance of the production season. In some cases such important players as George Bancroft and Clara Bow were featured in conjunction with an all-star cast. In others the title of the story predominated, and the cast of stars was featured as of secondary importance. Because of the impossibility of accurately measuring public opinion. Leader Specials were known to have exceeded more costly pictures in total box office receipts.

New Show World Specials were the Paramount Famous Lasky Corporation's extended-run pictures that commanded $1.50 and $2 admission prices when prereleased for roadshow purposes. "Glorifying the American Girl," a Ziegfeld production, assigned to a high-salaried director, cast with all star players, and staged on an elaborate basis, was typical of this type of picture. In that particular case, the use of Ziegfeld's name represented a large cost in itself. Because New Show World Specials required extensive preparations, as a general rule their production was started prior to the opening of the regular production season. . . .

Paramount pictures were released on an average of one each week, with two released during one week in every four. This system did not always operate as planned, but as a general rule changes were infrequent. During the 1929-1930 season every fifth picture released by the company was a costly special. In the president's opinion this was an unwise plan. He believed that the market could not absorb so many costly cinemas, and that as a result none of them would return the maximum possible income.

. . .

As a general rule, box office receipts varied during the four seasons of the theatrical year. The first quarter, September, October, and November, was fair, gaining momentum in late October. In the winter season receipts were greatest. In the early part of the spring season, receipts equalled those of late fall; in the late spring, they were approximately the same as in September. The summer season usually was the least profitable. In 1929, however, the introduction of talking pictures, a decline in the popularity of legitimate plays except in New York City, and the widespread use of theater refrigeration forecast a leveling out of boxoffice receipts. . . .

Appendix D
Selected Companies of the Silent Period:
A Chronological List

EDISON (Thomas A. Edison Inc.) 1894-1918. Provided kinetoscope and later theater films from West Orange, N.J., "Black Maria" studio. Edison took leadership in forming Motion Picture Patents Company and General Film Company. In 1908, he built a studio in the Bronx.

BIOGRAPH (American Mutoscope and Biograph Co.) 1895-1918. Founded by W. K. L. Dickson, Herman Casler, Harry Marvin, Elias Koopman. During the time D. W.Griffith was directing for Biograph, the N.Y. studio was at 11 East 14th Street.

PATHÉ (Pathé Exchange Co.) 1896 (1910)-1931. Bound Brook, N.J., studio for American production opened in 1910. Taken over by RKO in 1931.

SELIG (Selig Polyscope Co.) 1896-1918. Founded by William N. Selig in Chicago. May have made first Los Angeles film in 1908-09. Later specialized in jungle adventure films. Also worked in New Orleans.

VITAGRAPH (Vitagraph Co. of America) 1897-1925. Founded by J. Stuart Blackton and Albert E. Smith. First studio at 140 Nassau Street, New York City, later in Flatbush and California. Sold to Warners.

LUBIN (Lubin Film Manufacturing Co.) 1897-1917. Founded in Philadelphia by Sigmund Lubin, noted for his laboratory work.

KALEM (Kalem Co.) 1907-1917. Named from initials of founders, George Kleine, Samuel Long, Frank J. Marion. Produced in N.Y. and Florida.

ESSANAY (Essanay Film Manufacturing Co.) 1907-1917. From initials of founders, George K. Spoor and Gilbert M. ("Broncho Billy") Anderson. Headquarters in Chicago. Traveling companies worked the west; a studio was set up in Niles, California.

MOTION PICTURE PATENTS CO. 1908-1917. The "trust," headed by Jeremiah J. Kennedy, including all the companies listed above, plus Méliès and Gaumont (represented in the U.S. by Kleine).

IMP (Independent Moving Picture Co.) 1909-1912. Formed by Carl Laemmle. Some constituent companies reshuffled to form Universal.

AMERICAN (American Film Manufacturing Co.) 1910-1921. Founded by John R. Freuler and Samuel Hutchinson, with two companies in Chicago and one traveling. Studio in Santa Barbara, California, built in 1912.

GENERAL FILM COMPANY 1910-1919. Distributor for Patents Co. (above).

KEYSTONE (Keystone Film Co.) 1912-1933. Founded by Adam Kessel and Charles Bauman as subsidiary to their N.Y. Motion Picture Co. to be production company for Mack Sennett. Part of Triangle briefly.

MUTUAL (Mutual Film Exchanges Inc.) 1912-1918. Distribution company formed by Harry Aitken and John Freuler, serving many producers, notably Reliance, Majestic, American, also Griffith (1913-1914) and Chaplin (1916-1917). Later absorbed by Film Box Office, which became RKO.

UNIVERSAL (Universal Film Manufacturing Corp.) 1912– . Successor of IMP. Laemmle built a studio at Universal City, California, in 1915.

WARNERS (Warners Feature Film Co.) 1912– . Production and distribution company, set up by Harry, Albert, Sam, and Jack. Warner Brothers Pictures Inc. absorbed Vitagraph in 1925, First National in 1929.

FOX (Fox Film Corp.) 1912-1935. Production company first called "Box Office Attractions." Started by William Fox eight years after buying his first penny arcade. Combined with his distribution and exhibition activities in 1915.

FAMOUS PLAYERS (Famous Players Film Co.) 1912-1914. Formed by Adolph Zukor and Daniel Frohman for film production.

JESSE LASKY FEATURE PLAY CO. 1913-1914. Founded by Lasky, Samuel Goldfish, and Cecil B. DeMille. First feature made in Hollywood: *The Squaw Man*.

FAMOUS PLAYERS-LASKY 1914-1927. Lasky and Zukor companies' merger.

PARAMOUNT (Paramount Pictures Corp.) 1914– . Founded by W. W. Hodkinson. Financing distributor for Famous Players and Lasky. Taken over by Zukor acquiring control of stock, 1917.

VLSE 1915–1917. Brief combination of Vitagraph, Lubin, Selig, and Essanay for feature film production.

TRIANGLE (Triangle Film Corp.) 1915–1918. Aitken, Kessel, and Bauman combined to employ Griffith, Ince, and Sennett at Ince's new studio in Culver City (later to be M-G-M).

METRO (Metro Pictures Corp.) 1915–1918. Richard Rowland, president, assisted for a time by Louis B. Mayer. A group formed after Alco, a group of small Eastern distributors, failed. Production in New York and Hollywood. Sold to Loew's Inc. in 1920.

GOLDWYN (Goldwyn Pictures Corp.) 1916–1924. Formed by Samuel Goldfish (after he was ousted from Famous Players-Lasky) and Edgar and Archibald Selwyn. Studios in Fort Lee, N.J. Triangle's Culver City studio leased in 1918. Sam Goldwyn (having taken the name of the company as his own) resigned in 1922. Joseph Godsol sold out to Loew and M-G-M in 1924.

FIRST NATIONAL 1917–1929. An exhibitors' group initiated by Thomas Tally, J. D. Williams, and others to compete with Famous Players-Lasky by making and distributing films. Warner Brothers took over the company and its new Burbank studios at the end of the silent era.

LOUIS B. MAYER PRODUCTION CO. (1918–1924). Studio at 3200 Mission Road in Los Angeles after Mayer moved to the coast from Boston.

UNITED ARTISTS 1919– . Formed by Mary Pickford, Douglas Fairbanks, Charlie Chaplin, and D.W.Griffith to distribute their pictures.

LOEW'S INC. 1919– . Marcus Loew's theater company, formed with new capital, reorganizing Loew's Theatrical Enterprises (1910) after his original investment in an arcade in 1904.

METRO-GOLDWYN-MAYER 1924– . Subsidiary of Loew's Inc. combining Metro and Goldwyn companies under Louis B. Mayer's management.

SAMUEL GOLDWYN INC. LTD. 1924– . Goldwyn without partners.

COLUMBIA PICTURES 1924– . Reorganization of CBC Film Sales Co, headed by Harry and Jack Cohn and Joseph Brandt. A low budget production company in the 1920s.
PRODUCERS DISTRIBUTING CORP. 1925–1928. Cecil B. DeMille's production company after he was forced out of Famous Players-Lasky, to which he later returned as an independent. PARAMOUNT-FAMOUS-LASKY 1927–1930.

Appendix E
Brief Biographies of Early Film Executives

Harry E. Aitken (1870–1956). Born in Waukesha, Wisconsin, he was a real estate man who became associated with John R. Freuler in a film exchange company in Milwaukee and later the Mutual Film Corporation (1912). Mutual released the films of various production companies, including Reliance and Majestic, in competition with both the Edison patents trust and Universal. D. W. Griffith became a producer and director for these Mutual companies when he left Biograph in 1913, and Aitken became primarily responsible for financing *The Birth of a Nation* and its release through Epoch Corporation. Separating from Freuler and Mutual, he founded the Triangle Corporation (1915–1918) which attempted to provide a constant flow of product at top prices from D. W. Griffith, Thomas H. Ince, and Mack Sennett. Aitken retired from movies in 1920, retaining rights to *The Birth of a Nation* and occasionally offering it for re-release and even planning a new production.

Robert H. Cochrane (1879–1973). Educated in Toledo, Ohio, he became reporter and city editor for the Toledo *Bee* before joining his brothers' advertising agency in Chicago. Carl Laemmle, then a clothing store manager in Oshkosh, Wisconsin, had been in correspondence with him as an advertising consultant. When Laemmle came to Chicago and decided to enter the motion picture business, Cochrane joined him (1906) as his advertising director and was active in the campaign against the patents trust. Vice president of Universal Pictures from 1912 to 1936, he was briefly president, after Laemmle's departure (April 1936 to December 1937).

Appendices 247

Thomas Alva Edison (1847-1931). A sixth-generation American, born in a small town in Ohio, he had little schooling, but as a telegraph operator experimented with new improvements. Edison patented a stock ticker in 1868 and in 1871 began manufacturing some of his devices for Western Union. Later, Menlo Park, N. J., was his headquarters, where he invented the phonograph and perfected the incandescent light bulb. At Orange, N.J., after 1887, he began work on a motion picture machine, delegating much of it to W. K. L. Dickson. Although the Kinetophone (1889) offered film plus a disc recording, the silent peep-show Kinetoscope was more successful, along with the Kinetograph camera which supplied the content for it. Dickson built a darkened studio (dubbed "the black Maria") and the Edison company began to make films. Contracting for rights to the Jenkins-Armat projector, Edison showed films on a large screen at Koster & Bial's Music Hall on April 23, 1896. After arduous efforts, he brought together the leading film companies in the Motion Picture Patents Company in 1909, intended to keep all production and exhibition under their control. When this was put out of business by antitrust prosecution in 1917, the Edison company also closed down.

William Fox (1879-1952). Born in Hungary, he came to the U.S. with his parents (the original name was Fried) at the age of nine months. The oldest of six children, he sold newspapers and candy after school to help the family and quit school when he was 11 to work long hours in a garment factory. Young William later set up a processing plant for sponging and shrinking cloth, and at 21 he was doing well. But he discovered movies in 1904 and soon assembled a chain of 15 theaters in the New York City area, as well as a rental company. He refused to sell out to the Patents Company and went into production in 1912, combining production, distribution, and exhibition in the Fox Film Corporation in 1915. Depending for a while on such stars as Theda Bara and Tom Mix, Fox made a bid for both quality and quantity production in the late 1920s and also tried to build an empire of theaters, including a failed attempt to buy control of Loew's Inc. after Marcus Loew's death. Badly hurt in a car accident, he was unable to recoup his losses after the stock market crash of 1929 and lost control of his own company. Although he had the right technical answer for the sound revolution (sound on the film itself instead of on a synchronized record) he was unable to take full advantage of his patents and eventually declared bankruptcy. Jailed for bribing a judge in his bankruptcy case, he was paroled in 1943.

Samuel Goldwyn (1882-1974). Born in Warsaw, Poland, Sam Goldfish ran away to relatives in Manchester, England, when he was eleven. He turned up in the United States at 14, worked in a glove factory, became a salesman and developed his own glove business. Dismayed by a lowered tariff on imported gloves (1912), he looked into the new business of moving pictures and helped persuade his brother-in-law Jesse Lasky to get into movies in 1913. Ousted soon after Adolph Zukor joined forces with Lasky, he formed the Goldwyn Pictures Corporation with the Selwyn brothers (1916) and adopted this new name himself in 1918. Divorced from Blanche Lasky in 1919, he married actress Frances Howard in 1925; she played an important role in his very independent production status in Hollywood thereafter. He had resigned twice from his own company, after attempting to provide his board of directors with new faces like Lee and J. J. Schubert and Frank Joseph Godsol. In 1924, Samuel Goldwyn, Inc. Ltd., was formed, with no directors and no partners. From then on Goldwyn personally financed his studio, his contracts with stars and with famous writers, and his pictures. Famous for dignified, high quality adaptations of literary works, his most notable films probably were those directed by William Wyler in the early sound era.

Carl Laemmle (1867-1939). When he came to the U.S. from Germany at the age of 17, Laemmle was already a good bookkeeper, and that was one of many jobs he tried in New York, Chicago, and Oshkosh, Wisconsin, where he became manager of a clothing store in 1898. Seeking to set up a store of his own in Chicago, he noticed the steady business being done by a nickelodeon. He promptly went into movie exhibition (1906) and the next year set up the first of several exchanges. When the Patents Company tried to buy or force him out in 1909, he refused and set up his Independent Motion Picture production company (IMP), which eventually became Universal Pictures. Universal City, a separate town/studio, was opened in 1915 north of Hollywood. After a period when his son was placed in charge of production (1929) the company was sold to new owners in 1935.

Jesse L. Lasky (1880–1958). Grandson of a German immigrant and son of a shoe salesman, Lasky was born in San Francisco. His father died while the boy was in his teens, and young Jesse tried hunting for gold in Alaska and several other gambles, including a tour of America with his sister Blanche in a cornet duo act, before settling down as a vaudeville promoter. In 1913 his then brother-in-law, Samuel Goldfish (later Goldwyn) persuaded him to give his name to a feature film production company. Its first movie, *The Squaw Man*, was directed by Oscar Apfel and Cecil B. DeMille on the west coast and was successful enough to entice him into the business to stay. The Lasky Feature Play Company and Adolph Zukor's Famous Players were combined in 1916, with Lasky as vice president in charge of production in Hollywood and Zukor as president in N.Y. – a typical arrangement, as it turned out, for motion picture companies. Famous Players-Lasky (to be known later as Paramount) became the strongest company in the movie business, but in the depression year of 1932, with Zukor himself in the minority on the board, Lasky was forced out. He thereafter produced a dozen pictures independently at various studios.

Marcus Loew (1870–1927). Born and brought up in a lower East Side tenement in New York City, the son of Austrian immigrants, Loew had to start earning money at the same time he started school. At six, he spent his evenings selling newspapers; at nine, he was working full time, first as a laborer in a printing plant, then as a partner in an advertising venture. Before long, he was in the fur business, first in a factory, then on his own as a trader (an enterprise which foundered), later again as a successful traveling salesman, with real estate interests on the side. Another such salesman, Adolph Zukor, had already invested in a penny arcade, complete with moving pictures. In 1904, Loew invested in this new business. By 1907 he owned 40 nickelodeons. By 1912 Loew's Theatrical Enterprises included 400 movie theaters. In 1920, in possession of some of the best downtown theaters in the biggest cities, he followed the example of his former friend Zukor and got into production, buying Metro Pictures in 1920, the Goldwyn company and Louis B. Mayer Pictures in 1924: result, Metro-Goldwyn-Mayer.

Benjamin P. Schulberg (1892-1957). Born in Connecticut, educated in New York City and the College of the City of New York, he spent two years as reporter on the New York *Evening Mail*, one year as associate editor of a magazine, *Film Reports*. After a year as publicity director and scenario editor for Rex Pictures, Schulberg joined Famous Players in the same capacities when Adolph Zukor formed the company in 1912, planning the publicity for *Queen Elizabeth, The Prisoner of Zenda*, and many other films. "B. P." tried his hand at independent production after World War I and introduced Clara Bow to the screen. From 1925 to 1932 he was head of production for Famous Players-Lasky in Hollywood under Jesse Lasky. Replaced by Emanuel Cohen in the shakeup of 1932, he was successively an independent producer releasing through Paramount, Columbia, and Selznick and director of advertising for Enterprise Studios, but found no work in Hollywood after 1946.

Lewis J. Selznick (1870-1933). Born in Kiev, Russia, and sent by his family to England at 12, he worked to earn his passage to America. Starting in Pittsburgh as a jewelry apprentice, he owned a chain of stores at 24, but became attracted to the movie business. After a high-comedy period of pretended affiliation with Laemmle's then embattled group at Universal, he joined World Film Corporation, and later set up his own company in association with the star, Clara Kimball Young. Coming into conflict with Adolph Zukor, he began to experience difficulties in distribution, and a so-called partnership deal with Zukor effectively forced him out of business in 1923. He lived to see his sons revive the Selznick name in Hollywood—David as a producer, Myron as an agent.

Winfield H. Sheehan (1883-1945). Born and educated (St. Canisius College) in Buffalo, N.Y., and active in a New York volunteer regiment in the Spanish-American war (1896-1899) he was a reporter for the Buffalo *Courier* (1901), New York *World* and *Evening World* (1902-1910), secretary to the New York City fire commissioner (1910) and police commissioner (1911-1914). Sheehan became personal secretary for William Fox in 1914 and in his biography in the *International Motion Picture Almanac* he credits himself with organizing the Fox studios in Hollywood (1914) and the American and foreign distribution branches (1914-1921). As vice president and general manager of Fox from 1916 on, he had a direct influence on film production, especially in the late 1920s, until the formation of 20th Century-Fox in 1935. He produced two films at M-G-M, 1939-1940.

Adolph Zukor (1873-1976). An orphan immigrant from Hungary at 15, he found the fur business a good place to develop his salesmanship and before long he had his own company. Penny arcades attracted him, and he invested in one in 1903. After spending some time studying the audiences in nickelodeons he decided to cast his lot with feature length films. His production ventures came near the end of the Patents Company era, and his fortunate contract with Mary Pickford made his Famous Players company a leader in the new film world. Merging with Lasky's company, absorbing W. W. Hodkinson's Paramount distribution company, buying and building chains of movie houses, Zukor became the most powerful of the silent era tycoons, surviving competitive thrusts from First National and United Artists and less dangerous encounters with the Federal Trade Commission and the bankruptcy courts. When he died at the age of 103, he was still chairman of the board emeritus at Paramount.

Appendix F
A Few Business Events Covered by the *New York Times*

11 Feb 1908 "To Control Entire Moving Picture Business of World" (Edison patents agreement: "Mr. Edison will receive from the combination $200,000 a year royalty")

17 Aug 1912 "Motion Picture Men Sued as a Trust" (Sherman Act)

12 Apr 1914 "New Strand Opens; Biggest of Movies"

18 Jun 1915 "$2 Theatre Chain of Movie Features" (Aitken/Triangle)

21 Jul 1915 "Triangle Film Formed" (at LaJunta, California)

29 Jun 1916 "$12,500,000 Merger of Film Companies" (Famous Players to make 48 films, Lasky 36)

16 Aug 1916 "For Mary Pickford Films" (new Artcraft Pictures Corp.)

10 Nov 1918 "Mary Pickford Signs" (with First National "to be her own manager")

1 Sep 1921 "Attacks Big Firm as Film Monopoly" (Federal Trade Commission formal complaint)

29 Nov 1922 "Famous Players Sued for Millions" (by Vitagraph)

18 Apr 1924 "$65,000,000 Movie Merger Completed" (M-G-M Corp.)

29 Jan 1925 "Vitagraph Quits Hays Movie League"

23 Apr 1925 "Pioneer Vitagraph Sold to Warners"

18 Sep 1925 "700 Movie Houses Under One Control" (Famous Players-Lasky plus Balaban & Katz)

16 Jul 1927 "Famous Players Guilty of Film Trust Conspiracy" (Federal Trade Commission: in 60 days report to be filed promising no more conspiracy, block booking or coercion of exhibitors; divestment not required)

The above news stories are reproduced in the *New York Times Encyclopedia of Film*, Volume I, 1896–1928 (N.Y., Times Books, 1984).

Appendix G
Bibliography

A good deal of work remains to be done, certainly, in writing and interpreting motion picture history. Studio chronicles, by and large, have not lived up to the standard of Bosley Crowther's lively, opinionated, well-researched report on M-G-M, *The Lion's Share*. The history of Paramount, above all, is a major mountain which awaits exploration. Biographical material here seems to be less available than in the case of Metro. The Adolph Zukor autobiography and the praising biography by Will Irwin, like the John Drinkwater biography of Carl Laemmle, were written long ago and by today's standards are inadequate. Jesse Lasky's autobiography, on the other hand, is one of the richest in the whole range of film sources for understanding the contribution of a single individual to a studio program.

Although there has not been for many years any adequate single volume about American movies, there are at least three books specifically about the silent period in the United States which must be ranked as special treasures by the film history student.

The first in point of time is *A Million and One Nights*, by Terry Ramsaye, who was assigned to interview motion picture pioneers by the editor of *Photoplay*. The material is indeed "anecdotal," therefore more revealing than any statistical study could be. However fictional the dialogue, however worshipful of Edison's role in the earliest days, Ramsaye's book bears the marks of immediacy. It is the best we have for detail and coverage. Ramsaye did an enormous amount of checking and digging, and he added an irrepressible sense of humor which is both enjoyable and suitable for the age of innovation he was reporting.

Ramsaye's history of the early inventions and the silent film production companies carries the story up to 1926. Benjamin Hampton, in *A History of the Movies*, takes it very little farther (to 1931), but his approach is rather more serious and restricted to major business trends. He is trying to be an objective writer at the same time he is more of a participant than Ramsaye. As a representative of the American Tobacco Company, he was assigned to look into the investment possibilities of the film industry. He might have become one of the movers and shapers had he not leaned to the ideal view of W. W. Hodkinson that production, distribution and exhibition should remain separate. As it was, he looked on with much admiration and some impartiality as Adolph Zukor moved toward greater power in the industry.

In our own day, the most notable researcher has been Kevin Brownlow, who followed, in a way, the path of Ramsaye in searching out survivors of the silent era. He taped many interviews and regardless of the dangers of depending on self-serving and hazy memories, *The Parade's Gone By* is a remarkable evocation of the way it was, with emphasis on production processes and individual contributions to it. The title of Brownlow's book comes from a jibe by a skeptic on the sound stage who wondered why anyone should care about the silent days. The author's own staunch view is that silent films represent a unique period of greatness in the visual arts. He has added more to our knowledge of the first thirty years in *The War, the West, and the Wilderness* and a companion to his British TV series, *Hollywood: The Pioneers*.

Two other books of broader range are of special value to the student of silent films. *The Movies,* by Richard Griffith and Arthur Mayer (with updating in recent editions by Eileen Bowser) is more than half concerned with the silent era. It is a picture book, and for that reason especially belongs on the film student's shelf. If one were limited to a single book to survey the whole range of American film history, this would be the best and liveliest to start with.

Lewis Jacobs wrote the first comprehensive national film history, *The Rise of the American Film*. While his chronicle extends only to 1939, the greater part of it focuses on Griffith and other directors of the silent days. He makes a point of covering the art and the industry in separate chapters and also adds his judgments on the social content of the films. Later histories have drawn on Jacobs, and his pioneering work is still a first-rate usable textbook, partly because of his personal qualities as critic, teacher, and experimental film maker, and partly because he witnessed so much of what he describes.

The understanding of film history will continue to grow as new writers offer new views. Any interpretation, however objective it tries to be – or however close it tries to come to the natural history of the period – is only another contribution to that continuing chain of investigation which attempts to recapture and refurbish the moving images of the past, together with all the energies behind the scenes which made them happen.

Appendices 255

Balio, Tino. *The American Film Industry*. Madison, University of Wisconsin, 1976, 1985.
Balio, Tino. *United Artists*. Madison, University of Wisconsin, 1976.
Conant, Michael. *Antitrust in the Motion Picture Industry*. Berkeley, University of California, 1960.
Crowther, Bosley. *The Lion's Share*. N.Y., E. P. Dutton, 1957.
Drinkwater, John. *The Life and Adventures of Carl Laemmle*. N.Y., G. P. Putnam's Sons, 1931.
Frohman, Daniel. *Daniel Frohman Presents*. N.Y., Lee Furman Inc., 1935.
Goldwyn, Samuel (with Corinne Lowe). *Behind the Screen*. N.Y., George H. Doran Co., 1923.
Grau, Robert. *The Theatre of Science*. N.Y., Broadway Publishing Co., 1914.
Griffth, Richard and Arthur Mayer. *The Movies*. N.Y., Simon and Schuster, 1957.
Hall, Ben M. *The Best Remaining Seats*. N.Y., Clarkson N. Potter Inc., 1961.
Hampton, Benjamin B. *A History of the Movies*. N.Y., Covici Friede, 1931. Reprinted as *History of the American Film Industry*. N.Y., Dover Publications, 1970.
Henderson, Robert M. *D. W.Griffith: The Years at Biograph*. N.Y., Farrar, Straus, Giroux, 1970.
Huettig, Mae D. *Economic Control of the Motion Picture Industry*. Philadelphia, University of Pennsylvania, 1944.
Irwin, Will. *The House That Shadows Built*. N.Y., Doubleday Doran, 1928.
Kennedy, Joseph P. (ed.) *The Story of the Films*. N.Y., A. W. Shaw Co., 1927.
Knight, Arthur. *The Liveliest Art*. N.Y., Macmillan, 1957.
Lasky, Jesse (with Don Weldon). *I Blow My Own Horn*. N.Y., Doubleday, 1957.
Lewis, Howard T. *Harvard Business Reports, Volume 8: Cases on the Motion Picture Industry*. N.Y., McGraw-Hill, 1930.
Macgowan, Kenneth. *Behind the Screen*. N.Y., Delacorte Press, 1965.
Pratt, George. *Spellbound in Darkness*. Rochester, N.Y., University of Rochester, 1966. Reprinted, Boston, N.Y. Graphic Society,1973.
Ramsaye, Terry. *A Million and One Nights*. N.Y., Simon and Schuster, 1926.

Sklar, Robert. *Movie-Made America.* N.Y. Random House, 1975.
Spehr, Paul C. *The Movies Begin.* Newark Museum/Morgan Press, 1977.
Smith, Albert E. (with Phil A. Koury). *Two Reels and a Crank.* N.Y., Doubleday, 1952.
Zierold, Norman. *The Hollywood Tycoons.* N.Y., Coward McCann; London, Hamish Hamilton, 1969.
Zukor, Adolph (with Dale Kramer). *The Public Is Never Wrong.* N.Y., G. P. Putnam's Sons, 1953.

Bliven, Bruce. "The Covered Wagon," *The New Republic,* April 25, 1923.
Harrison, Louis Reeves. "The Squaw Man," *Moving Picture World,* Feb 28, 1914.
Mayer, Arthur, "The Origins of United Artists," *Films in Review,* Aug-Sep 1959.

Citations above refer to books and articles from which extracts are reprinted in this volume. Following are additional useful materials on early business practices.

Aitken, Roy. *The Birth of a Nation Story.* Middleburg, Va., William Denlingers, 1956. As told by Al P. Nelson.
Brownlow, Kevin. *The Parade's Gone By.* N.Y., Knopf, 1968.
Bryan, George S. *Edison: The Man and His Work.* N.Y., Knopf, 1926.
Ceram, C. W. *Archaeology of the Cinema.* N.Y., Harcourt, Brace, 1965.
Cook, David A. *A History of Narrative Film.* N.Y., W. W. Norton & Co., 1981.
DeMille, Cecil B. *The Autobiography of Cecil B. DeMille.* Englewood Cliffs, N.J., Prentice-Hall, 1959. Donald Hayne, editor.
Eames, John Douglas. *The Paramount Story.* N.Y., Crown, 1985.
Edmonds, I. G. *Big U: Universal in the Silent Days.* Cranbury, N.J., A. S. Barnes, 1977.
Edmonds, I. G., and Reiko Mimura. *Paramount Pictures and the People Who Made Them.* Cranbury, N.J., A. S. Barnes, 1980.
Everson, William K. *American Silent Film.* N.Y., Oxford, 1978.

Fell, John. *Film Before Griffith.* Berkeley, University of California, 1983.
Fielding, Raymond. *A Technological History of Motion Pictures and Television.* Berkeley, University of California, 1967.
French, Philip. *The Movie Moguls.* London, Weidenfeld and Nicolson, 1969; Pelican Books 1971.
Hendricks, Gordon. *Origins of the American Film.* N.Y., Arno Press, 1972. Includes *Beginnings of the Biograph* and *The Edison Motion Picture Myth.*
Jacobs, Lewis. *The Rise of the American Film.* N.Y., Harcourt, Brace, 1939.
Jobes, Gertrude. *Motion Picture Empire.* Hamden, Conn., Archon Books, 1966.
Kanin, Garson. *Hollywood.* N.Y., Viking, 1974. Brief dialogue with Laemmle.
Klingender, F. D. and Stuart Legg. *Money Behind the Screen.* London, Lawrence & Wishart, 1937.
Lahue, Kalton C. *Dreams for Sale: The Rise and Fall of the Triangle Film Corporation.* Cranbury, N.J., A. S. Barnes, 1971.
———. *Motion Picture Pioneer: The Selig Polyscope Company.* Cranbury, N.J., A. S. Barnes, 1973.
Lauritzen, Einar and Gunnar Lundquist. *American Film Index 1908-1915.* Stockholm, Akademibokhandeln, 1976.
Lyons, Timothy J. *The Silent Partner: The History of the American Film Manufacturing Company, 1910-1921.* Ph.D. dissertation, University of Iowa, 1972.
Niver, Kemp R. *The First 20 Years.* Los Angeles, Locare Research Group, 1968.
Quigley Jr., Martin. *Magic Shadows.* Washington D. C., Georgetown University Press, 1964.
Rosenberg, Bernard and Harry Silverstein. *The Real Tinsel.* N.Y., Macmillan, 1970. Interview with Adolph Zukor.
Sinclair, Upton. *Upton Sinclair Presents William Fox.* Published by the author, Los Angeles (West Branch) California, 1933.
Slide, Anthony. *Aspects of American Film History Prior to 1920.* Metuchen, N.J., Scarecrow Press, 1978.
———. *The Big V: A History of the Vitagraph Company.* Metuchen, N.J., Scarecrow Press, 1976.
———. *Early American Cinema.* N.Y., A. S. Barnes, 1970.
Tibbetts, John. *The Triangle Film Corporation, 1915-1918.* Unpublished M.A. thesis, University of Kansas, 1975.
Trimble, Marian B. *J. Stuart Blackton.* Metuchen, N.J., Scarecrow Press, 1985.

Weaver, John T. *Twenty Years of Silents.* Metuchen, N. J., Scarecrow Press, 1971. Actors, directors, producers, studios and distributing companies listed.

Busch, Niven, "Adolph Zukor," *New Yorker,* Sep 7, 1929.
"The Case of William Fox," *Fortune Magazine,* May, 1930.
Currie, Barton W., "The Nickel Madness," *Harpers Weekly,* 24 Aug 1907. The nickelodeon.
Dunn, Angela Fox, "When the Eagle Swallowed a Lion," *Los Angeles Times* Sunday 21 May 1978. About William Fox and MGM.
Merritt, Russell. "Nickelodeon Theaters: Building an Audience for the Movies." *Wide Angle* vol. 1, no. 1, 1979.
Parsons, Louella O., "The Essanay Days," *Theatre Arts,* July 1951.
Rogoff, Rosalind, "Edison's Dream: A Brief History of the Kinetophone," *Cinema Journal,* Spring 1976.
Staiger, Janet, "Combination and Litigation: Structures of U.S. Film Distribution, 1896–1917," *Cinema Journal* 23 (No.2, Winter 1984).
Stanbrook, Alan. *"The Covered Wagon." Films and Filming* May 1960. "Great Films of the Century – No. 1." Historical profile and critique.
Talmey, Allene. "Mr. Zukor." *Doug and Mary and Others.* N.Y., Macy-Masius, 1927. An acid view of "anaconda Adolph."

Every film scholar is greatly in debt to Ephraim Katz for his accurate, lucid, and extensive *The Film Encyclopedia* (N.Y., Putnam, 1979; Perigee, 1982). Especially useful for biographies and national histories; does not cover individual films.

For American films of the 1920s the basic source is *The American Film Institute Catalogue of Motion Pictures Produced in the U.S. Feature Films 1921–1920.* N.Y., Bowker, 1971. A volume on the 1910s is believed to be in preparation.

Another extensive resource for this period, drawn from trade press and other periodicals and prepared as a set of files by the WPA and Museum of Modern Art in 1935–940 but only recently published: *The Film Index: Film as Industry* (N.Y, Kraus, 1985). The

Film Index: Film as Art was published in 1941. This industry material is fairly rich and suggests another, quite different, anthology based on the contemporary articles made known by these annotated titles, some ephemeral, many still of interest.

Filmography

Ben Hur. Ramon Novarro and Francis X. Bushman. Directed by Fred Niblo. M-G-M 1926. 128 minutes. Rental, MGM United.

The Covered Wagon. Ernest Torrance and Lois Wilson. Directed by James Cruze. Paramount 1923. 98 minutes. Rental (with musical score) Films Inc., Kit Parker, Mogull Films. Rental, silent version, Films Inc., Museum of Modern Art, Mogull.

A Fool There Was. Theda Bara. Directed by Frank Powell. Fox, 1914. Rental, Museum of Modern Art, EmGee Film Library.

Origins of the Motion Picture. U.S. Naval Photographic Center, 1955. Based on Martin Quigley, Jr., *Magic Shadows: The Story of the Origin of Motion Pictures.* 21 minutes. Rental, Museum of Modern Art.

Queen Elizabeth. Sarah Bernhardt and Lou Tellegen. Directed by Louis Mercanton. France 1912; Famous Players release in U.S. 45 minutes. Rental, EmGee Film Library, Festival Films, Museum of Modern Art.

The Squaw Man. Dustin Farnum. Directed by Oscar Apfel and Cecil B. DeMille. Lasky Feature Play Co., 1913. Available for scholars, Library of Congress.

Vitagraph Comedies: *Stenographer Wanted. Goodness Gracious, or, Movies as They Shouldn't Be* (with Sidney Drew and Clara Kimball Young, shown at opening of Vitagraph Theater). *Professional Patient.* Program 56 minutes. Rental, Museum of Modern Art.